C0-ATU-362

THE REMINISCENCES OF CARL SCHURZ

CARL SCHURZ IN 1906

THE
REMINISCENCES
OF
CARL SCHURZ

VOLUME ONE

1829–1852

ILLUSTRATED WITH PORTRAITS AND
ORIGINAL DRAWINGS

NEW YORK
THE McCLURE COMPANY
MCMVII

Published, October, 1907

LIST OF ILLUSTRATIONS

THE REMINISCENCES OF CARL SCHURZ

CHAPTER I

MANY years ago I began at the desire of my children to write down what follows. In the domestic circle, partly from myself and partly from relatives and old friends, they had heard much about the surroundings and conditions in which I had grown up, as well as about the strange and stirring adventures of my youth, and they asked me to put that which they had heard, and as much more of the same kind as I could give them, into the shape of a connected narrative which they might keep as a family memorial. This I did, without originally contemplating a general publication.

The circumstance that this narrative was first intended only for a small number of persons who might be assumed to take a special interest in everything concerning the subject, may explain the breadth and copiousness of detail in the descriptions of situations and events, which perhaps will occasionally try the reader's patience. To soften his judgment he should imagine an old man telling the story of his life to a circle of intimates who constantly interrupt him with questions about this and that of which they wish to know more, thus forcing him to expand his tale.

However, I have to confess also that while I was writing, the charm of story-telling, the joy of literary production, came over me, and no doubt seduced me into diffusenesses which I must ask the kind reader to pardon.

Until recently it was my intent not to publish these reminiscences during my lifetime, but to leave it to my children to decide after my death how much of them should be given to the general reading public. It appeared to me that such a publication during the lifetime of the author might easily acquire the character of self-advertisement, especially in the case of a man who had been active in public life, and might, perhaps, continue to be so. But after ample consultation with judicious friends I have concluded that in consideration of my advanced age and of my retirement, which manifestly exclude all political ambition, I could not be suspected of such designs.

It is hardly necessary to say that in telling the story of my youth I had to depend largely upon memory. I am well aware that memory not seldom plays treacherous pranks with us in making us believe that we have actually witnessed things which we have only heard spoken of, or which have only vividly occupied our imagination. Of this I have myself had some strange experiences. I have therefore been careful not to trust my own recollections too much, but, whenever possible, to compare them with the recollections of relatives or friends, and to consult old letters and contemporary publications concerning the occurrences to be described. It may be indeed that in spite of such precautions some errors have slipped into my narrative, but I venture to hope that they are few and not important.

When I began to write these reminiscences of my youth, I attempted to do so in English; but as I proceeded I became conscious of not being myself satisfied with the work; and it occurred to me that I might describe things that happened in Germany, among Germans, and under German conditions, with greater ease, freedom, and fullness of expression if I used the German language as a medium. I did so, and thus this story of my youth was originally written in German. It was translated by my friend, Mrs. Eleonora Kinnicutt, and I cannot too strongly express my obligation to her, who not only did for me the more or less dry work of turning German phrases into English, but was in a large sense my coworker, aiding me throughout with most valuable counsel as to the tone of the narrative, and as to passages to be shortened or struck out, and others to be more amply elaborated.

I was born in a castle. This, however, does not mean that I am of aristocratic ancestry. My father was, at the time of my birth, a schoolmaster in Liblar, a village of about eight hundred inhabitants, on the left bank of the Rhine, three hours' walk from Cologne. His native place was Duisdorf, near Bonn. Losing his parents in early childhood, he was adopted into the home of his grandfather, a man belonging to the peasant class, who possessed a small holding of land upon which he raised some grain, potatoes and a little wine. Thus my father grew up a true peasant boy.

At the period of his birth, in 1797, the left bank of the Rhine was in the possession of the French Republic. The years of my father's youth thus fell in what the Rhine folk called "The French Time," and later in life he had much to tell me of those stirring days; how he had seen the great Napoleon, before the Russian campaign, passing in review a body of troops in the neighborhood of Bonn; how, in the autumn of 1813, the French army, after the battle of Leipzig, defeated and shattered, had come back to the Rhine; how, while standing in the market-place at Bonn, he had seen General Sebastiani dash out of his headquarters in the "Hotel Zum Stern," leap upon his horse and gallop around with his staff, the trumpeters sounding the alarm and the drums beating the long roll, because of the news that a band of Cossacks had crossed the Rhine between Bonn and Coblenz; how the French troops, stationed in Bonn, had hurriedly formed and marched off in the direction of France, many disabled soldiers dropping out of the columns; how, one morning, several bands of Cossacks, dirty, long-bearded fellows, on small, shaggy ponies, had swarmed over the country, and chased the French stragglers, killing many of them; how they had also forced themselves into the houses, stealing everything that took their fancy; and how, when the Cossacks had disappeared, the peasants hid their few remaining possessions in the woods, to save them from the oncoming Russians.

Soon after, the troops belonging to the allied powers marched through the country, on their way into France to fight the campaign of 1814, which ended in the occupation of Paris and Napoleon's exile to the Island of Elba. A short period of apparent peace followed; but when Napoleon, in 1815, suddenly returned from Elba and again seized the government of France, the Prussians levied fresh troops on the Rhine; all able-bodied young men were obliged to enlist; and so my father, who was then eighteen years of age, joined an infantry regiment and marched off to the seat of war in Belgium. The troops were drilled on the way thither in the manual of arms and in the most necessary evolutions to fit them for immediate service. My father's regiment passed over the field of Waterloo a few days after the battle, on its way to a small French fortress which they were to besiege, but which soon capitulated without bloodshed. Later he was transferred to the artillery and raised to the dignity of a corporal, an honor which gratified not a little his youthful ambition. He regretted never to have been in actual combat, and later in life, when his contemporaries told the stories of their deeds and dangers, he was always obliged to admit, with reluctance, the harmless character of his own war experiences.

Upon his discharge from military service my father entered, as a pupil, a teachers' seminary at Brühl, and was soon appointed schoolmaster at Liblar. He had received a little instruction in music at the seminary and had learned to play the flute. This enabled him to teach simple songs to the school children and to form a glee club, composed of the youths and maidens of the village. In this glee club he made the acquaintance of my mother, Marianna Jüssen, whom he married in 1827. My mother was the daughter of a tenant-farmer, Heribert Jüssen, who occupied part of a seignorial castle called "Die Gracht," near Liblar. My father and mother lived, for several years after their marriage, with my grandparents; and so it happened that I, their firstborn, came into the world on March 2, 1829, in a castle.

This castle, the ancestral seat of Count Wolf Metternich, was not very old—if I remember rightly it was built between 1650 and 1700—a large compound of buildings under one roof; surrounding on three sides a spacious courtyard; tall towers with pointed roofs, and large iron weather vanes at the corners, that squeaked when moved by the wind; a broad moat, always filled with water, encircling the whole; spanned by a drawbridge, which led through a narrow arched gateway into the court. In the wall above the massive gate, which was studded with big-headed nails, there was a shield bearing the count's coat-of-arms, and an inscription, which I puzzled out as soon as I could read, and which has remained in my memory through all the vicissitudes of my life. It read:

"*In the old days in Hessenland,*
I was called the Wolf of Gutenberg;
Now, by the Grace of God,
I am Count Wolf Metternich of the Gracht."

This large group of buildings contained the dwelling of the tenant and his retainers, the steward's officers necessary for the management of the estate, the granaries and the stables. On the fourth side of the court a second bridge spanned a branch of the moat and led to a small but more pretentious building, also surrounded on all sides by water. This was the residence occupied by Count Metternich and his family during the summer and the shooting seasons. It also had its tall towers and spreading wings, containing a chapel and household service rooms. It was situated on somewhat higher ground, and seemed to dominate the other buildings. This residence, standing apart, was called "The House." A third drawbridge united "The House" with a park of about sixty acres, of which one-half resembled the Versailles gardens, with its straight pebble walks, labyrinths and trimmed hedges, and here and there statues of Greek gods and nymphs, fountains and ponds. Large orange trees, in green tubs, stood, like sentinels, in rows along the walks.

The grounds were enlivened by flocks of guinea hens and stately moving peacocks. Another part of the grounds was laid out like an English park, with lawns, ponds and groups of tall trees and shrubbery, and here and there a small summer house or a pavilion. The estate as a whole was called by the people "Die Burg," and my grandfather was known in the village and surrounding country as "Der Burghalfen." "Halfen" was the name given originally to the farmer-tenants who went halves with the lord of the estate in the proceeds of the crops. This has in some parts of the Rhineland given way to the payment of a fixed rent to the landlord, but the old name "Halfen" remains.

My grandfather, the Burghalfen, had, at the time of my first recollection, attained his sixtieth year. He was a man of huge proportions: over six feet in height, with powerful chest and shoulders, and massive features to correspond; square chin; a firm mouth and full lips; large straight nose; fiery dark eyes with bushy eyebrows; a broad forehead, shadowed with curly brown hair. His strength of muscle was astounding. Once, at a kirmess festival, when several other halfen were his guests, my grandfather accepted a challenge to lift in his arms the great anvil which stood in the blacksmith's forge on the other side of the moat, and to carry it over the drawbridge, through the gate, into the house, up the stairs to the loft, and back again to the forge. I can see him now, striding along, up and down the creaking stairs, with the heavy block of iron in his arms, as though he were carrying a little child.

Wonderful were the stories told about him: that once a mad bull which had broken loose from the barn into the court-yard and driven all the stablemen under cover, was confronted by him, single-handed, and felled to the ground with one blow of a hammer; and that when heavily laden wagons were stuck in the ruts of bad country roads he would lift them up and out with his shoulders; and various other similar feats. It is not unlikely that such tales, as they passed from mouth to mouth, may have gone a little beyond the boundary line of fact, and swelled into legendary grandeur; but they were recounted with every assurance of authenticity; and certain it is that the Burg-halfen was the strongest man of his day in the neighborhood of Liblar.

His education had been elementary only. He could read and write, though with books he had little concern. But he was a man of great authority with the people. From the village and surrounding country men and women came to seek the Burghalfen's advice, and to lay their troubles before him; and whenever report reached him of a quarrel among neighbors, or between husband and wife, he would start forth with a stout stick in his hand for the seat of war. He would hear the case both for plaintiff and defendant, and after making up his mind which side was in the wrong he would pronounce judgment and deal out the punishment on the spot, which not seldom consisted in a sound thrashing. Against his verdict and its immediate execution—a somewhat patriarchal form of judgment—no one ever ventured to protest.

When the harvest-time came and the Burghalfen needed laborers for his fields, he had only to walk through the village street, and old and young flocked to his service and worked for him with zeal until the harvest was safely garnered. But the spirit of helpfulness was mutual; whoever was in distress would say, "I will go to the Burghalfen," and he would do so, confident that no sacrifice would be too great, no service too burdensome to him, when the welfare of others was concerned. "Live and let live" was his principle and his habit. Every parish in the Rhineland had its yearly kirmess, with feasting, drinking, games and dances. These festivals lasted always three days, and were not infrequently carried over into a fourth. At such times relatives and friends visited one another, bringing along their families; so that for those who had many brothers, sisters, cousins and intimate friends, opportunities for enjoyment were not wanting throughout the summer. At every kirmess gathering that he visited the Burghalfen was the central figure. He was pleasure-loving—perhaps a little too much for his own good. There were few whom he could not "drink under the table"; and he was a terrible fighter, too, when it came to blows; but fortunately this did not happen often, for he was a man of peace by nature. I have been told that when under strong provocation he would, in his wrath, seize a chair, dash it to pieces with a mighty foot thrust, grasp one of the legs for a weapon, and, like Samson with the ass's jawbone, charge upon and drive the Philistines irresistibly before him.

It was the custom in each parish to hold an annual "Schützenfest," or bird-shooting. An imitation bird, made of a block of wood, strengthened with iron bands and plates, was fastened to a tall pole, from sixty to eighty feet or more from the ground. The shooting was done with rifles, and he who brought down the last bit of the wooden bird won the prize and was crowned king. This custom still exists to-day in many parts of Germany. If, upon such occasions, in the neighborhood of Liblar, the Burghalfen failed to appear, the festival was incomplete; but he seldom did fail. With his big rifle he was almost always among the first on the spot. This rifle, called "der Ferkelstecher" (the pigsticker), was a most remarkable and formidable weapon. Why it was so called I do not remember. It discharged a good handful of powder and a ball weighing fully eight ounces, and was so heavy that the strongest man could not hold it horizontally from his shoulder without support. Even my grandfather always placed one of his tallest yeomen behind him to grasp the weapon upon its heavy recoil. Innumerable were the birds brought down with this formidable instrument. Every victory was followed by a feast at the tavern, which not only swept away all the prize-money, but a goodly sum besides; and not seldom did the victor return home with a hot and heavy head.

But the Burghalfen was also a thorough husbandman; intelligent, energetic and indefatigable. Bright and early in the morning he was up and joined his laborers in the field, not only giving directions, but when occasion required setting a good example by doing himself the most arduous task. I still see him before me as, according to custom, he drove the first harvest load into the barn, whip in hand, sitting on one of the four gayly decorated horses, which were harnessed tandem fashion to the wagon; and I have often heard that his counsel about questions of husbandry was frequently sought and highly esteemed by his fellow-farmers.

In his own home, of course, he was king, but a king who was loved as well as obeyed, and whose very faults were accepted by others as a kind of necessity of nature which had to be submitted to, and would suffer no change.

At his side, in remarkable contrast, stood my grandmother, a small, slender woman, with a thin, once pretty face; delicate, devout and domestic; always active and full of cares. The household which she conducted was, indeed, sufficiently large and onerous to allow her but little rest. At dawn of day in summer, by lamplight in winter, she was busy superintending the preparation of breakfast for the working people and starting them at their various occupations. They numbered, men and girls, over twenty, without counting the day laborers.

The "Folk," as they were called, assembled for meals in a hall on the ground floor, which had a vaulted ceiling resting on thick stone columns. On one side was a huge hearth, with an open-mouthed chimney; large pots hung over the fire on iron hooks and chains. This was the "commons" of the house. On the other side of the hall stood a long table, with wooden benches, at which the folk took their meals. Before sitting down—standing with their backs to the table—they all said a prayer; then the "meisterknecht," or foreman, struck a loud rap with the handle of his knife on the table, which was the signal for all to sit down. They ate their soup or porridge with wooden spoons out of big wooden bowls, which were arranged along the center of the table within easy reach. There were no individual plates or platters; meat and vegetables were served upon long, narrow strips of board, scoured white. The house

HERIBERT JÜSSEN

FRAU JÜSSEN

provided three-pronged iron forks; for cutting, the folk used their own pocketknives. The foreman dealt out the black bread in large chunks; white bread was given only on festive occasions. During the meal not a word was spoken, and when the foreman laid down his knife it was the signal that the repast was over. It goes without saying that he always allowed the people a sufficiency of food. They arose, again turned their backs to the table, repeated a prayer and separated, each to his or her task.

During the time that the servants were taking their meal my grandmother busied herself with the help of a scullery maid at the big fireplace, preparing breakfast for the family. On one side of the hall a few steps led up into a smaller, though spacious, room, also with a vaulted ceiling. A long table stood in the middle, surrounded by chairs, of which several were upholstered in leather and adorned with bright copper nails. A wide window, with a strong outward-curved iron grating, opened into the courtyard and allowed a full view of whatever took place there. This apartment was the living-room of the family, and served also as a dining-room, except upon great occasions, when the feast was spread in "The Saal," on the opposite side of the servants' hall. This living-room was my grandmother's headquarters. It had a small window, cut through the wall into the folk-hall, for the purpose of enabling her to oversee whatever happened there; and through it her voice was at times to be heard instructing or reproving. When the autumn and winter evenings came she gathered around her the maid servants, of whom there were a dozen or more, with their spinning wheels. Then the flax was spun which supplied the house with linen; and while the wheels whirred the girls sang, my grandmother encouraging them by setting the tunes. The men, meanwhile, came in from the stables and workshops and seated themselves on benches around the great hearth in the hall, to tell stories and to indulge in what passed with them for wit. In the summer evenings they sat around in the courtyard, or leaned upon the bridge-railing, chatting or singing. Two or three times during the year, in accordance with ancient custom, all assembled in the folk-hall for a romp; blindman's-buff and other games were played, and there was no end to the tumbling and pulling, shrieking and laughing, until, at a fixed hour, the foreman stalked in, like stern fate, and sent them all off to bed.

Such were the surroundings in which I first became aware of existence, and in which the earliest years of my childhood were passed. It is remarkable how memory can hark back to the time of the first development of consciousness. So I have still before me a picture of myself, when I could not have been much more than two years of age. On the road, bordered with horse-chestnut trees, leading from the castle to the village, there was a pit enclosed in masonry, in which the count kept some wild boars. I can see myself distinctly, a small child in petticoats and a little white bonnet on my head, sitting upon the wall, looking down with a mixed feeling of delight and terror upon the great black monsters, with their terrible white tusks. As I sat there, an old man with shining buttons on his coat approached, talked with the woman who had charge of me, and gave me some cake. My mother, to whom in later life I recalled this, told me that the man wearing the castle livery must have been old Bernhard, the count's body-servant, who died when I was in my third year.

Another picture I see before me: A large flock of sheep, with the lambs, returning home from the pasture in the dusk of the evening, bleating and crowding with impatient haste through the gateway into the court. Sitting on my mother's arm, I watched them; the old shepherd approaches to allow me to touch the shining little shovel on the end of his long staff, toward which I had stretched out my hand; but the old man's grim and wrinkled face frightens me; I shrink back and cling closely to my mother's shoulder.

With special pleasure do I recall the great cow stable, built like a church, with a central arched nave and two lower side naves, in which the cows stood—about forty in number. My mother, who interested herself in the work of the dairy, took me with her sometimes when she went to see that the animals were properly cared for. How warm it was there of a winter's evening! Sitting on a bundle of hay or straw, in the dim light of the lantern, suspended from the high arch of the central nave, I used to listen to the softly murmuring sounds of the kine chewing their cud, which filled the great space with a peculiar sense of comfort, and to the chatter and the songs of the dairy maids as they busily moved to and fro, calling the cows by their names.

My mother told me later that when I was between three and four years old I had a very exciting love affair. The count had a daughter, who was then about eighteen or nineteen, and very beautiful. The young Countess Marie, when she met me on her walks, sometimes stroked my red cheeks with her hands, as young ladies do now and then with very little boys. The consequence was that I fell ardently in love with her, and declared frankly that I would marry her. My intentions were quite determined, but the young Countess Marie did not seem to look at the matter as seriously as I did, and that led to a catastrophe. One day I saw her standing with a young man at one of the windows of the house, busy catching carp with a hook in the moat of the castle. A furious fit of jealousy seized me; I demanded, screaming, that the young man should leave the adored Countess Marie at once, in default of which I insisted that someone should throw him into the water. I grew still more furious when the young gentleman not only did not leave, but even seemed to be laughing at me. I made such a noise that the castle folk came running from all parts, to see what was the matter. I told them, with hot tears; and then they also laughed, making me still more furious. At last the count's good old cook hit upon a successful idea; she took me into the kitchen, where she gave me a small jar of quince jelly to eat. Quince jelly was then to me an entirely new form of human happiness, and it had a remarkably quieting effect upon my distressed feelings. So far the tale my mother told me; and I will confess that quince jelly has ever since remained my favorite sweet.

"The Burg" had also its terror for me; it was the head of a roe buck, with black antlers and very large eyes, which adorned the wall at the end of a long corridor. I do not know, and probably never knew, why this head of a roe buck was so terrible to me; but certainly it was so; and when I had to pass it I ran as fast as my little legs would carry me.

I can still hear the horn of Hermann, the count's huntsman, who, on fine evenings, sat on the bridge-railing and played merry tunes that reverberated from the walls and the towers of the castle. This huntsman was a great personage in my eyes, for on festive occasions he, arrayed in brilliant uniform with gold lace, a hunting-knife at his side, and a waving bunch of feathers on his hat, accompanied the count. He came to a sad end, poor Hermann! One day he was found in the forest, dead; probably shot by poachers. This was the first tragic sensation of my life. We children, for a long time afterwards, would point to this man or that, with a shuddering suspicion that, perhaps, he might have been the murderer of Hermann.

I must have been a little over four years old when my

parents left the castle to establish a home of their own in the village of Liblar. The village consisted of one street. Midway on an elevation stood the parish church with its pointed steeple and cross. The houses, mostly one-storied and very small, were of whitewashed plaster, with frames and beams exposed, and tiled roofs. There were perhaps half a dozen brick buildings in the village, belonging to the count. The inhabitants of Liblar, small farmers, laborers, mechanics and a few inn- or shop-keepers, took an especial pride in their village because its street was paved with cobblestones. Notwithstanding our house had two stories, it was very small, with ceilings so low in the upper story that my grandfather when standing upright almost touched them with his head.

Although we no longer lived at the castle, I continued to be my grandfather's favorite, and he wished me to come to him as often as possible. My mother had to take me almost every day to the Burg, and I accompanied my grandfather sometimes even at his work. At harvest time, when he took the loaded wagons into the barn, I had to sit with him in the saddle. In the late autumn, when the slaughtering of the fat swine,—a work which he insisted upon performing himself,—took place, the honor fell to me of carrying the big, leathern knife-case, the bright buckled straps of which were wound around my neck so that they should not drag along the ground. And the more important I believed myself to be on such occasions the greater was my grandfather's delight. On rainy days he lent me an old gun with a flint lock, and taught me how to cock and snap it so that it gave out sparks. Then I was allowed to go hunting in the sitting-room and the adjoining chambers, and to shoot as many deer and wild birds as my imagination could scare up. This would amuse me for hours; and my grandfather then took me on his knees and listened to the wonderful tales about the game I had bagged and the adventures in the forest and field I had encountered.

Suddenly a terrible misfortune befell the family. My grandfather had a stroke of paralysis. The upper part of his body remained sound, but he could no longer walk or stand. And thus, alas! the Burghalfen's bustling activity came to a sudden end; no more feats of strength; no more merry rides to the bird-shooting and to the kirmess. The robust man, yesterday still proud of his vigor, was now obliged to sit still from morning until night, his legs swathed in flannel. During the daytime his great armchair stood at the sitting-room window with the outward-curved grating, so that he might overlook the courtyard. He attempted to conduct farm affairs in this way, but he soon had to delegate his authority to a younger brother. And now the suddenly aged man did not know what to do with himself nor with his time. The *Cologne Gazette* was daily brought to him, but reading had never been much to his liking. It being summer and fly-time, a movable table attached to his armchair was sprinkled with sugar to attract the flies that swarmed into the room. He would sit for hours with a short leathern-flapped stick in his hand killing flies, now and then giving the table a terrible whack.

"This is all that I am still fit for," sighed the once useful man. Often I was taken to him to entertain him with my boyish prattle and to make him laugh. Then he began to tell me about bygone days, especially about the "French times," and the experiences of landed proprietors and peasants during those terrible years of war and pillage. As he talked I could see the merry "sans-culottes" swarming over the land, indulging in their wild pranks. I saw, as they approached, Count Wolf Metternich one night flying from the castle in a hurry, after having buried and walled his treasures, including the family archives, deep down under one of the towers, and confided all the belongings he left behind him to my grandfather's safe-keeping. I could see one of the great Napoleon's generals ride through the gate, filling the court with brilliantly uniformed horsemen, and take up his quarters in the great house. When my grandfather's narrative reached the period of the departure of the French and the arrival of the Cossacks he became specially animated. Then it was that the castle people had to hide in the depths of the forest all their horses and wagons, cows, sheep and pigs, lest they should fall a prey to either the retreating French or to the advancing Russians. Time and again I made him describe the Cossacks. They ate tallow candles and ransacked the house and stables for spirits. Finding none, they threatened to use force with my grandmother; whereupon my grandfather knocked a few of them down, and was much surprised that none of their comrades came to their help. When the search for "schnapps," however, continued, my grandmother hit upon the happy idea of filling a barrel with vinegar, to which she added a large quantity of mustard and pepper-seeds and a little alcohol. This brew, which would have burned like fire in the throats of ordinary mortals, the Cossacks praised highly; moreover, it seemed to agree with them. With all their devilishness they possessed a God-fearing sense, for whenever they were planning an especial mischief they would carefully cover the eyes of the crucifix on the wall so that the good Lord might not see the sin that they were about to commit.

Stories like these were told me over and over, and elaborated to suit my endless questions and my insatiable craving to know more; so that before I could read or write my grandfather's stirring recollections had etched into my mind a very fair impression of the Napoleonic wars, so closely complicated with the future history of Germany, and laid a foundation for my future political opinions and sympathies.

In the winter evenings the Burghalfen's great armchair was rolled up to the center-table for a game of cards; but in spite of all efforts made for his entertainment, the sad contrast between the past and the present soon undermined his cheerfulness. He tried to appear content, and not to be a burden to his loved ones, but the old life of bustle and gayety at the Burg, of which he had been the soul and center, was forever gone; and soon other clouds loomed upon the horizon.

CHAPTER II

BEFORE I was six years old my father took me into the village school of which he was the teacher. I remember that I could read and write very early, but not how I acquired those arts. Much I owed to the instruction which my father gave me at home. I had frequented the village school hardly a year when my father resigned his position as schoolmaster. The salary, about $90 a year, was too pitiably small to support the family, to which in the meantime two little girls had been added.

My father, like all who feel within themselves a yearning for knowledge with few opportunities for satisfying it, had the earnest ambition to give to his children the education that fate had denied to him. With this object in view he made a start in a new direction, and opened a hardware-shop, for which he appropriated a part of the house which had once been a cow-stable, hoping that the business would gradually yield an income sufficient for the family needs. In me he believed that he had discovered an aptitude for study. He therefore decided that at the proper age I should go to the " gymnasium " and later to the university, to be fitted for one of the learned professions. For the time being I continued to attend the village school, but the instruction I received there was early supplemented in various directions. It was my father's especial wish that all his children should study music. To this end, when I was about six years old, a queer little piano was procured which had neither pedals nor damper, and possessed several peculiarities incident to old age. But it served well for my first finger exercises, and to me the instrument was very beautiful. Now we had to find a music teacher. The organist who played in our village church possessed an ear for harmony, but, devoid of training, he could hardly decipher the simplest composition on paper. The village folk had accustomed themselves to his performances, and when there occurred in his interludes some strange entanglements nobody was much disturbed. After the organist frankly admitted to my father, with entire preservation of his dignity, that his musical talents did not include an ability to impart knowledge to others, it was decided that I should go twice a week to Brühl, a town four miles distant, to receive lessons from the well-equipped organist living there. The broad turnpike leading to Brühl passed through a great forest. It was a mailcoach road; and whenever the postilion happened to see me trudging along he would invite me to a seat with him on the box, which was a great favor cheerfully accepted. After a while my younger brother Heribert joined me in taking music lessons, and this enabled me to enlarge the scope of my studies; for while Heribert was taking his lessons with the organist I had time to lay the foundation of a knowledge of Latin with the parish priest. Thus we wandered twice a week to Brühl and back, singing duets on the way, and as we were both blessed with a good ear, and were not wanting in voice, it may have sounded well enough. At least we attracted the attention of many passers-by. Once a pleasure party, stopping their traveling carriage, and dismounting, invited us to sit with them under the trees, where they made us go through our entire repertoire and rewarded us with good things from their provision hamper.

My brother Heribert, fifteen months younger than I, was a charming boy; blue-eyed, blond, of a most cheerful tem-

CHRISTIAN SCHURZ

perament and an exceedingly amiable disposition. He liked to occupy himself with animals and flowers more than to sit still and pore over books; so it was decided that he should become a florist gardener. We two clung fondly to one another, and my mother later in life often told me that she had no greater joy than to see us together when, clothed alike and in many ways recognizable as brothers, we were the most cordial comrades in work and play. Nor were wild pranks wanting, though there were none of a vicious nature. The worst adventure made at the time a profound impression upon me and has remained vivid in my memory. The old halfen of an estate near Liblar died, and as he belonged to our extensive kinship, we two brothers had to carry lighted tapers in his funeral procession. After the burial, according to Rhenish custom, the relatives and friends attending sat down to a funeral feast. Such repasts, however solemn at the start, were apt to degenerate into merry carousals. And, so it happened this time. The feasting lasted long and the excellent wines pleased the mourners mightily. A thoughtless uncle had the unfortunate idea that this would be a good opportunity for giving my brother Heribert and me a practical lesson in wine-drinking. He filled and refilled our glasses, constantly urging us to empty them. The result was that first we became very jolly and finally slipped from our chairs under the table in an unconscious state; whereupon, profoundly sleeping, we were put into a haycart and taken home. When we woke up the following morning and heard what had happened we were heartily ashamed. I do not know whether at that time I resolved never to allow the like to happen again; but certain it is that this occurrence gave me a profound loathing for drunkenness, which I have carried with me through life; and although I have always taken wine or beer whenever it pleased me, that excess at the funeral-feast has remained to the present hour my only one.

Of intellectual stimulus our village did not offer much, except that which I found within our home walls and in the larger family circle. My mother's opportunities for cultivation had never extended beyond the parish school and intercourse with relatives and friends. But she was a woman of excellent mental qualities—in a high degree sensible, of easy and clear perception and discernment, and apt to take a lively interest in everything deserving it. But the chief strength of her character lay in her moral nature. I know no virtue that my mother did not possess. Nothing, however, could have been farther from her than assumption of superiority, for she was almost too modest and self-effacing. Rectitude, which is as it is because it cannot be otherwise, was in her joined to the gentlest judgment of others. Her disinterestedness in every trial proved itself capable of truly heroic self-sacrifice. The sorrows of those around her she felt more deeply than her own, and her constant care was for the happiness of those she loved. No misfortune could break her courage, and the calm cheerfulness of her pure soul survived the cruelest blows of fortune. When she died, nearly eighty years old, she had even in the last moments of consciousness a bright smile for the children and grandchildren standing at her bedside. Her figure was slender and well-formed and her features somewhat resembled those of our grandfather. We children always admired her curly golden-brown hair. Whether in the blossom-time of her life she would have been called beautiful or not we never knew; but her countenance was to us all love and goodness and sunshine. The customs and forms of the great world were of course unknown to her, but she possessed the rare grace of noble naturalness which goes far to supply a deficiency in social training. Her handwriting

MOTHER OF SCHURZ

was awkward and her spelling by no means faultless. Of literature she knew little, and with grammar and style she had never been troubled. But many of her letters, written to me at different times and in different situations of life, were not only filled with noble thought and sentiment, but possessed rare poetic beauty of expression; the unconscious greatness of her soul found its own language. Her very being exercised a constantly elevating and stimulating influence, although she could aid her children but little in the acquisition of what is commonly called knowledge.

All the more zealous was my father in this direction. The low whitewashed walls of the small, modestly furnished living-room of our house, in which we also took our meals, were hung with the portraits of Schiller, Goethe, Wieland, Körner, Tasso and Shakespeare; for poets, historians and scientists were my father's heroes, and he early told me of their creations and achievements. He read every book he could lay his hands upon and had collected a few of his own, among them Becker's "Universal History," some German classics and some translations from Voltaire and Rousseau. But these books were still beyond my childish comprehension; and so others were obtained for me from a circulating library at Brühl. There we found a series of folklore tales, pretty well-told old legends of Emperor Octavianus, and the four Haimons children, and the horned Siegfried, and strong Roland, etc., and some of the popular knight-stories, the contents of some of which I still could tell.

Then a new world opened itself to me. The old head gardener of the count, who had observed my love of reading, gave me one day that most magnificent of juvenile books, "Robinson Crusoe." It may be said without exaggeration that to "Robinson Crusoe" the youth of all civilized peoples have owed more happy hours than to any other one book. I can still see it before me, as I grasped it eagerly as soon as school hours were over; I can see the worn edges of the binding, the woodcuts, even the inkspot which to my extreme annoyance disfigured one of them; and I can still hear myself telling the schoolmaster about the wonderful contents of this book and begging him to read it aloud to the class, which he did on two afternoons in the week, his own interest increasing so much with every reading that the hours gradually lengthened, to the detriment of other studies. Next to "Robinson Crusoe" came the "Landwehrmann," a popular history of the war of liberation in 1813, for which my interest had been excited by my grandfather's and my father's reminiscences, and from the reading of which I emerged a fiery German patriot. And finally I was led up to higher literature by my father's reading aloud to me while I was ill with the measles some of Schiller's poems, and even the "Robbers."

There were still other stimulating family influences. My mother had four brothers. The oldest, "Ohm Peter," as we children called him, had served in a French regiment of grenadiers during the last years of Napoleon's reign, and was rich in recollections of that eventful period. The wars over, he married the daughter of a halfen and became himself the halfen of a large estate in Lind, near Cologne. In body and mind he resembled my grandfather, and we children loved him heartily. The second was "Ohm Ferdinand." He was the superintendent of extensive peatworks belonging to Count Metternich, and lived in Liblar in comfortable circumstances. He had risen in the Prussian military service to the dignity of a "Landwehr-lieutenant," and when he turned out at the periodical musters in his fine uniform, a sword at his side and a "tschako" with a high bunch of feathers on his head, we children looked at him with awe and admiration. This uncle had read much and was the free-thinker, the Voltairian, of the family. He also belonged to a Freemasons' lodge in Cologne, of which it was whispered among the village-folk that the members had sold themselves body and soul to the devil, and that at their frequent night-meetings the devil appeared in the guise of a black goat and demanded homage of them. The fact that "Ohm Ferdinand" never went to church on Sunday seemed to confirm the worst rumors with regard to him. The third brother, "Ohm Jacob," lived at Jülich, a fortified town not far distant, where he married the daughter of a merchant and established himself in mercantile business. He was an extraordinarily handsome man in face and figure; of fine, amiable qualities, and of distinguished personality. His admirable character won for him the respect and liking of the community to such a degree that he was elected burgomaster, an office which he held for many years with great dignity and with popular approval. Once a year he visited the great fair at Frankfurt-on-the-Main, from which he returned by way of Liblar, bringing to us pretty little gifts and also interesting tales about the remarkable men and things he had seen and heard there.

The fourth and youngest brother was "Ohm Georg," who had served in a regiment of cuirassiers in Berlin and then had come home to aid my grandfather in his husbandry. He had lived three years in the capital of the kingdom, and therefore had looked far beyond the shadow of the church-steeple of his home. He, too, was a handsome man, and had the chivalrous trait of the family. Each one of the four brothers was over six feet in height, and together they formed a stately group. Not in stature only, but in intelligence and breadth of view they towered far above the ordinary people of their surroundings. In addition to them there were two brothers-in-law—my father and "Ohm Rey," the husband of a sister of my mother's, a wideawake and jovial man, who owned a large farm about an hour's walk from Liblar. This circle met often in happy social intercourse. The conversation at such times was by no means restricted to local topics, nor to the transaction of every-day business. These men read newspapers, took an interest in all that happened in the outer world, and discussed, if not with thorough knowledge, at least with eager interest and sympathy, the events that moved humanity at large. Not seldom was I present at these talks, leaning against the arm of my father's chair or crouching unnoticed in the corner of the room, a silent and receptive listener. Here it was that I first heard of the struggles of Abdel-Kader in Algiers and of the hero Schamyl in the Caucasus; of the repeated attempts upon the life of Louis Philippe in France and the Carlist wars in Spain, with the generals of high-sounding, musical names, and—what especially excited me—of the imprisonment of the Archbishop of Cologne for Jesuitic conspiracies against the Prussian Government. And so on. Much of what I heard was at first to me little more than mere sound. Still I asked many questions, which were answered by my father and by my uncles as well as they could. And although perhaps the mind of the boy thereby acquired but little clear understanding of things, the feeling took early root in me that we in our little village were a part of a great world, the affairs of which concerned us, too, and demanded our attention and sympathy.

In this family circle I also heard for the first time about America. A peasant family of our village, by the name of Trimborn, emigrated to the United States. I still have before my eyes the picture of their departure. One afternoon a wagon loaded with trunks, boxes and household utensils started from a neighboring cottage; the village-folk wished good luck to the emigrants, and a large crowd followed them until the wagon disappeared in the forest on the road to Cologne. Another family, by the name of Kribben, who were particular friends of ours, soon followed the Trimborns to settle in Missouri, where I saw them many years later. Meanwhile, things American were eagerly discussed by my father and my uncles. Then I heard for the first time of that immeasurable country on the other side of the ocean, its great forests, its magnificent rivers and lakes—of that young republic where the people were free, without kings, without counts, without military service, and, as was believed in Liblar, without taxes. Everything about America that could be got hold of was eagerly read, and I saw for the first time in a penny magazine the picture of George Washington, whom my father called the noblest of men in all history, because he had commanded large armies in the war for the liberation of his people and, instead of making himself a king, had voluntarily divested himself of his power and returned to the plow as a simple farmer. By this example my father explained to me what it was to be a true patriot.

The men in our family circle fairly reveled in that log-cabin romance, which is so full of charm to the European unacquainted with the true conditions of American life; and it wanted but little to induce the men of the family to try their fortune in the new world at once. Although the resolution was not taken in a hurry, America always remained a favorite topic of conversation with them; and in the course of time every member of my family did emigrate, some to remain in America, others to return to Germany.

Among grown-up people outside of the family, too, I found a friend who stands out in my memory in bold relief. He was a singular character. His name was George van Bürk, and as he had been a master shoemaker, he generally went by the name of "Master George." Feeble sight obliging him to renounce his trade, he made a living as an errand man, and was so frequently employed by my father in that capacity that he almost seemed to belong to our house. He was then a man in middle life, tall and thin, with a haggard and sallow but pleasant face, to which, however, a whitish spot in one of his eyes gave a peculiar expression. He was one of that class of persons who with good natural endowments have had but little education, but whom that little has served to lift out of the rut of the commonplace. He had read all the books that had come in his way, and although many of them went beyond his comprehension, they had helped shape his thoughts and notions. He had all sorts of droll conceits, which he gave forth with facility of expression and sometimes in piquant terms of speech, and as he was, withal, an amiable soul, everybody liked him.

The whole population of the village and surrounding Rhine country, my own family included, was Roman Catholic. So was Master George; but upon many points he could not agree with the church. "Why," he argued, "if we are to believe blindly and never think for ourselves, why did the all-wise Creator give us our reason?" This view he applied with especial acuteness to the sermons of the parish priest. Also with the Apostle Paul he had various differences of opinion. I was still a mere child, but he confided his religious scruples and philosophical contemplations to me, thinking that as I was to become a learned man, the sooner I formed opinions of my own on serious subjects the better. With especial earnestness he warned me against studying theology with the intention of entering the priesthood—for "these divines are obliged to say too many things which they do not themselves believe." And then he attacked with great eloquence the miracles of which the Bible tells us, and which he confessed he could not understand.

Sometimes, however, he seemed to remember that after all I was only a child. He would then take me upon his knee and tell me fairy-stories, such as one tells to children, but he never omitted to add that the stories were not true and that I must promise not to believe them. This I did promise, but always asked for more. The child's mind has a craving for the supernatural, and although terror taken by itself is an uncomfortable sensation, still the shudders produced by the thought of the monstrous and awful have for it a strange fascination. The village people among whom I lived were for the most part superstitious to a degree. They firmly believed in the personal devil with horns and tail, and in witches who were in intimate league with him; and there were even two or three old women in our village to whom the finger of suspicion pointed as being "not quite right." I also heard some of our neighbors tell of "men of fire" whom they had seen with their eyes walking about the fields at night. These were said to be lost souls condemned for their misdeeds in the flesh to wander about forever in fiery torment. Although I knew perfectly well from my talks with my parents and uncles and Master George that there were no such creatures as witches, and that the "men of fire" were only will-of-the-wisps arising from the vapors of the moorland, nevertheless I found it delightfully gruesome to stare at these old women and cautiously to visit the morass where these terrible "men of fire" were said to hover.

To my friend, Master George, I am also indebted for my first understanding of the word philosopher. There stood in our village street an old deserted house which must once have been a more aristocratic dwelling than its neighbors. It was larger, the beams of its framework were more artistically fashioned and ornamented, and the entrance had a porte cochère, jutting out into the street. At the time of which I write the house was empty and dilapidated, and we village children tore up and down its rickety stairs and passageways and found its vacant rooms, with their dark corners, well adapted for hide-and-seek and robber plays.

This uncanny place interested me deeply, and from Master George I learned that its last owners and occupants had been two old bachelors by the name of Krupp, then long dead. The older of the two, so Master George told me, was a very peculiar gentleman. He wore his hair braided in a cue and on his head an old-fashioned three-cornered hat. He had but one eye and he wore spectacles with only one glass. These were sewed to the front corner of his hat so that the one glass should drop into place over the one eye the instant that he put his hat upon his head. He possessed a large library and was a very learned man. He would often wander through the village street, absorbed in thought, his hands behind his back, not noticing anyone. He never went to church, and before he died refused to receive extreme unction. Krupp, so Master George always wound up his talk about him, was " a true philosopher." I asked my father whether this queer man had really been a philosopher. My father thought so beyond a doubt. This, then, was my first conception of a philosopher, and frequently in late life, when I heard philosophy and philosophers spoken of, has the picture of the three-cornered hat with the one-eyed spectacle attached to it risen up in my mind.

Master George had strange peculiarities. One day, while he was entertaining a company with amusing talk, which kept his hearers in the merriest mood, he suddenly heard a clock strike. Master George stopped abruptly in the middle of the sentence, jumped to his feet, exclaiming in a solemn tone: "One hour nearer death." The next moment he sat down and after a short silence continued his talk as merrily as before. My father, to whom I described this scene, said that he had often seen Master George do the same; that his mind was filled with a presentiment of impending death, and with all kinds of thoughts about the hereafter which sometimes came suddenly to the surface in this strange way. My friend never spoke to me about his dark premonitions. To me he disclosed only the cheerful side of his nature and of his "philosophy of life," although he never used so pompous an expression as this. He frequently endeavored to show me how little one requires to be happy in this world, and made his own life serve as an example. He was a very poor man, according to the usual understanding of the term. Fate had not only refused him favors, but had in a certain sense persecuted him. He did not deny that he had within himself the making of something better than a mere cobbler, but his parents thought they could make nothing else of him. And yet the weakness of his eyes had robbed him even of the fitness for cobbler's work and he had been obliged to become an errand runner in order to earn the daily bread for his wife and children. But what would it avail to torment himself with dark broodings over that which he might have been and was not? The world was a beautiful world even for him, the poor errand runner. He had enjoyed the good fortune of associating with people who knew much more and were much cleverer than himself. And every new idea thus opened to him was a new delight. If he thought only of the pleasures that life had given, instead of the sufferings that it had inflicted upon him, he saw reason to be content. In fact, all that was required for earthly happiness was few wants and a good conscience.

"If," he would say with emphasis, "you are ever overtaken by misfortune, or oppressed by poverty, you must think of your friend Master George."

And so I have very often done. The counsel that he gave me upon every occasion was always mixed with jests and droll descriptions of men and things which never permitted the admonitions to become dull sermons. He also endeavored to stimulate my ambition by painting to me in glowing colors the good fortune of the liberal education which was in store for me; and when he spoke of my future career he gave full rein to his ardent imagination.

His presentiment of an early death proved true. My good friend did not long survive those days. While I was at the gymnasium he died of consumption. I have always kept him in warm remembrance.

The impression of what Master George had said to me about religious things was deepened by an occurrence of a different nature.

I fully resolved, so far as a child could make such a resolution, that when I studied it would not be for the ministry. True, among the Roman Catholic population of the lower Rhine country, a family that counted a priest among its members was proud of the distinction. But this was mainly the case with the women of our home circle; the men were more or less affected by the free-thinking spirit of the age, and my uncle Ferdinand, the Voltairian, even went so far as to indulge in bold jests and scoffings upon religious subjects. This jarred upon me painfully. It seemed to me audaciously wicked to speak in flippant words about things which I had been taught in church, and at my mother's knee, were high and holy. My father, who, as already mentioned, had read his Voltaire and Rousseau and been influenced by them, never fell in with that tone of talk. On the other hand, he made no effort to hold me by means of counteracting influences to strict adherence to the faith. From the pulpit as well as in private religious instruction I had repeatedly heard the priest say that the Catholic religion was the only saving one, and that all of different belief—Protestants, Jews and heathen—were hopelessly doomed to everlasting hell-fire. There was not a single Protestant in Liblar; in fact, we children could hardly imagine what a "Calvinist," as the Protestants were called, was like; and when one day a stranger, a Prussian official, passed through our village and we heard that he was a Protestant, we looked at him with a mixture of pity and fear, and were much surprised to find him a man of dignity and agreeable presence. How could he be cheerful? we wondered; for, of course, he too must know of his doom. There was one Jew in the village, a butcher who supplied the neighborhood with meat. In no other way did we come into contact with him. But I saw sometimes in our house another Jew by the name of Aaron, who lived in a neighboring village, and I observed that my father always talked with him in a friendly and interested way upon various subjects. This astonished me. But my father told me that old Aaron, whose face had always appeared to me very serious and of great dignity, was not only a very good and honest, but also a very enlightened, even a wise, man—more honest and virtuous and wise than many a Christian. The question whether so good a man as old Aaron must necessarily be doomed to eternal hell-fire troubled me very much. I could not make this agree with my idea of the all-just God. Soon my father read to me Lessing's "Nathan der Weise," setting before me the lesson of tolerance which this dramatic poem so attractively teaches, and which I most heartily enjoyed, without being conscious how dangerously those teachings shook the pillars and undermined the fundamental dogmas of the only true church.

Another event brought further shock. The schoolmaster who had succeeded my father had taken some liberties with one of the pupils, a relative of ours, and was called to account for it. He denied the accusations, and the community soon split into two parties: on the one side the schoolmaster defended by the parish priest, and supported by the count's family and a large part of the population; on the other our family and friends. The quarrel waxed very bitter, as is always the case with such village warfare, and led to violent disputes, once even to a bloody riot, which the one constable of the place was unable to suppress. "There is revolution in the village," people said. This was the first time that I had heard this fateful word. The priest made himself especially conspicuous by repeating slanderous tales about members of our family. This went so far that even my mother, the gentlest of women, became greatly excited, and one day I overheard her tell the priest to his face that he was a wicked man and a reckless defamer of character—whereupon the clerical gentleman tamely slunk away. To my mind the priest, as the vicar of God and the mouthpiece of His word, had been a holy man. And now to hear my mother, the very embodiment of truthfulness and piety, tell the priest that he was wicked, could not but be to me a dangerous revelation. It tormented me greatly after this not to be able to listen to his Sunday sermons with unshaken faith, and it distressed me beyond measure when I stood near him as a choir-boy to see him perform the holy office of the mass. But my religious observances went on as before.

The unhappy conflict caused by the schoolmaster episode had unforeseen consequences. The schoolmaster indeed had to quit Liblar, but he left the quarrel behind, and it affected the relations between my grandfather and the count, which down to this time had been most friendly. Count Wolf Metternich was older than my grandfather—a stately and stalwart figure over six feet high and unbent by the burden of his years; his hair and whiskers silver white and his countenance most benignant. He was a nobleman of the old school, proud to have old servants and old well-to-do and contented tenants. The farm-rents were low, and when the crops failed the count was always willing to make reductions. On the other hand, when the crops were plentiful, he did not at once seize the opportunity to advance rents, but rejoiced in the prosperity of his people. His old business manager, the rent-master, as he was called, looked grim and exacting, but he conducted affairs in the spirit of his lord. Thus the relation between the count and my grandfather had been one of easy-going contentment on both sides, cemented by the common remembrance of the hard times of the "French War," during which the count had often been obliged, under the most trying circumstances, to entrust to my grandfather the care of his ancestral home. Of course, the difference in the worldly position between the count and the halfen was never overlooked. My grandfather, according to the ideas of those days, was a well-to-do man and could allow himself some comforts and luxuries. But I remember hearing it spoken of in the family circle that this or that could not be had or done, because the castle people might consider it presumptuous and take offense. For instance, my grandfather could go to town or pay visits in a two-wheeled chaise, but not in a four-wheeled carriage; and his wife and daughters might wear as pretty caps or hoods as they pleased, trimmed with lace ever so costly and even adorned with precious stones, but they could not wear bonnets such as were worn in Cologne. The count when he gave his great annual hunt always invited the men of our family. I vividly remember the stately old nobleman as he went on foot with his company into the forest—he himself in a gray hunting coat armed with an out-of-date flintlock gun—for such new-fangled things as percussion-caps he would not trust. Upon such occasions he treated his guests, whether noble or not, as friends. But when my grandfather leased for himself a hunting preserve in the neighborhood, to shoot his own hares and partridges, it was considered doubtful at the castle whether the Burghalfen had not gone a little too far. However, the matter was fortunately allowed to remain in doubt. The old countess was generally regarded as a very proud lady, but in her intercourse with my grandfather's family she always showed the friendliest spirit. We children were invariably invited on Christmas eve to the Christmas tree at the castle and presented with gifts, and whenever there was illness in our household practical helpfulness as well as genuine concern was shown by the count and his family. The count's sons were on a friendly footing with the sons of the Burghalfen, and on festive occasions they danced right merrily with the daughters.

In this long-established happy relation the quarrel about the schoolmaster, in which, I do not know why, the count's family took a lively part, sounded like a discordant note. As so often happens, when irritated feelings are at play, one cause after another bred mutual misunderstanding and discontent. Then the old count died, and soon after the old rent-master. The estate passed into the possession of the eldest son, and with him began a new régime. The young count was a man of a good and kindly character, but the time-honored principles in regard to old servants and old tenants were not a part of his nature, as they had been of his father's. The high-bred patriarchal simplicity, so characteristic heretofore of the house, seemed to him antiquated and not a little dull. He found more pleasure in his English racehorses and his smart jockeys than in the fat, heavy bays that had formerly drawn the family coach, with a sleepy gray-headed coachman on the box. He was not bound to the Burghalfen by any memories of the hard French times, and thus their relations gradually became merely those of business interest. He appointed a new rent-master, a young man with brusk manners and entirely unsentimental views of life, and when he explained to the count that the income from the estate could be considerably increased, the information was by no means unwelcome in view of growing expenditures. Under these circumstances the breach between the young count and the Burghalfen rapidly widened, and finally—the precise particulars I no longer remember—the rupture came, the lease of the estate was cancelled and my grandfather, a year or two later, left the Burg. There was a public auction of the house and farm-belongings lasting several days, which I once attended for a few hours. The jokes of the auctioneer sounded harshly offensive to my ears and there was a deep resentment in my young heart as though a great wrong were being done. My grandparents then took a house in the village, but they did not long survive the change from the castle. My grandmother died first and my grandfather twelve days later. Many tears of heart-felt sorrow were shed for them both.

Meanwhile a great change had taken place with me, too. When I was in my ninth year my father thought I had outgrown the village school in Liblar. He therefore sent me to a school of a somewhat higher order in Brühl, which was connected with the teacher's seminary there, and was regarded as a model institution. The schoolrooms were in an old Franciscan monastery, and I remember with a shudder the tortures to my sensitive musical ear when my father, in order to present me to the principal, led me through a long corridor, in each window-recess of which stood a young man practising finger-exercises on the violin, so that at least a dozen instruments giving out discordant sounds were to be heard at the same time. The instruction I received from the well-equipped master was excellent, and at the same time I continued my lessons in Latin and my musical studies. I also began to live among strangers, boarding during the winter in the modest home of a butcher's widow. In the summer I walked to school from Liblar to Brühl and back every day of the week—a walk of about eight miles.

And then came a heavy blow. One gloomy winter's day, returning from school to my lodging, I found my father awaiting me with tears in his eyes. Several times his voice failed in attempting to tell me that my brother Heribert, after an illness of only a few days, had died. Only the Monday before I had left him a picture of health. This was a dreadful shock. My father and I wandered home through the forest holding one another by the hand and weeping silently as we walked. For a long time I could not console myself over this loss. Whenever I was alone in the woods I would call my brother loudly by name and pray God, if He would not give him back, at least to allow his spirit to appear to me.

Then I felt a want of mental occupation on my lonely way between Brühl and Liblar and so I accustomed myself to reading while I walked. My father, whose literary judgment was somewhat determined by current tradition, counted Klopstock among the great German poets, whom one " must have read," and so he gave me the " Messiah " as appropriate reading. To read the whole of Klopstock's "Messiah" is considered to-day an almost impossible test of human perseverance, and there are probably few Germans now living who can boast of having accomplished the feat. I am one of the few. On the long walks between Brühl and Liblar I studied the whole twenty cantos, not only with steadfastness, but in great part with profound interest. It is true that among the pompous hexameters I hit upon many that sounded very mysterious to me. I consoled myself with the thought that probably I was too young fully to understand this grand creation. Other parts really impressed me as transcendentally beautiful. I must confess that in the literary studies of my later life I have never been able to rise again to this appreciation of Klopstock's greatness. After having finished the "Messiah," I was told by my father to learn by heart Tiedge's "Urania" and a series of poems by Gellert, Herder, Bürger, Langbein, Körner and others. Thus I became acquainted with a good many products of German literature, and was in point of reading well prepared to enter the lowest class of the gymnasium.

Here I must mention an occurrence which in a truthful narrative of my life should not be suppressed. My father, who loved me dearly and took pride in me, was extremely exacting in the performance of duty. He examined carefully the weekly reports of my teachers and was never satisfied with anything short of the best. These reports were always good. Only once, tempted by a robber play with my school-fellows, I had omitted the learning of the Latin lesson, which crime the priest, my teacher, duly recorded. Whether shame or fear prevented me from telling my father I do not remember, but returning home on Saturday afternoon, I tried to make him believe that accidentally the report had not been written. My hesitating manner at once convinced him that something was amiss, and a few direct questions brought me to full confession. Then the following conversation took place:

"You failed to do your duty and you tried to conceal the truth from me; don't you think that you deserve a whipping?"

"Yes, but do please let us go into the cow-stable, so that nobody can see or hear it."

The request was granted. In the solitude of the cow-stable I received my punishment, and nobody knew anything about it; but for many a day I carried with me a bitter consciousness of well-deserved humiliation, and for a long time I would not put foot into the cow-stable, the theater of my disgrace.

But my childhood was on the whole sunny and happy, and if my memory fondly dwells upon it and I am a little diffuse in describing it, I must be pardoned. I consider myself fortunate to have spent my early life in the country, where one feels himself not only nearer to nature, but nearer to his kind than in the confinements and jostling crowds of the city. I also consider myself fortunate in having grown up in simple and modest circumstances which knew neither want nor excessive affluence, and which did not permit any sort of luxury to become a necessity; which made it natural to me to be frugal and to appreciate the smallest pleasures; which preserved my capacity of enjoyment from the misfortune of being blunted and blasé; which kept alive and warm the sympathy, that feeling of belonging together, with the poor and lowly among the people, without discouraging the striving for higher aims.

Our village was so small that only a few steps led into field or forest, and every inhabitant was a near neighbor.

Although, after I could read, my books consumed much of my time, I had my full part of the games with the peasant and tradesmen's children in the village, and their faces and names are still quite familiar to me. My most intimate friend was the youngest of the three sons of a well-to-do merchant—a boy of amiable disposition and good parts. We were exactly of the same age and pursued the same studies. So we believed ourselves destined to walk through life side by side. We separated in early boyhood and did not meet again until late in life. He had studied law, had served his country with honor in the wars of 1866 against Austria and of 1870 against France, had risen to the dignity of a major of Uhlans and been decorated with the Iron Cross, an order bestowed only for personal bravery. After the French war he had been appointed a judge in Alsace, and later he retired from that place to his native village, an old bachelor in very comfortable circumstances. He inhabited a fine house on the very spot where many years before the queer old philosopher Krupp had lived. Here, in 1889, the dear comrade of my boyhood, now a portly man of years, welcomed me and my children who accompanied me with radiant heartiness and hospitality. A repast was quickly improvised, and when the dear old friend pressed his arm around my neck and in his best wine proposed my health, our eyes, like our glasses, were full to the brim.

My father interested himself greatly in the care of animals and flowers. Plants and song birds were in every room of our house. He taught me how to set snares for the field-fares which passed over our country in the autumn, and were regarded as a great table delicacy. Those snares were distributed along the hunters' trails in the forest, and I used to go before sunrise and again at twilight in the evening into the depth of the woods and secure the birds that had been caught

—a form of sport which I confess I no longer approve. In these lonely walks, when roe, fox, rabbit and now and then a wild boar rustled past me, I learned to love the woods and to feel the fascination of the forest-solitude, with its mysterious silence under the great leaf-roof and the whisper of the winds in the treetops. Soon I cared less for the bird-trapping than for the enjoyment of that woodland charm, and even on the way to and from school I learned to avoid the highroad and to strike into the shade on the right or left, wherever I could find a path. This love for the woods has never left me, and often in later life, at the aspect of a beautiful spreading landscape or of the open sea, I have asked myself whether what I had seen and felt in the forest did not surpass all else.

Summer was for us a period of festivities. Already in May occurred the kirmess in Lind, Ohm Peter's home, and late in the autumn the kirmess in Herrig, where Ohm Rey lived; and between those there were still a great many more kirmesses on the farms of uncles and cousins. To most of them the whole family went, including the children. For such occasions a two-wheeled chaise was not sufficient. So the kirmess-car, an ordinary two-wheeled cart, covered with tent cloth and furnished with seats that consisted of wooden boards or bundles of straw, was put into requisition, and the number of human beings which the kirmess-car could take seemed beyond calculation. The horse, or when the roads were bad, the horses, shone in their most resplendent brass-ornaments, and the vehicle was decorated with green boughs and flowers. We found at the kirmess a crowd of boys and girls of our kin, who, like ourselves, during these festive days, enjoyed full freedom. At the midday-meals, at which the older guests usually spent from four to six hours, we children did not sit very long. Only when for the entertainment of the company a juggler appeared, as for example the great "Janchen of Amsterdam," who on the farms of that region enjoyed the reputation of being a true sorcerer, we would stand transfixed until he was gone. Then we ran to the booths on the village street with their honey-cakes, cheap toys and little roulettes, and in the evening we went "to the music." From the dance the older people as well as the children usually retired early—the older people to begin their game of cards, which frequently lasted until sunrise next day—and the children to go to bed. Even this going to bed was a festivity. As the house on such occasions always had many more guests than beds, a room for the boys was fitted out with straw, blankets, linen sheets and pillows laid on the floor. When such a sleeping apartment was offered to a dozen or more boys as their domain for the night, the main frolic of the day began, which was continued with boisterous hilarity until one boy after another sank down utterly overcome by fatigue.

To us children in Liblar the greatest day of the year was Whitsun Monday, when the annual bird-shooting, "the Schützenfest," took place. How grand appeared to me this "Fest," which in truth could hardly have been more modest! Such excitement! On the Saturday afternoon before Whitsuntide five or six men were seen striding through the village, bearing upon their shoulders a pole forty or fifty feet long, at the point of which a wooden bird was fastened. The village youth joined the procession, which slowly moved up the street to a meadow shaded by elms and linden-trees. The wooden bird was decorated by the children with flowering broom-twigs, and then the pole was hoisted upon one of the trees and lashed to the branches with ropes and chains. As this was done by hand, it was hard work not without danger. We children always watched it with no little trepidation. I came very near losing my life on one such occasion. The pole, having been hoisted up the tree, slipped the rope and knocked one of the men from the branch on which he sat. Standing just under the tree, I suddenly heard above me the crash of a branch and the cry "Jesus Maria!" I sprang away to see the body of a man fall exactly upon the spot on which I had stood. The poor fellow broke his spine and died shortly after he had been carried into the village. Usually, however, the raising of the pole passed without accident, and we children marched back with bouquets of blooming broom in our hands, conscious of having helped in accomplishing a great work, and with the anticipation of still greater things to come.

How slow Whitsunday was in passing! But the fun began all the earlier on Monday morning. Already at daybreak the drummer—an old bow-legged little man—had marched through the village, beating the reveille; but it was afternoon before the head men of the San Sebastian society—that was the name of the sharpshooters-corps, to which belonged almost all the grown-up inhabitants of the village, male and female—came to our house, where at that time the flag and the other treasures of the society were kept, to take them from there to the dwelling of the last year's "king." Finally, the procession started: first the old drummer with a bouquet of flowers and many colored ribbons on his breast and hat; next, bearing the flag, Master Schäfer, a tailor, white-haired and spindle-legged. He was called the "young ensign," because his father had before him carried the banner, upon which was painted in loud colors St. Sebastianus, the patron-saint, pierced with an incredible number of arrows; then the captains, carrying ancient spears, also decorated with flowers and ribbons, accompanied by all the solemn-visaged directors of the society, and then the "Schützenkönig" of the previous year. The king wore upon his hat a crown of gold tinsel and artificial flowers, and around his neck a silver chain, from which were suspended silver shields, the size of a hand, with the engraved names of the kings of at least a hundred years back. The shields covered the king's shoulders and breast and back, giving him a gorgeous appearance. His Majesty was followed by the marksmen, with their rifles on their shoulders, the remainder of the population, old and young, bringing up the rear. Arrived at the green, the procession marched three times around the tree upon which the pole was fastened, halted, knelt down and repeated the Lord's Prayer. Then the drummer beat the roll, the ex-king hung his crown and chain upon the branch of a tree, and after the old men and the women members of the society, who could not themselves fire rifles, had chosen among the sharpshooters present those who were to represent them, the shooting began. The drummer watched each shot with close attention, for it was his duty to beat a roll every time that the bird was hit. When that roll was particularly vigorous the rifleman who had fired the shot rewarded the drummer with a glass of wine, and it must be confessed that with every glass the good man's face grew redder and his drumbeats wilder. The multitude, which meanwhile had scattered among the booths where sweetmeats, wine and beer were sold, crowded again around the marksmen as soon as the wooden bird began to splinter. From minute to minute the excitement rose; ancient-looking telescopes were raised to discover the weak spots on the bird, and the suspense became breathless when, as often happened, only a small ragged bit of wood remained on the top of the pole and the next well-aimed shot might decide the day. Finally, when the last bit fell, the drummer beat the most terrible of his rolls, the crowd, with deafening cheers, pressed around the victor, who now, as the new king, was adorned with the crown and chain of shields. Then the moment had come for the "young ensign" to show what he could do. He swung the flag so violently around himself that those standing nearest stepped back in alarm; he waved it over his head and around his breast like a wheel, then around his legs, then up and down, back and forward, until the veins in his forehead threatened to burst, and all this to the accompaniment of the drummer's most passionate beats. I always watched him with admiration, convinced that nothing greater in this line was possible, until, alas! one day I overheard an old peasant, shaking his head, remark: "He is nothing to what the old man was!" Again the procession marched three times around the tree and back to the village, the drummer at the head, making remarkable zigzags with his bowlegs, the gray-headed "young ensign" still waving his colors furiously and the marksmen punctuating the triumphal march with occasional blind shots. Happy was the boy to whom one of the men was willing to entrust the carrying of his rifle, thus allowing him to take part in the great event!

Then came the royal feast at the tavern, at which the new king entertained his predecessors in office and the directors of the society, with ham, white bread and wine. Finally, in the evening followed a dance, the music for which was originally furnished by the drum, which in my time, however, had been superseded by an orchestra consisting of a violin, clarionette and double bass. The reason why this festival remained so vivid in my memory, even to the minutest detail, is that it excited in me for the first time something like a real ambition. It was the great public contest of skill in the arena of the world in which I lived; and when I saw the victor with the crown on his head and the resplendent chain of shields upon his shoulders and breast, surrounded by a cheering multitude, it seemed to me something very great, to which I too some day might aspire. And this honor was indeed to come to me in later days when I no longer appreciated it so highly.

Although the summer was thus rich in joy, our winter was no less so. It not only brought skating on the castle moat and battles with snowballs, but to me the first enjoyment of the stage; and of all the joyous excitements of my childhood none surpassed that into which we were thrown by the arrival of the puppet theater in Liblar. With eagerness we boys regularly accompanied the crier through the village, who by means of a drum brought the people to their doors and announced to the honored public the coming of the drama. Oh, the fear that I might not be allowed to visit the theater, and the impatience until the final moment came! The stage was erected in a small dance-hall. The price for front seats ranged from one cent for children to five cents for adults. The lighting of the hall consisted of a few tallow candles. But the center of the dark curtain was decorated with a rosette of transparent paper in different bright colors, and was lighted from behind by a lamp giving a suggestion of marvel and mystery. A shiver of expectation crept over me when at last a bell rang three times, sudden silence fell upon the hall, and the curtain lifted. The stage scenery was arranged in perspective and the puppets were moved from above by wires.

The first play that I saw was "Die Schöne Genovefa." It was a splendid piece. The fair Genovefa is the wife of Count Siegfried. The count rides to the Holy Land to wrest the Holy Sepulchre from the infidels. He entrusts the countess and the castle to the care of his castellan Golo, in whom he reposes absolute confidence. Hardly has the count ridden away, when Golo conceives the plan of making himself master of the castle and of marrying the fair Genovefa. She repels him with disgust. The wicked Golo then locks her into a dark dungeon and orders his man-at-arms to kill her. This the servant promises to do, but moved by pity he leads her out of the dungeon into a great lonely forest after telling Golo that the murder has been accomplished. The fair Genovefa lives upon herbs and berries and finds shelter in a cave. Here she gives birth to a child, a boy, the son of Count Siegfried, whom she calls "Schmerzenreich"—dolorosus. Fearing that both she and the boy will starve to death, the poor mother fervently prays to God for help, and behold! a doe appears and provides them both with milk. Every day the doe returns and Schmerzenreich grows up to be a strong boy. Suddenly Count Siegfried arrives from the Holy Land to the dismay of the wicked Golo, who had been hoping that his master would be killed in the far-away country.

The castle folk at once recognize the count; Golo turns over the castle to him, and tells him that Genovefa is dead. The count is very sad. He goes into the forest to hunt, and happens to see a doe, which leads him to the cave. Husband and wife are reunited and the whole truth comes to light. Mother and child are taken back in triumph to the castle, and the horrid Golo is condemned to die of hunger in the same dungeon into which he had cast the fair Genovefa.

The puppet show had other plays, one—the great warrior-prince "Eugene"—a heroic drama in which great battles were fought and whole rows of paper Turks were shot down. And then a fairy play with every kind of marvelous transformation and other surprises. All these things were very pretty, but to my mind they could not be compared to the fair Genovefa. The impression that this play made upon me was simply overpowering. I wept hot tears at the leave-taking of Count Siegfried from his wife and even more over their reunion, and could hardly restrain a cry of delight when husband and wife returned to the castle and the wicked Golo met his well-deserved fate. I do not believe that ever in my life at a play was my imagination so active and the effect on my mind and emotions so direct and overwhelming. This doll with a plume on its hat was to me the real Count Siegfried; that one there with the red face and black beard the real treacherous Golo; this one with the white gown and the yellow hair the beautiful Genovefa, and the little red thing with the wriggling legs a real live doe. The impression was the same when I saw the play a second time. I knew the whole story and how it was to end; but when the count took leave of his wife and departed for the Holy Land I could hardly refrain from calling out to him not to go, for if he did, something terrible was sure to happen. How happy that naïve condition of childhood in which the imagination surrenders itself so unresistingly, without being in the least disturbed by the critical impulse!

But this faculty of naïve enjoyment received with me an early and a vicious shock. When I was about nine years old I saw for the first time live human beings on the stage in a play called "Hedwig, the Bandit Bride," by Körner. It was played in Brühl by a traveling company. The chief character, that of the villain Rudolph, was acted with all the teeth-gnashing grimaces customary on a little provincial stage. But as I still took this to be the genuine thing, it did not fail to make a strong impression, although not nearly as strong as that at the puppet-show when the fair Genovefa was played. I began to criticise, and this inclination received a tremendous impulse when in the company of my father I saw this "Bandit Bride" for the second time. In the last act, according to the text, Hedwig, the heroine, has to kill the villain by hitting him a vigorous blow on the head with the butt of a gun while he is crouching over a trapdoor. On the Brühl stage this, however, was changed: Hedwig was to shoot the villain instead of striking him. When the actress who played this part pointed her weapon and tried to fire, it refused to go off and gave only a faint click. The villain remained in his bent posture over the trapdoor, hoping every moment to be killed. Hedwig again pulled the trigger, but in vain. The poor woman looked around utterly helpless. In the audience there was the deepest silence of expectation. Then from behind the side-scene came the order, in that loud stage-whisper which can fill an entire house: "Bang him on the head with the butt; bang him quick!" Whereupon Hedwig with slow deliberation reversed the gun and struck the man who had been so patiently awaiting death a leisurely blow upon the head. He rolled over, the audience burst into uncontrollable shrieking laughter, in which the dead villain, lying upon the stage, could not refrain from joining. In the audience the merriment would not cease. But as for me, I would far rather have cried; the occurrence fairly stunned me. With it ended that complete surrender to illusion which had given me so much joy. It failed me, at least until I was fortunate enough to behold artistic performances of a higher order; and this happily came soon during my schooltime at the gymnasium in Cologne.

CHAPTER III

I WAS ten years old when my father took me to the gymnasium at Cologne, usually called the "Jesuit Gymnasium," although it had no connection with that religious order. In those days Cologne had about ninety thousand inhabitants, and was, as I supposed, one of the finest cities in the world. My grandfather had taken me there several years before on a visit, and well do I remember the two things that then interested me most: the cathedral tower with the huge crane on top, and the convict chain-gangs sweeping the streets—sinister-visaged fellows in clothes striped dark gray and yellow, with heavy iron chains on their feet that rattled and clanked dismally on the pavement stones, one or more soldiers standing guard close by, gun in hand. I remember also how my grandfather reproved me for taking off my cap to everybody whom we met in the streets, as was the custom in our little village at home; for he said there were so many people in Cologne that were one to attempt to bow to them all there would be no time left for anything else; that one could never become acquainted with all those persons, and many of them were not worth knowing; and finally, that such deference on my part would mark me at once as a country boy and make me appear ridiculous.

This "making myself ridiculous" was something I greatly dreaded, and I would have taken any pains to avoid it; yet it happened that my first appearance at the gymnasium was an occasion of amusement to others and of mortification to myself. In the schools at Liblar and Brühl we had been in the habit of using slates for our arithmetic and dictation exercises. Not dreaming that a slate was incompatible with the dignity of a ten-year-old pupil at the gymnasium, I carried mine under my arm into the class-room and thus unwittingly exposed myself to the scoffs and giggles of the boys, not one of whom I knew. There was a loud burst of laughter when one boy shouted: "Look at that fellow; he has got a slate!" I should have liked to reply to this remark with my fists, but just at that moment the instructor entered, and all was respectful silence.

My scale of living at Cologne was, of necessity, extremely modest. Board and lodging had been provided for me by my parents at the house of a locksmith. I slept in the same bed with the locksmith's son, who was also a mechanic, and took my meals at the family table with the journeymen and apprentices. Severe decorum was exacted of all; the master led the conversation, and only the foreman occasionally took part in it. I had no social intercourse whatever with persons of good education outside of school; but within school many helpful influences surrounded me.

At the present day the question "What should be the course of study in an educational institution of the rank of a gymnasium?" is being much discussed. This I shall return to later. But the question what the course of study should be seems to me by no means the only important, nor even the most important, one. What we learn in school is naturally but little, only a small portion of that which we have to learn for fruitful activity in after life. It is therefore of especial consequence that the things learned in school, whatever they may be, should be taught in such a manner as to awaken and encourage in the pupil the desire and enjoyment of learning more, and to enable him to seek and find for himself the means of further instruction, and to use them to the greatest possible advantage—in one word, that the pupil in school should learn how to learn. This requires not only appropriate methods of teaching, but also individual ability of the teacher to judge of the capacities of his pupil, to put those capacites into activity and to guide and inspire them. And just in these respects I was uncommonly fortunate in my years at the gymnasium.

The head master of the lowest class was, in my time, a young Westphalian, Heinrich Bone, whom I remember with especial gratitude. At a later period he became widely known as a teacher of exceptional ability. He instructed us not only in Latin, but also in German; and he strictly held to the principle that clearness and directness of expression are the fundamental requisites of a good style. Instead of wearying his pupils with dry grammatical rules, he gave them at once short compositions to write, not upon subjects like "The Beauty of Friendship," or "The Uses of Adversity," but simple descriptions of things actually seen—a house, a group of people, a picture, and the like. He required these compositions to be rendered in the simplest possible sentences, without any complication or ornament. The most important rule, however, which he enforced with especial emphasis was this: every noun, every adjective, every verb, must express some object or some quality, or some act perceptible to the senses. All that was vague or abstract or not perceptible to the senses was at first severely forbidden. In this manner he accustomed his pupils to see clearly whatever was before their eyes, and then to set forth the impression received in words so concise and clear-cut that their meaning was unmistakable.

When we had attained a certain degree of efficiency in this very simple exercise, we were allowed to enlarge the form of our sentences, but only for the purpose of presenting more clearly and fully some vivid picture. Thus we were led step by step to the construction of some complicated periods. Narrative compositions followed the descriptive ones, the teacher's requirement still being the utmost clearness of expression; and not until the pupil had proved himself competent to grasp and to present the actual, the sensually perceptible, was he permitted to indulge in abstractions and reflections. This method taught us not only to form correct sentences, but to exercise the faculty of correct observation, which, strange to say, is developed in a comparatively small number of people.

The fundamental idea underlying this method, applicable to all instruction, is that the principal aim of teaching should be to fit, equip and stimulate the mind of the scholar with a view to independent action. Herein lies the secret of all successful mental education. This is the way to learn how to learn. To be sure, the pursuit of this method demands teachers of ability and thorough training, to whom their calling is something more than a mere routine business.

I count it among the special favors of fortune in my life that such a man as Professor Bone continued to be my principal teacher in the three lowest classes of the gymnasium. The instruction I received from him in the class room was supplemented by frequent private conversations, for I was among those favored with his personal friendship. My first little composition attracted his attention and won his approval. I vividly remember my proud satisfaction when once he read one of my writings to the class. He invited me to visit him in his quarters. At that time he was occupied in compiling a reader, to be used at the higher institutions of instruction, and for this book he himself wrote a series of little descriptions and stories, as illustrations of his method. Several of them he read to me and asked me, probably to assure himself of the impression made upon the simple mind of a pupil, to criticise them, which privilege I exercised with frankness. He did me the honor of putting two or three of my little compositions, without essential change, into his book, as examples of his rules faithfully followed. From the thirty-fifth edition of Bone's "Lesebuch," received by me from Germany some years ago, I will quote one of them as illustrating the principles fixed by him for the beginner. It is a "Hunting Scene."

"The mountains and meadows were covered with glistening snow. The sky shone red with the rising of dawn. I saw three huntsmen standing under a tall oak. The large branches on the tree bore a heavy weight of snow; the small twigs sparkled with icicles. The huntsmen were clad in light green jackets, adorned wth shining buttons. At their feet lay a large stag; its red blood colored the white snow. Three brown dogs stood beside the dead body, their tongues hanging quivering out of their mouths."

In turning the pages of this reader, many delightful evening hours passed with my teacher arise in my memory. In many of those conversations he sought to guide my reading and especially to make me acquainted with the beauty of old German poetry. He also encouraged me to read historical works. I possessed Becker's Universal History. This I read from beginning to end, and reread what had especially interested me. Through the extracts given in Becker's work I first became acquainted with Homer. Those extracts in fluent prose stimulated my desire to learn more of that poet so much that I procured the translation of the "Iliad" and the "Odyssey," by Johann Heinrich Voss. Never until then, and I believe never since, has poetry moved me so tremendously as in the great passages describing Hector's leave-taking from Andromache at the city gate, when the hero lifts little Astyanax upon his arm and invokes the gods for him; or the prostration of old King Priam in the tent of Achilles as he implores the cruel victor for the dead body of his heroic son; or the meeting of Odysseus and Nausikaa, and the departure of the god-like sufferer from the house of the Phaiakian king, when Nausikaa, sad and bashful, hides behind a column and gazes after the departing stranger; or, after the terrible battle with the suitors, the meeting of Odysseus with the faithful Penelope, or the scene where the returning hero reveals himself in the garden to his old, sorrow-stricken father, Laertes. The reason why these scenes moved me so much more deeply than the descriptions of the battles in the "Iliad" and the fabulous adventures in the "Odyssey," although these, too, were most fascinating, I only learned to appreciate later; it is because they touch within us the purely human feeling which depends neither on time nor place; which is neither ancient nor modern, but universal and eternal.

After reading Homer in translation I began to long impatiently for the study of Greek, and the ease with which I acquired that language afterwards, was undoubtedly due to my desire to meet Homer in the full beauty of the original form.

Of course I was early introduced to the kings and to the republican heroes and sages of Roman history, and learned, through my own experience, to appreciate how greatly the study of a language is facilitated by studying the history of the country to which it belongs. This applies to ancient tongues as well as to modern. When the student ceases to look upon the book which he is translating as a mere pile of words to be brought into accord with certain rules of grammar; when that which the author says stimulates him to scrutinize the true meaning, relation and connection of the forms of expression and the eager desire to learn more of the story or the argument urges him on from line to line, and from page to page, then grammar becomes to him a welcome aid, and not a mere drudgery, and he acquires the language almost without knowing how.

I fully experienced this when under Bone's guidance I read Cornelius Nepos and Cæsar's Gallic wars, and still more in translating Cicero's Orations. Most of these appear to the student at first rather difficult. But if he begins each time by examining the circumstances under which the oration was delivered, the purpose it was to serve, the points upon which special stress was to be laid, and the personalities which were involved in the proceeding, he will be imperceptibly hurried along by the desire to discover with what representations and arguments, what attacks and defenses, what appeals to reason, honor, or passion, the orator has sought to carry his cause, and the quickened interest in the subject will soon overcome all the linguistic difficulties. I remember that, so stimulated, I usually exceeded in my translations the task set to me for the next recitation, and, besides, by this zealous reading a sense was created for what I may call the music of the language, which later greatly helped me in the idiomatic construction of my Latin compositions.

Professor Bone ceased only too soon to be my teacher, for his extraordinary capacities attracted wide attention outside of the gymnasium, and he received a call to undertake the directorship of an educational institution founded by some Rhenish noblemen for the education of their sons. He left the gymnasium in compliance with this call. I did not see him again for many years. When traveling in 1888 through Germany I heard from an old school fellow that Bone, in failing health, had retired to Wiesbaden. I resolved at once to seek him out.

I found him living in a very modest house, the interior of which looked almost like a convent—for Bone had always been a devout and strict Roman Catholic. An elderly nun-like person ushered me into a small parlor hung with pictures of saints and adorned with crucifixes. She carried my card into an adjoining room, from which instantly issued a cry of delight; and the next moment, dragging himself hurriedly along, my good old teacher appeared. Time had changed him from a vigorous young man into a shriveled, fragile little body, clad in a long dressing gown, his feet in large gray felt slippers, and a black skull-cap covering his thin white hair. We embraced, and the dear old man seemed beside himself with joy.

"There, I knew I was right," he exclaimed: "I heard that you had come to Germany, and I was sure that if you went to see the great people in Berlin you would certainly also come to see me. I recognized your voice at the front door; yes, yes, I knew it at once, although I have not heard it for more than forty years."

We sat down close together, and there was much asking and answering of questions. His eyes shone with pleasure when I told him that I had sent to Germany for the latest edition of his reader; that I had often explained to my children and friends the method by which he taught me how to write German, whereupon he reminded me of our evenings in Cologne and how he had liked me as a boy, and so forth. Thus a few delightful hours slipped by. When finally I rose to go, he exclaimed:

"What, not going already! We must have a glass of wine together. Good heavens! there isn't a drop of wine in the house. What shall I do?"

Then he added, thoughtfully:

"I have some excellent stomach bitters; shall we drink one another's health in bitters?"

I was quite content. The bottle was taken from the cupboard, the black liquor poured out, we drank one another's health in stomach bitters, and the glasses rang. Another embrace, and we parted never to meet again.

But to return to my school days. The quiet life of the first years in Cologne was not without its excitements. Two occurrences of this time made a deep impression upon me. My daily walk to school led past the great Cathedral, which, now in its finished state the admiration of the world, looked in those days much like a magnificent ruin. Only the choir had been nearly finished. The great central part between the choir and the towers stood under a temporary roof and was built partly of brick. One of the two towers was not more than some sixty feet above the ground, while the other, surmounted by the famous century-old crane, had reached perhaps three or four times that height. The tooth of time had gnawed the medieval sculptures on the walls and arches and turrets, and the whole hoary pile, still unfinished, yet decaying, looked down, sad and worn, upon the living generation at its feet.

One morning when I was wending my accustomed way to school I saw fall from the top of the crane tower an object which looked like a cloak, and from which in its descent something detached itself and floated away in the breeze. The cloak shot straight down and struck with a heavy thud upon the stone pavement below. The passers-by ran to the spot; the cloak proved to contain a man, who, without doubt, had sought his death by jumping down. He had fallen upon his feet, and lay there in a little heap; the bones of the legs had been pressed into the body; the head, encircled by a fringe of gray hair, was much disfigured; the face, pale and distorted, was that of an elderly man. The object which had floated away in falling proved to be a wig. When the winds had played with it for a while it settled down quietly beside its dead owner.

This shocking spectacle filled my mind with uncanny imaginings. I made every effort to discover who the unfortunate man was, and what the cause could have been to drive him to such desperation; but all rumors were uncertain and contradictory. Then fancy conjured up to my mind all possible turns of fortune and conditions of life which could drive a human being into self destruction—hopeless poverty; lost honor; disappointed affections; torments of conscience—and soon my head was filled with plots of stories or tragedies, all of which ended with the self-destructive plunge from the cathedral tower.

Another tragic scene which agitated my mind in a similar way is photographed upon my memory. A young man in Cologne had murdered his sweetheart and been condemned to death. The execution, by the guillotine—for the left bank of the Rhine was still under the "Code Napoleon"—was to take place at dawn of day on a public square between the Cathedral and the Rhine, and before the eyes of all who might choose to witness it. The trial had excited the whole population to a high degree; now the people looked forward to the final catastrophe with almost morbid interest. My locksmith guardian was of the opinion that neither he nor I should miss the opportunity of beholding so rare a spectacle. Long before sunrise he awoke me, and together we went to the place of execution in the gray morning light. We found there a dense crowd, numbering thousands, of men, women and children; above them loomed the black scaffold of the death machine. Deep silence reigned; only a low buzz floated over the multitude when the condemned man appeared on the scaffold, and then all was silence again. My sturdy locksmith held me up in his arms, so that I might look over the heads of the crowds in front. The unfortunate culprit stepped forward; the assistant of the executioner strapped him to a board which extended from his feet to his shoulders, leaving his neck free; the victim glanced up at the ax, suspended from a cross beam; the next instant he was pushed down so that his neck lay under the gleaming blade; the ax fell like a flash of lightning, severing the head from the shoulders at a whisk. A stream of blood spurted into the air, but the hideous sight was quickly concealed from the gaze of the public by a dark cloth. The whole deed was done with the rapidity of thought. One scarcely became conscious of the terrible shock before it was over. A dull murmur arose from the onlooking throngs, after which they silently dispersed; the scaffold was taken down and the blood on the ground covered with sand before the first rays of the morning sun shone brightly upon the Cathedral towers. I remember walking home shuddering and trembling, and finding it impossible to eat my breakfast. Nothing could have induced me to witness another execution.

The good locksmith was an enthusiastic play-goer, and allowed me sometimes to accompany him to the theater—to be sure only on the topmost gallery, where a seat cost five groschen (twelve and a half cents). The theater of Cologne occupied, as I learned later, in the world of art a very respectable place. To me it was a dream of the marvelous and magnificent. I was beside myself with astonished delight when, for the first time, I saw, before the lifting of the curtain, the painted ceiling over the auditorium part in the middle and through this mysterious opening a brilliantly lighted chandelier slowly descend, the ceiling thereupon closing again. The performances I witnessed also moved me powerfully.

Indeed I did not follow them with the same naïve illusions with which I had lived through the adventures of the fair Genovefa; but what I saw in the theater in Cologne was on so much higher a level that I could surrender myself again to full enjoyment. Thus I saw one or two knight dramas, popular at the time; also "Wallenstein." These pleasures did not come in rapid succession, for frequent visits to the theater could hardly have accorded with the principle of economy that governed my locksmith as well as myself. But the drama took profound hold upon me, and what I saw of it created an almost irresistible desire to write a play myself. I searched through Beckers' Universal History for a good subject, and finally fell upon the Anglo-Saxon King Edwy, who ruled in England in the middle of the tenth century and who brought upon himself, through his love for the beautiful Elgiva, a struggle with Saint Dunstan, and an unhappy fate. It seemed to me that if I took some liberties with history, as dramatic poets not seldom do, this subject—a royal lover battling with the power of the church—might be capable of being worked up into a fine tragedy. Of course the play as I wrote it amounted to nothing; but in weaving the plot through successive scenes, and in writing out some of the dialogues, I enjoyed the full bliss of literary creation. Never to have tasted this delight is never to have known one of the greatest joys of life.

Lyric poems and ballads also figured among my "early works." One of my ballads originated in this wise: Under a clump of tall trees not far from the castle at Liblar were some crumbled ruins of masonry that had an uncanny look. Nobody seemed to know their history. Imagination pictured to me a variety of possibilities, out of which I wove a romantic tale. The Knights of the Gracht had on this spot kept wild animals in a big pit. A beautiful maiden had somehow got into this pit and had been rescued by a noble youth after a heroic fight with the monstrous beasts. This adventure, not very original to be sure, I worked up in pompous eight-line stanzas, the sound of which delighted me so much that I could not refrain from sending a copy of my poem to my father. He, even prouder of it than I, hastened to show the verses to Count Metternich. The count, who probably took little interest in any kind of poetry, pronounced them fine, but said that he had never heard of this occurrence as a part of his family history—which did not surprise me in the least.

At prose, too, I tried my hand. Once, after having written a composition on " Schiller's Maid of Orleans," which struck me as especially good, I found it difficult to resist the ambitious desire of seeing myself in print. I made a clean copy of the composition and carried it to the office of the *Cologne Gazette,* with a letter addressed to Levin Schücking, a well-known novelist of the time, and the literary editor of that great journal. In my letter I begged the privilege of a personal interview. A courteous answer fixed the day and hour of my visit, and soon I stood, with loud heart-beats, at the great man's door, who, so I believed, held my literary future in the hollow of his hand. I found in him an amiable gentleman, with pleasant features, and large, blue, benevolent eyes. He received me very kindly, talked upon a variety of subjects and finally returned my manuscript to me with the remark that it contained much that was excellent, but that I would do well to regard it only as a " study." I departed completely crushed with disappointment and mortification; but after all I lived to become sincerely grateful to good Mr. Schücking for his timely counsel. Much that I have since written has, in pursuance of his sound advice, been quietly treated as a " study " by myself.

When I had reached the "Tertia" of the gymnasium, fortune favored me again by bringing me into close relations with another admirable instructor, Professor Pütz, who had become distinguished as the compiler of excellent historical text-books. He could not boast of great historical researches made by himself, but he possessed a rare skill in exciting the interest of the pupils in the subjects of instruction, and in pointing out the way to further studies. His method of teaching history was to devote the greater part of the hour to a presentation, in free speech, of the particular period with which he wished to make us familiar. He enlivened his subject by exhibiting it in a variety of lights and by adding sufficient detail to make his lecture not only instructive, but also dramatic and picturesque, and thus easily remembered.

In the next lesson the pupils were expected, whenever called upon, to reproduce, out of themselves, in their own language, what they had learned in the previous lessons, the short recitals of the hand-book serving as a framework to the historical structure. From time to time the professor would deliver a comprehensive discourse, grouping together the events of certain historic periods, and thus giving us bird's-eye views over wide fields. In this way history was impressed upon our memory as well as our understanding, not in the form of tabulated statements or columns of figures, nor merely by means of anecdotes, but in panoramic views and prospects full of life and philosophical light. To me, the class lesson and the study connected with it, for which I had always an especial liking, became, instead of hard, dry labor, a genuine joy which could not repeat itself too often. It was largely owing to these methods of instruction that, when a few years later at my final examination Professor Pütz asked me whether I thought I could from my memory describe the conquests of

Alexander the Great and draw a map thereof on the blackboard, I felt myself able to undertake the task, and accomplished it satisfactorily.

Soon after I had become his pupil Professor Pütz drew me nearer to him, and something like relations of confidential friendship grew up between us. He had traveled much during his long vacations, had seen many foreign countries and made acquaintance with many remarkable personalities. Thus he had widened his mental horizon beyond the limits of that of the ordinary teacher of the gymnasium. There was something cosmopolitan in his conceptions, and in regard to theological, as well as political things, he passed for a man of advanced ideas.

In addition to history, he also taught us German composition, and as in my writings he discovered something akin to his own views, he treated me almost like a young comrade, whom he permitted in his presence to forget the schoolboy for the moment. He liked to tell me about his travels and about the social and political institutions and affairs of the world; and when our conversation turned upon church and state, he talked not seldom with a certain touch of irony, which was to make me understand that in his opinion many things ought to be different from what they were. He also encouraged expressions of opinion on my part, and it gave him pleasure to see that I had thought of this and that which was not just within the circle of a schoolboy's ideas; and when, so encouraged, I gave expression to my boyish criticisms of existing conditions, he would sometimes listen with an approving smile, at the same time remarking that we might talk unreservedly between ourselves, but that it would be advisable for us to be more circumspect in conversation with others.

In other ways also he enlarged my horizon. From his

private library he lent me several volumes of Goethe and of works of writers of more recent times. Even foreign literatures he opened to me; he gave me, for instance, the translations of Shakespeare by Schlegel and Tieck, which I devoured with avidity, and he made me acquainted with Cervantes and Calderon. He also taught me some Italian, and read with me the "Prisons" of Silvio Pellico in the original, and parts of Tasso and Ariosto in translation. Thus he disclosed to me a new world; and I think of him with gratitude, as one of the benefactors of my youth. It was a great pleasure to me to meet Professor Pütz again in later life. It must have been in 1873, when I was a member of the Senate of the United States, that I received one day, by European mail, a package containing a letter from Professor Pütz, with some printed pages. "I have frequently corrected your tasks," he wrote, "and now you have to correct mine." Then he informed me that he was preparing a new edition of his historical handbooks, and wished to have my judgment about that part which treated of the latest events in America. And this he laid before me on the proofsheets that accompanied the letter. With pleasure I complied with his request, and found his work so correct in every detail that it did not call for the slightest amendment. On my next journey to Germany I sought him out in Cologne. He had retired from his office, and lived in comfortable surroundings. I found him, to be sure, very much aged, but still young in spirit. Our meeting was a hearty joy to us both, and we celebrated it with a delightful supper.

When I entered the higher classes of the gymnasium the influence of youthful friendship came powerfully into my life. I gave up my quarters at the locksmith's because there was no piano there for daily practice, and moved into more suitable lodgings. It now became possible for me to receive visitors and to lead a somewhat freer life. Among my schoolmates I always had friends of my own age, but none whose endeavors and ambitions accorded much with my own tastes. Now I became acquainted with a circle of youths who, like myself, wrote verses, and read them, and encouraged each other in the study of literature. The two with whom I came into closest intimacy were Theodore Petrasch, the son of a secretary of the provincial government, and Ludwig von Weise, a descendant of a patrician family of Cologne. Petrasch was an uncommonly bright youth of a most amiable, cheerful and exuberant nature. Weise, while possessing excellent abilities and a strong character, had developed rather the critical than the productive faculties of his mind. Both discussed political, as well as religious, subjects with far more freedom and assurance than I had dared to do, and their liberal utterances had already attracted the notice of the gymnasium authorities. Petrasch had been called to account by the instructor of religion and had made certain heretical confessions with such frankness that the shocked schoolmaster suspended him from all religious observances until a new light should break in upon him, and he invited him to further talks upon sacred subjects.

To me, questions of religious faith had for some time caused many hours of most serious reflection. I have already narrated how in earliest childhood my belief in the everlasting punishment of the heterodox, and in the infallibility and moral perfection of the priesthood, had been severely shaken. Since then I had pondered much upon kindred subjects, and the time had now come for me to be "confirmed." In preparation for this rite, the Roman Catholic priest, our instructor, especially indoctrinated us in the tenets of the church. I threw myself into this study with an earnest desire to overcome all doubts. It even seemed to me at times that this had been accomplished, and I went through the act of the "First Communion" in a state of religious exaltation. But very soon the old scruples and doubts returned stronger than before. What was most repugnant to me was the claim of the church to be not merely the only true church, but also the only saving one, and that there was absolutely no hope of salvation outside of its pale, but only damnation and eternal hell-fire. That Socrates and Plato; that all the virtuous men among the heathen; that even my old friend, the Jew, Aaron; nay, that even the new-born babe, if it happened to die unbaptized, must forever burn in unquenchable fire—yes, that I too, were I so much as to harbor the slightest doubt concerning their terrible fate, must also be counted among the eternally lost—against such ideas rebelled not only my reason, but my innermost instinct of justice. Such teachings seemed to me so directly to contradict the most essential attributes of the all-just Deity, that they only served to make me suspicious of other tenets of the creed. High authorities in the church have indeed not maintained teachings so extreme, but assigned to unbaptized, innocent infants and to virtuous heathen after death a mysterious state intermediate between heaven and hell. Yet certain it is that the religious teachings of my youth held to the immoderate tenets I have described, thus enforcing with a rude and relentless logic the dogma of original sin and the necessity of infant baptism. What a blessing it would have been to the church and to all within reach of its influence, if, not only some, but all of its teachers had opened its whole heaven, with the full countenance of God, not only to its believers, but to all innocent and virtuous human souls.

I was distressed beyond measure. Often I prayed fervently for light, but in answer to my prayers only the old doubts came back. I went to my teacher of religion and confided to him the condition of my mind with perfect frankness. We had a series of conversations, in which, however, he had little to say to me that I had not heard before. I confessed to him with the utmost candor, that while I should be glad to be convinced by what he said, he had not so convinced me; whereupon I also was relieved of the obligation of attending religious observances until I myself felt an urgent desire to resume them. I zealously studied ecclesiastical history and dogmatic writings, and availed myself of every opportunity to listen to preachers of renown; but the longer and more earnestly I continued those studies the less could I find my way back to the articles of faith which were so repugnant to my sense of justice. There remained, however, within me a strong religious want, a profound respect for religious thought. I have never been able to listen to a light-minded scoffer about religious subjects without great repugnance.

While my friends could not tell me much that was soothing on religious topics, they opened to me vistas in German literature—especially the political part of it—which were new and fascinating. Of Heine, my teacher, Professor Pütz, had told me, but I knew of him little more than his name; of Freiligrath, only a few of his pictures of the tropics; of Gutzkow, Laube, Herwegh, and so on, nothing at all.

Petrasch lent me Heine's "Book of Songs." This was to me like a revelation. I felt almost as if I had never before read a lyric poem; and yet many of Heine's songs sounded to me as if I had always known them, as if the fairies had sung them to me at my cradle. All the verses that I myself had written until then, and which were mostly of the declamatory kind, went at once into the fire, and I saw them burn with genuine relief. The reading and the rereading of the "Book of Songs" was to me an indescribable revelry. Then I read the pictures of travel, the various political poems, and "Atta Troll," with its acrid political satire, the wit of which did not do good to the heart, but sharply turned one's thoughts upon the condition of the fatherland. I read also with my friends the poems of such revolutionary stormers as Herwegh, Hoffmann von Fallersleben and others, most of which we possessed and circulated among us only in written copies.

The revolutionary passions expressed in many of those poems were in fact foreign to us, but their attacks upon the existing governments, especially upon the Prussian, struck a responsive chord which easily reverberated in the breast of every Rhinelander. Our Rhine country, with its gay, light-hearted people, had, within a comparatively short period, passed through a series of multi-colored experiences. Before the time of the French Revolution it had been under the easy-going, loose rule of the Archbishop Electors; then, conquered and seized by the French, it belonged for a time to the French Republic and the Empire. At last, after the French wars, it was annexed to Prussia. Of these three rulerships, following one another in too rapid succession for any sentiments of allegiance to take firm root, the Rhine folk liked the Prussian rule the least, although it was undoubtedly the best. The abrupt, stiff, exacting character of Prussian officialdom, with its rigid conceptions of duty and order, was uncongenial to the careless and somewhat too pleasure-loving Rhenish people. Besides, the population was throughout Roman Catholic, and the word Prussian was synonymous with Protestantism. Prussian officers in considerable numbers came to help govern the Rhine people, which of course created bad blood. All these things made Prussian rule on the Rhine appear like a sort of foreign rule, which was very repugnant to the feelings of the natives. In the course of time they recognized that the honest, orderly methods of administration by the Prussian officers possessed great merit; but the spirit of opposition, characteristic of the Rhenish population, once aroused, could not be easily overcome. The word Prussian served for an opprobrious invective, and when one schoolboy flung it at another it was difficult to find a more stinging epithet to fling back. All this was to become entirely changed in consequence of the revolutionary movement toward national unity in 1848; but at the time when I was a student at the gymnasium the hatred of Prussia was still in fullest flower on the banks of the Rhine.

We young people were indeed free from provincial, and especially religious, narrowness of sentiment, but we shared the prevailing impression that great changes were necessary; that it was scandalous to withhold from the people the freedom of speech and press; that the old Prussian absolutism must yield to a new constitutional form of government; that the pledges made to the German nation by the German princes in 1813 had been shamefully violated, and that the disintegrated fatherland must be molded into a united empire with free political institutions. The fermenting restless spirit permeating the minds of the educated classes, and finding expression in the literature of the day, aroused in us boys the warmest enthusiasm. By what means the dreams of liberty and unity were to be accomplished—whether, as Herwegh advised in one of his poems, which we all knew by heart, we were to tear the iron crucifixes out of the ground and forge them into swords, or whether there was a peaceable way of reaching the goal—we were not at all clear in our thoughts. But we eagerly read newspapers and pamphlets to keep ourselves informed of the occurrences and tendencies of the day. Neither could we altogether refrain from occasionally uttering our sentiments. I was in the Upper Secunda when our professor of German —it was no longer my friend Pütz—gave us, as the subject of a composition, a memorial oration on the battle of Leipzig. Believing it to be my duty to write exactly what I thought about that event, I expressed with entire frankness my feelings about the ill-treatment the German people had suffered after their heroic efforts on that battlefield, and my hope of a complete regeneration of the German fatherland. I was profoundly in earnest. I wrote that memorial oration, so to speak, with my heart's blood. When the professor, at one of the next lessons, returned the papers to us in the class room, with critical remarks, he handed mine to me in silence. It bore this footnote: "Style good; but views expressed nebulous and dangerous." After the adjournment of the class he called me to his side, put his hand upon my shoulder and said, "What you wrote has a fine sound; but how can such things be allowed at a royal Prussian gymnasium? Take care that it does not happen again." From that time on he refrained from giving subjects to the class which might tempt us to political discussion.

In the meantime I continued zealously my literary studies, and my creative impulses were constantly stimulated by the applause of intimate friends. I wrote a large number of short poems, and also some tragedies on historic subjects. No record of these sins of my youth have remained in existence to embitter my subsequent life—or perhaps also to contribute to its merriment. We are easily ashamed of our premature productions and of the sublime conceit that must have inspired them. But I cannot look back without a certain feeling of tender emotion upon the time when I surrendered myself to those poetic impulses with the hope, certainly with the desire, to give in the course of time, to my fatherland, something valuable and lasting.

It is needless to say that these literary efforts absorbed much of the time that should have been devoted to other studies. In the first years at the gymnasium I had always received, in the semi-annual examinations, the highest marks. I sacrificed these to my literary work, inasmuch as in some branches of instruction, especially in mathematics and natural science, I did only what was rigorously exacted of me.

My life outside of school was simple in the extreme and afforded me every opportunity to practise the virtue of frugality. My pocket-money allowance was very small; sometimes I had none at all; neither can I remember ever to have asked my parents for any money. They thought of it themselves and put a pittance into my pocket when, after my vacation, I returned to Cologne, or when they visited me there. Frequently I managed to get along for weeks with the sum of five groschen (twelve and a half cents). The occasional possession of a thaler (seventy-two cents) gave me the sensation of wealth. Even when I had nothing, which sometimes happened, I never felt poor. This mental habit, acquired early in life without much reflection, has subsequently proved of great value to me. It has spared me much heart-burning. I have always had to associate with persons possessing more than myself of the so-called good things of life—persons that could allow themselves many enjoyments that I had to do without. To this I accustomed myself, and I did it without the slightest self-depreciation or envy. Among all human passions envy is the one that makes a man the most miserable. Of course I do not mean by envy the mere wish to possess desirable things which we see others possessing, for such wishes are legitimate and not foreign to the noblest ambition. The envy I speak of is that jealous ill-will which begrudges others what they possess, and which would destroy their enjoyment of it. A long life has convinced me that the truest and most beautiful happiness of the human soul consists in the joyous contemplation of the happiness of others. The envious, consciously or unconsciously, wish to deprive others of that which makes them happy; and this is, of all imaginable dispositions of the mind and heart, the most wretched. Education can render young people no better service than to teach them how to make their pleasures independent of money. This is far easier than we commonly suppose. It requires only that we learn to appreciate the various good things which cost nothing and some of which are offered by almost every environment. In this way we discover how many enjoyments there are in life which usually remain hidden to those who are in the habit of purchasing their pleasures with silver and gold.

Although during my boyhood my means were extremely limited, my opportunities for enjoyment, even in æsthetic directions, were by no means few. I have already told how I went to the theater, not very often, but finding all the more pleasure in it the few times I could go. There were other opportunities no less valuable. On Sunday mornings sometimes I spent hours in the Walraff Gallery, some rooms of which were filled with pictures of the old Cologne school. Although I was then unable to appreciate their historic and artistic value, they attracted me greatly by their splendor of color and naïveté of composition. Particularly I recall a "Last Judgment," in which the humorous grimaces and sardonic smiles of a number of fantastic red, blue, and green devils amused me immensely. For many an hour I stood in dreamy contemplation before the "Sorrowing Jews on the Waters of Babylon," by Bendemann, a celebrated painter of the Düsseldorf school. As is usual, the boy in me was first fascinated by the subject of the picture, until repeated scrutiny gradually stirred my critical faculty and developed my taste as to composition and execution.

Nor were opportunities for musical delight wanting. On Sunday morning the so-called "Musical Mass" was celebrated in the cathedral, at which frequently the archbishop officiated and the church displayed its splendor. The principal charm of the service was the music, which attracted not alone the devout, but also the art-loving public. A full orchestra and a choir of selected voices rendered a Mass by some celebrated composer. These performances were sometimes of singularly marvelous effect. I have already mentioned that the cathedral at that period resembled a ruin as to its exterior. This was also true in great measure of the inside. Upon passing through the timeworn portals into the middle nave one was confronted at a distance, just beyond the transept, by a bare, gray wall shutting off the choir from the rest of the cathedral; this was the back of the great organ, placed temporarily in this position because the choir was the only really completed portion of the edifice. The organ therefore stood, so to speak, with its back to the larger part of the church. On the platform in front of the organ, facing the choir, were placed the orchestra and the singers. Thus the people standing in that part of the church between the back of the organ and the portals heard the music not directly, but as an echo wonderfully broken. The forest of pillars and the arches high as heaven, carried it back as from a far distance, aye, as from another world. It was a mysterious waving and weaving and surging and rolling of sound; the violins and 'cellos, and flutes and oboes, like the whispering and sighing of the spring winds in the treetops; the trumpets and trombones and the mighty chorus now and then like the roaring of the storm and the raging of the sea. Sometimes the echoes seemed to be silent for a moment and a melody or a succession of harmonies would ring clear through the immense space; or a soprano solo would detach itself from the magic confusion and float upon the air like an angel's voice. The effect was indescribably touching, and I remember how, not seldom, I stood leaning against one of the gigantic columns and something like devout tremors passed over me, and my eyes filled with tears. This, I thought, must be what I had heard called the "Music of the Spheres," or the "Concert of the Children of Heaven," as I had seen depicted on the old canvases of the Walraff Museum.

Sunday noon afforded still another treat. A part of the garrison paraded on the Neumarkt, and its excellent band played martial strains for the changing guard, afterwards entertaining the public with a well-selected programme. Their repertoire being large, these military concerts helped not a little to increase my musical knowledge.

The talks with my much traveled friend, Professor Pütz, together with books on architecture lent by him, excited in me an interest in ancient and mediæval architecture, and many happy hours were spent in studying the middle-age structures of religious and secular character of which Cologne is justly proud. My artistic studies were therefore by no means inconsiderable, although I had to confine myself to such as were accessible without cost.

Free afternoons were usually passed with my friends. Besides reading aloud, we philosophised together on everything above and below with that gravity characteristic of young, ardent and somewhat precocious persons. Sometimes I went to my uncle's house at Lind, a half-hour's walk from Cologne, to visit two cousins of about my own age. They were dear comrades. As they were not to prepare themselves for any learned profession, but were to be farmers, like their father, I had not so many interests in common with them as with my other friends; but they were boys of mental activity, excellent disposition and chivalrous spirits, and we amused ourselves together to our hearts' content. When the weather was bad we now and then resorted to a game of cards. And here, in order to be entirely faithful to truth, I must mention an occurrence which will prove that my youth was by no means free from serious blemish.

At first we played cards merely for the sake of passing time. Then as the taste for it grew, we staked small sums of money to increase the interest and excitement, which it did most effectually. The stakes were very small indeed, but the changing fortune in winning and losing stimulated the gambling passion until finally a catastrophe occurred. One particular afternoon I happened to have the money in my pocket with which to pay my tuition fees, which were due in a few days. I lost steadily in the game and was so carried away that at last I took out of my pocket the money entrusted to me by my parents. Of course, with it I expected to win back all that I had lost. We played on feverishly, but luck would not turn, and at last the entire sum of the tuition fee was swept away. It amounted only to a very few thalers, and my cousins helped me out of my immediate embarrassment; but my horror at what had happened was so great, my consciousness of guilt so painful, and the sense of mortification so acute—for I considered myself, and with reason, to be a criminal—that the inward suffering of those days, especially when I made a confession to my parents, has ever remained in my memory as a terrible lesson. I had gone through a very serious experience with myself. In playing for stakes the desire to win money had really not been my impelling motive, but the evil fascination which the demon of fortune always possesses had led me to commit an act which, committed under less favorable circumstances, and upon a larger scale, might have ruined my character irretrievably. Card-playing for money is often classed among the aristocratic passions; but I believe there is no form of amusement which, when it becomes a real passion, is so dangerous even to nobly cast natures. It was perhaps very fortunate in my own case that this lesson came so early in life and appeared in so drastic a shape.

Gay days we had during our summer vacations at home in Liblar. A crowd of cousins from various places found themselves together, reinforced by friends from Cologne. That was the time for merry pranks, which, as it seemed, gave as much pleasure to the old members of the family as to the young. One occurrence of my vacation life has remained especially vivid in memory. In a German village the "studying" boy, as he is called, is always regarded with interest and wonder, and upon the occasion of his visits family and friends are apt to take a pardonable pride in displaying his attainments. So it was with me. My father, who could not produce much effect upon his villagers with my Latin and Greek, took great delight in showing off my musical proficiency, especially my ability to improvise. He succeeded in persuading the old organist, a feeble musician, but one free from all artistic jealousy, to allow me to play a voluntary at the Sunday morning service. Once on a festive day when Count Metternich and his family occupied their private chapel attached to the church, and the congregation happened to be exceptionally large, I felt it incumbent upon me to do something extraordinary. So at the close of the mass I pulled out all the stops and played a military march that I had heard at one of the parades at Cologne with such effect that the departing congregation stood still in astonishment. Even the count stepped out from his chapel to see what was the matter. This was the climax of my musical career as an organist, which soon came to an abrupt end. One Sunday at vesper service I accompanied the choir, consisting of the sacristan and four other singers. It was the organist's custom to play a short interlude between the alternate verses of the hymn. This gave me an opportunity to give my faculty of improvising full swing. Beginning in the key in which the hymn was being sung, I moved up a tierce, intending to return to the original key by means of a bold transition. But the sacristan and the choir were not accustomed to such antics. They resumed their song in the higher key, shrieking themselves red in the face until the veins of their foreheads and temples threatened to burst. At the close of the service the sacristan declared with unmistakable emphasis that he would have no more improvising and thorough bass; that this nonsense must stop, and that for his part he liked the old organist far the better of the two. Thus was my glory as a performer on the organ in Liblar forever gone.

In another field an ambitious wish of mine found its fulfillment. I became a member of the Sanct Sebastianus Society, and resolved to take part in the annual bird-shooting. Having learned very early how to handle a rifle, I had myself inscribed in the list, and offered to several members, male and female, to shoot for them; and the offers were accepted. The casting of bullets on the Saturady before Whitsuntide was one of the most solemn acts of my life; and when I woke with sunrise on Whitsun Monday I felt as if for me a day of great decision had dawned. I have already described the different features of that popular festival. With profound seriousness on this occasion I marched behind the old bow-legged drummer and the master-tailor, our color-bearer, in the ranks of the marksmen to what my heroic enthusiasm called "the field of honor"; and when, after marching three times around the tree bearing the pole with the wooden bird, we knelt down for prayer I was one of the most devout. Not one of my first shots missed. The bow-legged drummer rewarded me with the customary roll, and I suspect I sometimes looked around with eyes that sought admiration. Only one shot more was mine, but the wooden bird was already much splintered, and with every moment it became more uncertain whether my last chance would yet be reached. My heart beat high; my last turn was really reached, and on the top of the pole there was only a little strip of wood left which a well-aimed bullet would surely bring down. I raised the rifle to my shoulder with the feeling as if this shot would determine the current of my future. With a mighty effort I kept cool, so that my eye should be clear and my hand firm. But when I had pressed the trigger I felt myself as if in a dense fog; I only heard how the drummer furiously belabored his instrument and how the surrounding multitude shouted. The great deed, therefore, was done. I had "shot down the bird." I was king. Not far from me stood my father; he laughed aloud and evidently was extremely proud. Now the great chain with the silver shields was put upon my shoulder, a tall hat with the old tinsel crown and flowers on top was fixed upon my head. It was a great moment; but I had won the prize merely as a substitute for another person, not for myself. Who was that person? A Sanct Sebastianus sister, an old washerwoman. She was brought forward and also adorned with ribbons and flowers. I was obliged to offer her my arm as my queen, and so we marched solemnly behind drum and flag back into the village. The riflemen made every possible noise with their guns; the children shouted, and the old people stood in their doorways, greeted me with their hands, and called out: " See the Schurz Karl! " But I felt as if we two, the old washerwoman and myself, presented a decidedly grotesque spectacle in that triumphant procession, which in my imagination had always been such a solemn affair. I thought I even saw some people indulge in a mocking smile about our unquestionably ridiculous appearance. But worse than this—I noticed on the faces of some of the old marksmen something like an expression of disapproval; my ear caught a remark that it was, after all, not quite proper to make the Schützenfest of the venerable old Sanct Sebastianus Society a boy's play. I could not deny within myself that this view of the case was not unjustified; and thus in the hour of that triumph which I had so often pictured in my dreams, a heavy drop of bitterness fell into the cup. It was the old, old experience, at that time still new to me, that we seldom are blessed with success or joy without some bitter admixture, and that the fulfillment of a wish usually looks very different from anticipation; and this experience has been repeated in my life again and again.

In the meantime dark clouds were gathering over our home. My grandfather's retirement from the Burg had been followed by evil consequences; it was as if the firm ground had been taken from under our feet. The proceeds of the sale of the inventory had been entrusted to my youngest uncle for investment. He groped about for a considerable time and finally hit at the idea of trading in grain. In connection with this plan my father, who was in need of a larger income than his little hardware business yielded, decided to erect a building of which the ground floor was to be a large amusement hall and the upper story a granary. In one of his many books he had read the description of some new method of construction which caught his fancy and which had the charm of novelty. The building was successfully erected, but it cost far more than had been anticipated. It appeared also that the festive occasions proved too few to make the letting of the amusement hall profitable, and the granary yielded even less. My uncle's grain business soon became highly speculative and he promised himself mountains of gold from it. When he drifted into embarrassment, of course his brothers and brothers-in-law came to the rescue, thus involving themselves also in affairs of which not one of them had any knowledge. My uncle Jacob, the burgomaster of Jülich, had indeed good qualities as a merchant; he was painstaking, orderly and exact, but the quick calculation of chance, the instinct of the trader, he, too, lacked entirely. So with my father; he was far more interested in his scientific books than in his ledger. Often I recall seeing him at his desk with a disorderly pile of papers before him and a helpless, impatient expression on his face. Sometimes he would then rise abruptly, push the papers into the desk, crowd them down with both elbows, and drop the lid upon their wild confusion. The various members of our family came to one another's financial assistance so often that after a little while not one of them knew accurately the condition of his own or of their common affairs. To bring order out of chaos they would occasionally meet at Liblar for the purpose of talking over business matters and "settling up." But this would have required the saying of many disagreeable things from which each in his amiability and brotherly affection recoiled. By way of beginning they would sit down together to a comfortable repast and recall happy bygone times; gradually the proposed business conference faded out of view; they ate and drank and were so happy together that it would have been a pity to disturb all by alluding to unpleasant subjects. After this had gone on for a day, or even a few days, they remembered that it was high time for them to return home; then they took leave in the most touching manner, kissed one another, sometimes even shedding tears at the parting, and each one went his way without having talked of the business matters which had brought them together. Of course their affairs drifted from worse to worse, and some further daring grain speculations only served to hasten on the final disaster.

My father was not directly implicated in those speculations, but he could not keep from getting entangled in the difficulties which sprung from them. Although youth is inclined to take matters of business lightly, I became gradually aware that my parents were often in pressing need of money, and I began to share their anxieties. I myself raised the question whether it would be possible for them to keep me any longer at the gymnasium. This was quickly answered by my obtaining a fellowship which covered a large part of my expenses; and besides I resolved to tutor junior pupils, thus earning the rest of the money needed. I threw myself into this new task with eagerness. The tuition fees amounted to about six and a half cents per hour, but they were sufficient to enable me to work my way up to the highest class but one.

Suddenly my parents were cheered by apparently more hopeful prospects. My father found an opportunity for selling his property in Liblar at a price which would enable him to discharge his obligations and furnish the means for a new livelihood. As soon as the sale was concluded he removed with the family to Bonn, where I was to go to the university after having absolved the gymnasium. In Bonn my father made arrangements with an old friend which put him in possession of a spacious house, the lower part of which was used as a restaurant for students, while in the upper stories were several rooms to be let. My friend Petrasch, who meantime had been matriculated in the university, took one of them. All this promised very satisfactorily.

But then a great misfortune fell upon us. The purchaser of the property in Liblar, with whom my father had made a very imperfect contract, declared that he had become dissatisfied with the arrangement and that he proposed to forfeit the little sum paid in advance, and not take the property. This was a hard blow. My father tried, unsuccessfully, to hold the purchaser to the bargain, and no other purchaser could be found. To return to Liblar was impossible, as my father was then bound to his new arrangements in Bonn. Now the bills of exchange became due, which in anticipation of the money coming to him from the sale in Liblar he had given to his creditors. He could not meet them; the bills were protested, and suddenly I received in Cologne the news that some of the creditors had thrown my father into the debtors' prison. This struck me like a clap of thunder. I ran to the prison house and saw my father behind an iron bar. It was a distressing meeting, but we endeavored to encourage one another as best we could. He explained to me his circumstances, and we considered what might best be done to extricate him from this humiliating situation.

I was then seventeen years old and on the point of passing into the highest class of the gymnasium, but evidently I could no longer remain in Cologne. I hurriedly took leave of my teachers and friends, and devoted myself entirely to the affairs of the family. My uncles would have been glad to assist us, but they themselves were involved in grievous embarrassments. Business matters were entirely foreign and repugnant to me; but necessity is a wonderful schoolmaster, and I felt as if in a day I had grown many years older. After much traveling to and fro I succeeded in making arrangements sufficiently satisfactory to the creditors to induce them to release my father. Those were very dark days.

When my father was thus enabled again to take our affairs into his own hands, the question arose, what was to become of me. Was I to abandon my studies and enter upon a new course of life? This idea was rejected at once; but circumstances did not permit my return to Cologne. I had to remain with my family. We therefore formed the bold plan that I should begin at once as an irregular student to attend lectures at the university, and at the same time to pursue those studies which would make it possible for me to pass the graduation examination in Cologne the next year. This plan was bold in so far as it was generally understood that when a young man left the gymnasium without having completed the course and then came back to pass the examination required for regular standing at the university, that examination was often made exceptionally severe in order to discourage like practice. But there was no hesitation in attempting the difficult task. Meanwhile, my mind had also settled upon a calling. I was fond of historic and linguistic studies, and believed I possessed some literary capacity. I therefore resolved to prepare myself for a professorship of history, and so began to attend philological and historical lectures.

My passing from the gymnasium to the university brings me back to the question already mentioned, whether the classical curriculum at the German gymnasium, as well as at corresponding institutions in other countries, has not become antiquated and unpractical. Is it wise to devote so large a part of the time and of the learning-strength of boys to the study of the Latin and the Greek languages and the classical literatures? Would it not be of greater advantage to a young generation to put in place of the Latin and Greek the study of modern languages and literatures, the knowledge of which would be much more useful in the practical business of life? This question is certainly entitled to serious consideration. Latin is no longer what it was in most of the countries of the so-called civilized world down to the beginning of the eighteenth century, and, in some of them, even to a much more recent period, the language of diplomacy, of jurisprudence, of philosophy, and of all science. Not even the ability to quote Horace in conversation is any longer required to give one the stamp of an educated man. The literatures of classical antiquity are no longer the only ones in which great creations of poetry in perfect beauty of form are found, or models of historical writing, or of oratorical eloquence, or of philosophical reasoning. Of all these things modern literatures contain rich treasures, and there is also an abundance of excellent translations to make the masterpieces of antiquity accessible to those who do not understand the classical tongues.

And yet, when I now in my old days, and after multifarious experiences of life, ask myself which part of the instruction I received in my youth I would miss with the most regret, my answer would not be doubtful for a single moment. Indeed, I have, I am sorry to say, lost much of the Latin and Greek that I knew when I was at the gymnasium. But the æsthetic and moral impulses that such studies gave me, the ideal standards they helped me in erecting, the mental horizons they opened to me, I have never lost. Those studies are not a mere means for the acquisition of knowledge, but, in the best sense of the word, an element of culture. And thus they have remained to me during my whole life an inexhaustible source of elevating enjoyment and inspiration.

If once more I had to choose between the classical studies

and the so-called useful ones in their place, I would, for myself at least, undoubtedly on the whole elect the same curriculum that I have gone through. I would do this the more readily as in all probability I should never have been able to begin or resume the classical studies had I not enjoyed them in my youth, and as the knowledge of the ancient languages has been of inestimable value to me in acquiring the modern ones in later life. He who understands Latin will not only learn French, and English, and Spanish, and Italian, and Portuguese much more easily, but also much better. I can say of myself that I have in fact studied only the Latin grammar quite thoroughly, but that this knowledge has divested my grammatical studies in modern Latin and Germanic languages of all wearisome difficulty. Therefore, while I recognize the title of the utility argument, now so much in vogue, to our serious consideration, I cannot but confess that I personally owe to the old classical courses very much that was good and beautiful, and that I would not forego.

To be a student at the university is the most entrancing dream of the German gymnasium boy. It had been mine. Now I was at the university. But how? As a mere intruder who had still to win his right to academic citizenship through a difficult examination still to pass; as a person of questionable standing hardly relieved of a most humiliating situation, troubled by bitter cares, with very uncertain prospects before me. Thus it happened to me that what I had hoped for came to me in depressing form. The wish could hardly be recognized in the appearance of the fulfillment.

CHAPTER IV

ALTHOUGH not yet regularly immatriculated at the university at Bonn, I received a warm welcome from a group of fine young men, the Burschenschaft Franconia—one of that class of students' associations which after the wars of liberation of 1813, '14 and '15 had been organized at various German universities, in obedience to a patriotic impulse. My admission to this fellowship I owed to my Cologne friends, Petrasch and von Weise, who had preceded me at the university and had spoken a good word for me to their brethren of the Franconia society, probably with an exaggerated account of my literary capabilities. This I discovered upon the occasion of my first appearance at the Franconia "Kneipe," when it was the evident intention of both my friends to make a show of my talents. But I was at that time an extremely bashful youth, always silent and awkward in the presence of strangers. I shall never forget the feeling of utter helplessness that came over me when Petrasch introduced me to the presiding officer of the society, Johannes Overbeck, a self-poised young man several years my senior, and a brilliant student who had already published a volume of original poems. All this I knew and it had impressed me greatly. In answer to the friendly greeting he gave me I blushed and stammered and only managed to articulate an occasional yes or no. I was quite conscious of the sorry figure I was cutting, and what was worse, aware that Petrasch and Weise were disappointed and ashamed of me. It was the first occasion in life when I was brought in contact with men from other parts of Germany; and they, especially the North-Germans, had something superior and deliberate in their ways that greatly impressed me.

My irregular standing at the university did not permit me to be received as a full member into the Franconia, but I was admitted as a guest to their convivial meetings. For a long time I sat a mute spectator at the jovial gatherings of my friends, but finally my hour came. One of the principal events of the convivial evenings was the reading aloud of the *Kneipzeitung,* a humorous paper, written and read in turn by different members. To write a good *Kneipzeitung* was the object of general ambition, and those papers not seldom possessed decided literary merit. As I sat or moved, a quiet observer among my friends, abundant opportunity was afforded me to study the peculiarities of my new companions. My observation finally took form in a parody of the "Auerbach cellar scene" in "Faust," in which I made the leading members of the Franconia the *dramatis personæ.* The satire was pointed, though of course not ill-natured. When I had finished the composition I showed it in confidence to Petrasch. He shouted with delight, and was certain that nothing better had ever been written by any member of the society. This of course I refused to believe, but yielded to his entreaties that I turn it into a *Kneipzeitung* and that he should be the one to read it aloud at the next reunion. I insisted that he keep its authorship strictly secret, which he promised. When finally the evening came for its presentation my heart was in my throat, and my face red with blushes, as the assembled company burst into repeated laughter and applause. The success of the paper was complete. Petrasch declared that the writer wished to remain unknown, but with this the audience would not rest content. Of course nobody suspected me. My friend, as proud of the achievement as if it had been his own, winked at me across the table and whispered audibly, "May I not tell?" This alone would have been sufficient to betray me, but another member sitting near recognized my handwriting. And now there was a great hurrah. From all sides they rushed upon me; there was no end of congratulation and handshaking; and Petrasch, looking around at the assembled company, called out: "There, now, what did I tell you?"

It has always been a relief to me that the poetic productions of my youth somehow disappeared; but I confess that I would like very much to see this one again, for at the time it rendered me an inestimable service. Its success aroused my dormant self-reliance and transformed me from an awkward country lad, who was in a good way to remain a ridiculous figure, into a respectable and respected young man. My shyness rapidly ceased in the intercourse with my comrades, and many delightful friendships were the outcome of it all.

Much time I could indeed not give to my friends during my first university year at Bonn, for the graduation examinations at the Cologne gymnasium, upon which my whole future depended, were still ahead, and they ever stood before me like a threatening specter. Aside from the historical and philological lectures by Aschbach and Ritschl, which I attended, I had to acquire all that was taught in the upper class of the gymnasium by way of self-instruction, and with the exception of higher mathematics and of natural science I succeeded in doing this, but, of course, not without much labor. At last, in September, 1847, the crisis came, and I journeyed to Cologne, accompanied by the prayers of my family and the cordial wishes of all good friends. Fortune favored me again, and all went well. I knew the sixth canto of the Iliad by heart, and it so happened that the examiner in Greek gave me a part of

UNIVERSITY AT BONN

that canto to translate, which I could do without looking at the book. In addition to this, the result of my examination in history and my compositions in German and Latin were sufficiently satisfactory to move the examiners to overlook my weakness in other branches. Upon the conclusion of the ordeal the government commissioner, who had before seemed to me the personification of grim fate, handed me my graduation papers with an especially cordial handshake, and he gave me many good wishes for future success on my way. I returned to Bonn in triumph.

Now at last, as a regularly matriculated student, I could take equal rank with my university friends. With ardor and with a feeling of assurance I threw myself into philological and historical studies, looking with greater calmness into the future, in which I pictured myself as a professor of history at some German university, devoting some of my time to literary work. I hoped that now the severest storms of life were behind me, and that I might look forward to a smooth career which would satisfy all my ambitions. How little did I dream of the strange vicissitudes of fortune which were soon to scatter all these plans and to hurl me into currents of life entirely different from those which I had anticipated!

The cheerfulness of temperament with which benign nature had endowed me and the capacity of frugal enjoyment which the conditions of my early youth had developed in me, rendered me highly susceptible to the fascination of free student-life. Again fortune had greatly favored me in opening to me at the very entrance into the academic world access to a most stimulating circle of young men.

Friedrich Spielhagen, in his memoirs, says that the Burschenschaft Franconia was in a sense the most distinguished among the student societies of that day. And this it was indeed. To be sure, it did not count among its members scions of noble houses nor men of exceptional wealth. At any rate rank and wealth did not count. But its scientific and literary tone was marked, and many of its members later made a name for themselves in various walks of life. Among these were Johannes Overbeck, the archæologist, of whom it has been said that he wrote the best book that has ever been written on Herculaneum and Pompeii, without ever having seen either spot; Julius Schmidt, an astronomer, who gave to the world various works of great scientific value, and died as director of the astronomical observatory at Athens; Carl Otto Weber, of Bremen, a young man of rare brightness of mind and the most charming sweetness of character, whose distinguished merit gave him a professorship of medicine at Heidelberg, where, like a soldier in battle, he died of diphtheritic poison in an heroic effort to save a human life; Ludwig Meyer, who became an expert in mental diseases and a professor at Göttingen, and director of various institutions for the insane; Adolph Strodtmann, the biographer of Heine, who also excelled as a remarkably able translator of French, English and Danish literature; Friedrich Spielhagen, in whom in spite of his somewhat distant and reserved character we all recognized a man of rare intellectuality and moral elevation, and who later became a star of the first magnitude among the novelists of the century. There were several other young men of uncommon capacity and sound ambition who afterwards rose to honorable if less conspicuous positions in life.

Although in this company there was earnest and hard work done, its members were neither priggish nor did they lack youthful exuberance of spirits. But these spirits only very seldom degenerated into those excesses which usually pass as characteristic of German student-life. There were indeed a

RATHAUS AT BONN

few capable of great things in beer-drinking. But beer-drinking was not cultivated as a fine art, in the exercise of which one had to seek honorable distinction. Nor would he who was temperate be exposed to any want of respect or derision. Moderation was the rule, and he who broke that rule too often made himself liable to a reprimand or even expulsion. Neither did we take part in the practice of dueling, in which various corps at German universities sought then as now their glory. I can recollect but two cases during my time at Bonn that a member of the Franconia fought a duel, and of those we were by no means proud. There is probably no civilized people to-day, except, perhaps, the French, in which enlightened public opinion does not look upon and condemn dueling as a remnant of medieval barbarity. While excuses may sometimes be offered in cases of exceptional insult, it is no longer accepted as evidence of true courage nor as the best means for a man to guard or avenge his honor; and the professional duelist who by frequent encounters creates suspicion that he is wantonly seeking an opportunity for a fight wins rather the reputation of being a rude if not a criminal ruffian than the renown of a hero. The true gentleman has ceased to be ashamed of invoking the law for the protection of his own or his family's or friends' honor when that honor may need protection; and the world has begun to suspect the man who for its defense breaks the law instead of appealing to it. Irresistibly this view is becoming public opinion among all truly civilized peoples.

In what light then, in the face of this public opinion, does that portion of the so-called educated youth in German universities stand, which, not making even injured honor an excuse, cultivates the duel as a form of social amusement, and finds glory in the number of scars won in causeless combats? The precautionary measures customary at German universities have made an ordinary duel so harmless that usually nothing more than a mere scratch on the face is the result. To fight in this way requires no more courage than to have a tooth drawn; perhaps not even so much. As a true test of courage, therefore, such a duel cannot be regarded. The cause for it mostly consists in nothing but some childish quarrel, wantonly brought on for the very purpose of provoking a challenge; and the student who in this way disfigures his face with a network of unsightly scars is truly foolish to think he can pose as a braver and better man than others who enjoy their youth in a more sensible way during the period when they are preparing themselves for the grave problems of life. It is said that the duel prevents personal quarrels from degenerating into vulgar brawls and fisticuffs, and that the sword is a more dignified weapon than the fist. But this defense appears utterly untenable when we look at the universities of other countries, where dueling is practically unknown and where common fights are as infrequent as they are in Germany. It is also asserted that dueling stimulates a nice sense of honor among young people. But what kind of honor is this? Is it honorable to fight without due cause? Is it honorable to treat with contempt those who object to dueling about silly nothings? Is not this so-called sense of honor mere shallow and rude rodomontade? It is in fact nothing but the cultivation of an entirely false standard of honor—a self-deception very dangerous to young people, because it confuses their moral principles, upon the clearness and firmness of which the character of the true gentleman rests. Such a notion of honor which consists only in cheap show induces one too easily to forget that the moral courage of a man who unflinchingly and unselfishly stands up in the struggle of opinions and of interests for that which he recognizes as true and right, rises far above all the glories of the dueling-field and all its pretended heroism. It is a matter of experience that not a few of the most bellicose students, devoid of just this genuine and higher courage, become the most servile sycophants of power in later life, always parading the scars on their faces as proof of their bravery. In this way a class of unprincipled climbers has developed itself, which depends in the competition for place and promotion, not on its real ability and true merit, but on social connections and the protection of the powerful, and which thus loses in the matter of character what it wins in the way of success.

Such were the views about the duel held in my time by the Franconians, although it is certain that they were not lacking in sense of honor nor of pride. Their principles, however, did not keep them from the fencing school; indeed several of them would have been conspicuously able to enforce respect sword in hand. I have to confess that I found especial pleasure in the fencing exercises, and Spielhagen praises me in his memoirs "for wielding a deft and powerful blade."

In other respects we followed the customs and enjoyed the pleasures of German student-life to our hearts' content. We wore with pride the society colors on our caps and the tricolored ribbon across our breasts. We celebrated our "commerses" and went through all the traditional ceremonies with becoming solemnity. We took long rambles into the country—and it was no pedantic affectation, but a real outflow of gay spirits that on such occasions some of us who had studied our Homer with especial assiduity conversed in homeric verses, which somehow we contrived to apply to what we were doing or observing. We also indulged in delightful excursions up and down the Rhine and into its lovely side-valleys; and blessed be the memory of the innkeepers who did not demand an immediate settlement of our accounts; blessed above all, that of the benign Nathan of Sanct Goarshausen, under the shadow of the Loreley-rock, who welcomed every Franconian under his roof as an own child. Oh, how we reveled in the poetry of those friendships, which more than all else made youthful years so happy! The mature man should never be ashamed of the emotions that once moved him to wind his arm around his friend's shoulder and to dream of inseparable brotherhood. Thus I shall never be ashamed of the feelings which I showed as exuberantly as my companions, whenever at the close of the semester some members dropped out of our circle never to return, and when at leave-taking our glasses rang to the echo of the farewell song:

"*Wohlauf noch getrunken*
Den funkelnden Wein,
Ade nun Ihr Lieben,
Geschieden muss sein."

Even now I cannot listen to this song without a throb in my heart, for I see before me the dear fellows as their eyes filled at the moment of parting and they again and again embraced. Oh, these careless, sunny, university days, with their ideals and enthusiasms, their sentimentalities and their felicities! How soon they were to be overshadowed for me by the bitter earnestness of life!

It was at the beginning of the winter semester of 1847-8, at Bonn, that I made the acquaintance of Professor Gottfried Kinkel—an acquaintance which for my later years became one of fateful consequence. Kinkel delivered lectures on literature and art-history, some of which I attended. I also participated in his course of rhetorical exercises. This brought me into close personal contact with him. He was at the time when I first

PROF. GOTTFRIED KINKEL

knew him thirty-two years of age; the son of an evangelical minister stationed in a village on the Rhine, and he himself also to be educated for the church. To this end he visited the universities of Bonn and Berlin. In the year 1836 he settled down at the university of Bonn as a teacher of church history. But on account of his health he made a journey to Italy in 1837, where he gave himself up to the study of the history of art. After his return he became assistant preacher of an evangelical church in Cologne, where he attracted large congregations by the eloquence of his sermons. In the meantime his poetical gifts, which by personal intercourse with Simrock, Wolfgang Müller, Freiligrath and others had been constantly stimulated, had attracted wide attention. Especially his romantic epic, "Otto der Schütz," won for him a prominent name in literature. In Cologne he became acquainted with the divorced wife of a bookseller, a woman of extraordinary mental activity. While rowing on the Rhine one day Kinkel saved her from drowning, the boat having capsized, and soon after, in the year 1843, they were married. This union with a divorced Roman Catholic woman would alone have sufficed to make his position as an evangelical clergyman untenable, had it not already been undermined by his outspoken liberal opinions. For this reason he abandoned theology and accepted a position of professor-extraordinary of art-history at the university of Bonn.

As a lecturer he proved himself exceedingly attractive by his interesting personality as well as by the charm of his delivery. Kinkel was a very handsome man, of regular features and herculean stature, being over six feet in height and a picture of strength. He had a wonderful voice, both strong and soft, high and low, powerful and touching in its tone, gentle as a flute and thundering like a trombone—a voice which seemed to command all the registers of the church organ. To listen to him was at the same time a musical and an intellectual joy. A gesticulation as natural as it was expressive and graceful accompanied his speech, which flowed on in well-rounded and not seldom poetic sentences.

When Kinkel offered to introduce his hearers in a special course to the art of speech, I was one eagerly to seize the opportunity. He did not deliver theoretical instruction in rhetorics, but he began at once to produce before us eminent models and to exercise our faculties by means of them. As such models he selected some of the great rhetorical passages in the dramas of Shakespeare, and for me he set the task to explain the famous funeral oration of Marc Antony, to point out the intended effects and the means by which these effects were to be accomplished, and finally to recite the whole speech. I accomplished this task to his satisfaction, and then Kinkel invited me to visit him at his house. I soon followed this invitation, and the result was the development between teacher and scholar of a most agreeable personal intercourse. He possessed in a high degree the genial unconventionality and the gay temper of the Rhineland.

He delighted to put the professor aside and to let himself go when in the circle of his family and friends in unrestrained hilarity. He drank his glass of wine—with moderation, to be sure—laughed heartily at a good jest and even at a poor one, drew from all circumstances of life as much enjoyment as there was in them, and grumbled little when fate was unkind. Thus one soon felt at home in his company. He had indeed also his detractors, who accused him of being what they called "vain." But who is not vain, each one in his way? Vanity is the most common and the most natural of all weaknesses of character—and at the same time the most harmless and the most pardonable if it stands under the influence of a sound ambition. Whenever it is carried too far it becomes ridiculous, and thus punishes itself.

Mrs. Kinkel was not at all handsome. Her stature was low, her features large and somewhat masculine and her complexion sallow. Nor did she understand the art of dressing. Her gowns were ill-fitting and usually so short that they brought her flat feet, clad in white stockings and black slippers, with cross-ribbons, into undue prominence. But the impression made by her lack of beauty vanished at once when one looked into her blue, expressive eyes, and when she began to speak. Even then she seemed at first to be neglected by nature, for her voice was somewhat hoarse and dry. But what she said almost instantly fascinated the hearer. She not only spoke upon many subjects of high significance with understanding, sagacity and striking clearness, but she also knew how to endow by her picturesque presentation commonplace things and every-day events with a peculiar charm. In conversing with her one always felt that behind what she said there was still a great wealth of knowledge and of thought. She also possessed that sparkling Rhenish humor that loves to look at things from their comical side and under all circumstances appreciates whatever there is enjoyable in life. She had received an exceptionally thorough musical education, and played the piano with a master hand. I have hardly ever heard Beethoven and Chopin compositions performed with more perfection than by her. In fact, she had passed far beyond the line that separates the dilettante from the artist. She had also written some exquisite compositions. Although her voice possessed no resonance and in singing she could only indicate the tones, still she sang with thrilling effect. Indeed, she understood the art of singing without a voice.

Whoever observed these two externally so different human beings in their domestic life could not but receive the impression that they found hearty joy in one another and that they fought the struggles of life together with a sort of defiant buoyancy of spirit. This impression became even stronger when one witnessed their happiness in their four children.

No wonder that Kinkel's house became the gathering place of a circle of congenial people, whose hours of social intercourse left nothing to desire in animation, intellectual vivacity and cheerfulness. It was composed throughout of men and women of rich mental endowments and of liberal ways of thinking in the religious as well as the political field—men and women who liked to utter their opinions and sentiments with outspoken frankness; and there was no lack of interesting topics in those days.

The revolt among the Roman Catholics caused by the exhibition and adoration of the "holy coat" in Trier had brought forth the so-called "German Catholic" movement, and had also given a vigorous impulse to the tendency for free-thinking and free-teaching among Protestants. Upon the political field, too, there was a mighty stir. The period of political discouragement and of national self-depreciation in Germany had given place to an impulse to strive for real and well-defined goals, and also to the belief that such goals were attainable. Everybody felt the coming of great changes, although most people did not anticipate how soon they would come. Among the guests of Kinkel's house I heard many things clearly uttered which until then were only more or less nebulous in my mind. A short review of the origin and development of the feelings with regard to political conditions, which at that time prevailed with the class of Germans to which he, and, in a more modest way, I belonged, may serve to make intelligible their conduct in the movements which preceded the revolutionary upheavals of the year 1848.

The patriotic heart loved to dwell on the memories of the "holy Roman empire of the German nation," which once, at the zenith of its power, had held leadership in the civilized world. From these memories sprang the Kyffhäuser romanticism, with its dreams of the new birth of German power and magnificence, which had such poetic charm to German youth: the legend telling how the old Kaiser Friedrich Barbarossa was sitting in a cave of the Kyffhäuser mountain in Thuringia, in a sleep centuries long, his elbows resting on a stone table and his head on his hands, while a pair of ravens were circling around the mountain top; and how one day the ravens would fly away and the old kaiser would awaken and issue from the mountain, sword in hand, to restore the German Empire to its ancient glory. While cherishing such dreams we remembered with shame the time of the national disintegration and the dreary despotism after the Thirty Years' War, when German princes, devoid of all national feeling, always stood ready to serve the interests and the ambitions of foreign potentates—even to sell their own subjects in order to maintain with the disgraceful proceeds the luxuries of their dissolute courts; and with equal shame we thought of the period of the "Rheinbund," when a number of German princes became mere vassals of Napoleon; when one part of Germany served to keep the other part at the feet of the hated conqueror, and when Emperor Francis of Austria, who had been also emperor of the hopelessly decayed empire of Germany, laid down in 1806 his crown, and German Emperor and German Empire ceased even to exist in name.

Then came, in 1813, after long suffering and debasement, the great popular uprising against Napoleonic despotism, and with it a period of a new German national consciousness. To this feeling appealed the famous manifesto, issued from the town of Kalisch, in which the king of Prussia, allied with the Russian Czar, after Napoleon's defeat in Russia, called the German people to arms, promising at the same time a new national union and participation of the people in the business of government under constitutional forms. The new birth of a united German national empire, the abolition of arbitrary government by the introduction of free political institutions—that was the solemn promise of the Prussian king as the people understood it—that was the hope which inspired the people in the struggle against Napoleonic rule with enthusiastic heroism and a self-sacrifice without limit, and ended in a final victory. It was one of the periods in history when a people proved itself ready to sacrifice all for the attainment of an ideal. But after the victories of Leipzig and Waterloo followed another time of bitter disappointment. Against the formation of a united Germany arose not only the jealous opposition of non-German Europe, but also the selfish ambitions of the smaller German princes, especially of those who, as members of the "Rheinbund," such as Bavaria, Würtemberg, Baden, etc., had been raised in their rank. And this opposition was strengthened by the intriguing policy of Austria, which, with her possessions outside of Germany, had also un-German interests and designs. And this Austrian policy was conducted by Prince Metternich, the prime minister of Austria, to whom every emotion of German patriotism was foreign, as he hated and feared every free aspiration among the people. Thus the peace was far from bringing to the German people the reward for their sacrifices which they had deserved and expected. From the Congress of Vienna, in 1814 and 1815, which disposed of peoples as of herds of cattle in order to establish a permanent

FREDERICK WILLIAM III

balance of power in Europe, nothing issued for the German nation but a treaty of alliance between German states, the famous "Deutsche Bund," the organ of which was to be the "Bundestag"; and this organ was to be composed of the representatives of the various German kings and princes, without any vestige of a representation of the people. There was no mention of any guarantee of civic rights, of a popular vote, of a free press, of the freedom of assembly, of a trial by jury. On the contrary, the "Bundestag," impotent as an organ of the German nation in its relations to the outside world, developed itself only as a mutual insurance society of despotic rulers—as a central police board for the suppression of all national and liberal movements. The king of Prussia, Frederick William III., the same who had made the promises to the people contained in the proclamation of Kalisch, had probably in the days of distress and of national uprising honestly meant to do what he promised. But his mind was narrow and easily disposed to consider autocratic authority on his part as necessary for the well-being of the world. Every effort among the people in favor of free institutions of government appeared to him as an attack on that absolute authority, and therefore as a revolutionary transgression; and the mere reminder on the part of the people of his own promises made to them in 1813 was resented by him as an arrogant self-assertion of subjects, and as such to be repelled. Thus he became, perhaps unconsciously, the mere tool of Prince Metternich, the evil genius of Germany. The outcome was a period of stupid reaction, a period of conferences of ministers for the concoction of despotic measures, of cruel persecutions of patriotic men whom they called demagogues, of barbarous press-gagging, of brutal police excesses. In some of the small German states some advance was made toward liberal institutions, which, however, was usually followed by more odious measures of repression on the part of the Bundestag. Such were the returns for the sacrifices and the heroism of the German people in the struggle for national independence; such was the fulfillment of the fair promises made by the princes. It was a time of deepest humiliation. Even the Frenchmen, who had felt the edge of the German sword, derided, not without reason, the pitiable degradation of the victor.

Hope revived when Frederick William III.'s son and successor, Frederick William IV., ascended the Prussian throne in 1840. He was regarded as a man of high intelligence and had, as crown-prince, excited fair expectations. Many considered him incapable of continuing the stupid and sterile policy of his father. Indeed, the first utterances of the new king and the employment of able men in high positions encouraged the hope that he harbored a national heart, in sympathy with the patriotic aspirations of the German people, and that the liberal currents of the time would find in him appreciative understanding. But fresh disappointment followed. As soon as the demand was publicly made, that now at last the old promises of a representative government should be fulfilled, the king's attitude changed. These demands were bluntly repelled, and the censorship of the press was enforced with renewed severity.

Frederick William IV. was possessed of a mystical faith in the absolute power of kings "by the grace of God." He indulged himself in romantic imaginings about the political and social institutions of the Middle Ages, which had for him greater charm than those befitting the nineteenth century. He had sudden conceits, but no convictions; whims, but no genuine force of will; wit, but no wisdom. He possessed the ambition to do something great and thus to engrave his name upon the history of the world; but he wished at heart to leave everything substantially as it had been. He thought he could satisfy the people with an appearance of participation in the government without however in the least limiting the omnipotence of the crown. But these attempts ended like others made by other monarchs in other times. The merely ostensible and insufficient things he offered served only to strengthen and inflame the popular demand for something substantial and effective. Revolutions often begin with apparent but unreal reforms. He called "provincial diets," assemblies of local representative bodies, with the expectation that they would modestly content themselves with the narrow functions he prescribed for them. But they petitioned vehemently for a great deal more. The experiment of appearing to give and of really withholding everything was bound to fail miserably. The petitions of the provincial diets for freedom of the press, for trial by jury, and a liberal constitution, became more and more pressing. The discontent gradually grew so general, the storm of petitions so violent, the repugnance of the people to the police-despotism so menacing, that the old parade of the absolute kingly power would no longer suffice, and some new step in the direction of liberal innovations seemed imperatively necessary.

At last Frederick William IV. decided to convoke the so-called "United Diet," an assembly consisting of the members of all the provincial diets, to meet on April 11, 1847, in Berlin. But it was the old game over again. This assembly was to have the look of a parliament and yet not to be one. Its convocation was always to depend upon the pleasure of the king. Its powers were circumscribed within the narrowest limits. It was not to make laws nor to pass binding resolutions. It was to serve only as a sort of privy council to the king, to assist him in forming his decisions, its wishes to be presented to him only by way of petition. In the speech with which the king opened the United Diet, he declared with emphasis that this was now the utmost concession to which he would ever consent; he would never, never permit a piece of paper, meaning a written constitution, to be put between the prince and his people; the people themselves, he claimed, did not desire a participation of their representatives in the government; the absolute power of the king must not be broken; "the crown must reign and govern according to the laws of God and of the country and according to the king's own resolutions"; he could not, and must not, "govern according to the will of majorities"; and he, the king, "would never have called this assembly had he ever suspected in the slightest degree that its members would try to play the part of so-called representatives of the people." This was now, he said, the fulfillment, and "more than the fulfillment," of the promises made in the time of distress in 1813, before the expulsion of the French.

General disappointment and increasing discontent followed this pronouncement. But the concession made by the king in fact signified more than he had anticipated. A king who wishes to govern with absolute power must not permit a public discussion of the policy and of the acts of the government by men who stand nearer to the people than he does. The United Diet could indeed not resolve, but only debate and petition. But that it could debate, and that its debates passed through faithful newspaper reports into the intelligence of the country—that was an innovation of incalculable consequence.

The bearing of the United Diet, on the benches of which sat many men of uncommon capacity and liberal principles, was throughout dignified, discreet and moderate. But the struggle against absolutism began instantly, and the people followed it with constantly increasing interest. What has happened in the history of the world more than once happened again. Every step forward brought to the consciousness of the people the necessity of further steps forward. And now, when the king endeavored to stem the growing commotion, repelled the moderate demands made by the United Diet with sharp words, and dismissed that assembly "ungraciously," then the public mind was, by the government itself, dragged into that channel of thought in which revolutionary sentiments grow.

There had indeed long been some revolutionary agitators who, in their isolation, had passed for dreamers and could win but a slim following. But now the feeling began to spread in large circles that the real thunder-storm was coming, although hardly anybody anticipated how soon it would come. In former days people had excited themselves about what Thiers and Guizot had said in the French chambers, or Palmerston and Derby in the English parliament, or even what Hecker, Rotteck and Welker had said in the little Diet of the grand duchy of Baden. But now everybody listened with nervous eagerness to every word that in the United Diet of the most important of German states had fallen from the lips of Camphausen, Vincke, Beckerath, Hansemann and other liberal leaders. There was a feeling in the air as if this United Diet, in its position and the task to be performed by it, was not at all unlike the French assembly of the year 1789.

We university students watched these events with perhaps a less clear understanding, but with no less ardent interest, than our elders. As I have already mentioned, the "Burschenschaft" had its political traditions. Immediately after the wars of liberation—1813 to 1815—it had been among the first in line to raise the cry for the fulfillment of the pledges given by the princes. It had cultivated the national spirit with zeal, although sometimes with exaggerated demonstrations. It had furnished many victims in the persecutions of so-called demagogues. The political activity of the old Burschenschaft had indeed not been continued by the younger associations; but "God, Liberty, Fatherland," had still remained the common watchword; we still wore the prohibited black-red-golden ribbon under our coats, and very many members of the new Burschenschaft societies still recognized it as their duty to keep themselves well informed of what happened in the political world and to devote to it as active an interest as possible. Thus the liberal currents of our time found among us enthusiastic partisans, although we young people could not give a very definite account of the practical steps to be taken.

In the prosecution of my studies I had taken up with ardor the history of Europe at the period of the great Reformation. I expected to make this my specialty as a professor of history. The great characters of that period strongly attracted me and I could not resist the temptation to clothe some of them in dramatic form. So I planned a tragedy, the main figure of which was to be Ulrich von Hutten, and I began to elaborate some scenes in detail. At the beginning of the winter semester of 1847-48 I had made the acquaintance of a young student from Detmold, who became not indeed a member, but a guest of the Franconia. His name was Friedrich Althaus. More than any young man of my acquaintance he responded to the ideal of German youth. His was a thoroughly pure and noble nature and richly endowed with mental gifts. As we pursued similar studies we easily became intimates, and this friendship lasted with undiminished warmth long beyond the university years. To him I confided my Hutten secret, and he encouraged me to carry out my plan. Happy were the hours when I read to him what I had written and he gave me his judgment, which usually was altogether too favorable. Thus passed the larger part of the winter in useful and enjoyable occupations. Then fate broke in with the force of a mighty hurricane, which swept me, as well as many others, with irresistible power out of all life-plans previously designed and cherished.

CHAPTER V

ONE morning, toward the end of February, 1848, I sat quietly in my attic-chamber, working hard at my tragedy of "Ulrich von Hutten," when suddenly a friend rushed breathlessly into the room, exclaiming: "What, you sitting here! Do you not know what has happened?"

"No; what?"

"The French have driven away Louis Philippe and proclaimed the republic."

I threw down my pen—and that was the end of "Ulrich von Hutten." I never touched the manuscript again. We tore down the stairs, into the street, to the market-square, the accustomed meeting-place for all the student societies after their midday dinner. Although it was still forenoon, the market was already crowded with young men talking excitedly. There was no shouting, no noise, only agitated conversation. What did we want there? This probably no one knew. But since the French had driven away Louis Philippe and proclaimed the republic, something of course must happen here, too. Some of the students had brought their rapiers along, as if it were necessary at once to make an attack or to defend ourselves. We were dominated by a vague feeling as if a great outbreak of elemental forces had begun, as if an earthquake was impending of which we had felt the first shock, and we instinctively crowded together. Thus we wandered about in numerous bands —to the "Kneipe," where our restlessness, however, would not suffer us long to stay; then to other pleasure resorts, where we fell into conversation with all manner of strangers, to find in them the same confused, astonished and expectant state of mind, then back to the market-square, to see what might be going on there; then again somewhere else, and so on, without aim and end, until finally late in the night fatigue compelled us to find the way home.

The next morning there were the usual lectures to be attended. But how profitless! The voice of the professor sounded like a monotonous drone coming from far away. What he had to say did not seem to concern us. The pen that should have taken notes remained idle. At last we closed with a sigh the notebook and went away, impelled by a feeling that now we had something more important to do—to devote ourselves to the affairs of the fatherland. And this we did by seeking as quickly as possible again the company of our friends, in order to discuss what had happened and what was to come. In these conversations, excited as they were, certain ideas and catchwords worked themselves to the surface, which expressed more or less the feelings of the people. Now had arrived in Germany the day for the establishment of "German Unity," and the founding of a great, powerful national German Empire. In the first line the convocation of a national parliament. Then the demands for civil rights and liberties, free speech, free press, the right of free assembly, equality before the law, a freely elected representation of the people with legislative power, responsibility of ministers, self-government of the communes, the right of the people to carry arms, the formation of a civic guard with elective officers, and so on—in short, that which was called a "constitutional form of government on a broad democratic basis." Republican ideas were at first only sparingly expressed. But the word democracy was soon on all tongues, and many, too, thought it a matter of course that if the princes should try to withhold from the people the rights and liberties demanded, force would take the place of mere petition. Of course the regeneration of the fatherland must, if possible, be accomplished by peaceable means. A few days after the outbreak of this commotion I reached my nineteenth birthday. I remember to have been so entirely absorbed by what was happening that I could hardly turn my thoughts to anything else. Like many of my friends, I was dominated by the feeling that at last the great opportunity had arrived for giving to the German people the liberty which was their birthright and to the German fatherland its unity and greatness, and that it was now the first duty of every German to do and to sacrifice everything for this sacred object. We were profoundly, solemnly in earnest.

The first practical service we had to perform turned out to be a very merry one. Shortly after the arrival of the tidings from France the burgomaster of Bonn, a somewhat timid man, believed the public safety in his town to be in imminent danger. In point of fact, in spite of the general excitement there were really no serious disturbances of the public order. But the burgomaster insisted that a civic guard must at once be organized, to patrol the city and the surrounding country during the night. The students, too, were called upon to join it, and as this forming of such a guard was also part of our political programme, we at once willingly obeyed the summons, and we did this in such numbers that soon the civic guard consisted in great part of university men. Our prescribed task was to arrest disturbers of the public order and suspicious individuals, and to conduct them to the guardhouse; to induce gatherings of a suspicious nature to disperse; to protect property and generally to watch over the public safety. But the public safety being really in no manner threatened, and the patrolling of the city and neighborhood meeting no serious need, the university men found in the whole proceeding an opportunity for harmless amusement. Armed with our rapiers, the iron sheaths of which were made to rattle upon the pavement to the best of our ability, we marched through the streets. Every solitary citizen whom we met late in the night was summoned with pompous phrases to " disperse " and to betake himself to his " respective habitation," or, if it pleased him better, to follow us to the guardhouse and have a glass of wine with us. Whenever we happened to run across a patrol not composed of students, but of citizens, we at once denounced them as a dangerous mob, arrested them and took them to the guardhouse, where with cheers for the new empire we drank as many glasses together as there were points of reform in the political programme. The good burghers of Bonn fully appreciated the humorous situation and entered heartily into the fun.

While all this looked merry enough, affairs elsewhere were taking a serious turn—as serious as we, too, felt at the bottom of our hearts.

Exciting news came from all sides. In Cologne a threatening ferment prevailed. In the taverns and on the streets resounded the " Marseillaise," which at that time still passed in all Europe as the "hymn of liberty." On the public places great meetings were held to consult about the demands to be made by the people. A large deputation, headed by the late lieutenant of artillery, August von Willich, forced its way into the hall of the city council, vehemently insisting that the municipality present as its own the demands of the people of Cologne to the king. The streets resounded with the military drumbeat; the soldiery marched upon the popular gatherings, and Willich, as well as another ex-artillery officer, Fritz Anneke, were arrested; whereupon increasing excitement.

The Rhenish members of the prorogued United Diet implored the president of the province to urge upon the king an immediate acceptance of the demands of the people as the only thing that could prevent bloody conflicts. In Coblenz, Düsseldorf, Aachen, Crefeld, Cleves and other cities on the Rhine similar demonstrations took place. In South Germany —in Baden, Hessen-on-the-Rhine, Nassau, Würtemberg, Bavaria—the same revolutionary spirit burst forth like a prairie-fire. In Baden the Grand Duke acceded almost at once to what was asked of him, and so did the rulers of Würtemberg, Nassau, and Hessen-Darmstadt. In Bavaria, where even before the outbreak of the French February revolution the notorious Lola Montez, favorite of King Ludwig I., had had to yield her place near the throne to the wrath of the people, uproar followed uproar to drive the king to liberal concessions. In Hessen-Cassel the "Elector" also succumbed to the pressure when the people had armed themselves for an uprising. The students of the university of Giessen sent word to the insurgent Hessians that they stood ready to help them. In Saxony the defiant attitude of the citizens of Leipzig, under the leadership of Robert Blum, quickly brought the king to terms.

Great news came from Vienna. There the students of the university were the first to assail the Emperor of Austria with the cry for liberty and citizens' rights. Blood flowed in the streets, and the downfall of Prince Metternich was the result. The students organized themselves as the armed guard of liberty. In the great cities of Prussia there was a mighty commotion. Not only Cologne, Coblenz and Trier, but also Breslau, Königsberg and Frankfurt-on-the-Oder, sent deputations to Berlin to entreat the king. In the Prussian capital the masses surged upon the streets, and everybody looked for events of great import.

While such tidings rushed in upon us from all sides like a roaring hurricane, we in the little university town of Bonn were also busy preparing addresses to the sovereign, to circulate them for signature and to send them to Berlin. On the 18th of March we too had our mass demonstration. A great multitude gathered for a solemn procession through the streets of the town. The most respectable citizens, not a few professors and a great number of students and people of all grades marched in close ranks. At the head of the procession Professor Kinkel bore the tricolor, black, red and gold, which so long had been prohibited as the revolutionary flag. Arrived on the market-square he mounted the steps of the city hall and spoke to the assembled throng. He spoke with wonderful eloquence, his voice ringing out in its most powerful tones as he depicted a resurrection of German unity and greatness and of the liberties and rights of the German people, which now must be conceded by the princes or won by force by the people. And when at last he waved the black, red and gold banner, and predicted to a free German nation a magnificent future, enthusiasm without bounds broke forth. People clapped their hands, they shouted, they embraced one another, they shed tears. In a moment the city was covered with black, red and gold flags, and not only the Burschenschaft, but almost everybody wore a black-red-gold cockade on his hat. While on that 18th of March we were parading through the streets suddenly sinister rumors flew from mouth to mouth. It had been reported that the king of Prussia, after long hesitation, had finally concluded, like the other German princes, to concede the demands that were pouring upon him from all sides. But now a whispered report flew around that the soldiery had suddenly fired upon the people and that a bloody struggle was raging in the streets of Berlin.

The enthusiastic elation was followed by a short time of anxious expectancy. At last came the report of the awful events that had taken place in the capital.

The king of Prussia, Frederick William IV., at first received the petitions rushing in upon him with sullen silence. He had so recently, and then so emphatically, even so defiantly, proclaimed his inflexible determination never to consent to any constitutional limitation of his kingly power, that the thought of yielding to popular pressure anything that he fancied should be only a free emanation of the royal will was well-nigh inconceivable to him. But the situation became more threatening from day to day. Not only the language of the deputations arriving from various parts of the kingdom constantly grew more and more impetuous and peremptory, but the people of Berlin began to hold mass meetings counting by thousands and to greet with thundering acclamations the political watchwords uttered by popular orators. The municipal authorities, too, were swept into the current and entreated the king to make concessions. At last he saw the necessity of yielding something. On the 14th of March he gave a " gracious " answer to an address presented by the city council, but that answer was still too evasive and indefinite to satisfy public opinion. Meanwhile bloody collisions occurred between the police supported by military detachments and the multitude thronging the public squares and streets, in which a merchant and a university student were killed. The bitterness of feeling caused by these events was somewhat assuaged by a rumor that the king had resolved upon further and more important concessions, which would be publicly announced on the 18th. He had indeed concluded to issue an edict opening a prospect of steps to be taken in favor of national unity and abolishing the censorship of the press.

FREDERICK WILLIAM IV

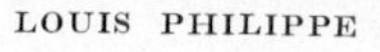

LOUIS PHILIPPE

On the afternoon of the fateful 18th of March an immense concourse of people assembled on the open square in front of the royal palace, hoping to hear the authoritative announcement that the popular demands had been granted. The king appeared on the balcony and was received with enthusiastic cheers. He attempted to speak, but could not be heard. In the belief, however, that he had granted all that was asked for, the people were ready for a jubilee. Then a cry arose for the removal of the bodies of troops surrounding the palace and appearing to separate the king from his people. It seemed to be expected that this would be granted, too, for an effort was made to open a passage for the soldiers through the dense crowd, when a roll of drums was heard. This was regarded as a signal for the departure of the soldiery; but, instead of the troops withdrawing, heavy bodies of infantry and cavalry pressed upon the multitude for the evident purpose of clearing the square. Then two shots rang from the infantry line and the whole scene suddenly and frightfully changed. Frantic cries arose: "We are betrayed! We are betrayed!" In an instant the mass of people who but a moment before had joyously acclaimed the king, dispersed in the adjoining streets with the angy shout, "To arms, to arms!" In all directions the thoroughfares were soon blocked with barricades. The paving-stones seemed to leap from the ground and to form themselves into bulwarks surmounted by black-red-gold flags, and manned by citizens, university students, tradesmen, artists, laborers, professional men—hastily armed with all sorts of weapons, from rifles and shotguns down to pikes, axes and hammers. There was no preparation, no plan, no system, in the uprising; everybody seemed to follow a common instinct. Then the troops were ordered to the assault. When, after a fierce fight they had taken one barricade, they were at short distances confronted by another and another. Behind the barricades women were busy bringing food and drink for the fighters and caring for the wounded. During the whole night the city resounded with the roar of cannon and the rattle of musketry.

The king seemed at first sternly determined to put down the insurrection at any cost; but as the street battle proceeded he became painfully conscious of its terrible character. Reports arrived in rapid succession. He would now give an order to stop the fight and then an order to go on. Shortly after midnight he wrote with his own hand an address to "My dear Berliners." He began by saying that the firing of the two shots which had caused the excitement had been a mere accident, that a band of miscreants, mostly foreigners, had taken advantage of this misunderstanding to goad many of his good subjects into this fratricidal fight. Then he promised to withdraw the troops as soon as the insurgents would remove the barricades, and he implored them "to listen to the fatherly voice of their king, to which the grievously suffering queen joined her affectionate and tearful prayers." But the address failed to produce the desired effect. It was accompanied with the roar of cannon and the rattle of musketry, and the fighting citizens rather resented being called "a band of miscreants."

At last, on the afternoon of Sunday, the 19th of March, when one of the high commanders of the troops, General Möllendorf, had been captured by the citizens, the withdrawal of the troops was resolved upon. Peace was concluded on the understanding that the army should leave Berlin, that there should be freedom of the press, and that Prussia should have a constitution on a broad democratic basis. When the soldiery had marched off something happened that in dramatic force and significance has never been surpassed in the history of revolutions. From all parts of the city solemn and silent processions moved toward the royal palace. They escorted the bodies of those of the people who had been killed in the battle; the corpses of the slain were carried aloft on litters, their gaping wounds uncovered, their heads wreathed with laurel branches and immortelles. So the processions marched into the inner palace court, where the litters were placed in rows in ghastly parade, and around them the multitude of men with pallid faces, begrimed with blood and powder smoke, many of them still carrying the weapons with which they had fought during the night; and among them women and children bewailing their dead. Then the king was loudly called for. He appeared in an open gallery, pale and dejected, by his side the weeping queen. "Hat off!" the multitude shouted, and the king took off his hat to the dead below. Then a deep voice among the crowd intoned the old hymn, "Jesus, meine Zuversicht"— "Jesus, my Refuge," in which all present joined. The chorus finished, the king silently withdrew and the procession moved away in grim solemnity.

This was a terrible humiliation to the crown, but at the same time a pointed answer to the king's address in which the fighters had been denounced as a band of miscreants, or as the seduced victims of such a band. Had there really been such miscreants, or persons answering our present conception of anarchists, among them, Frederick William IV. would hardly have survived that terrible moment when he stood before them, alone and defenseless, and they fresh from the battlefield with guns in their hands. But at that moment their cry was not "Death to the king!" nor "Down with royalty!" but "Jesus, my Refuge!"

Nor was the history of those fateful days tainted by any act of heinous crime; indeed, two private houses were sacked, the owners of which had been caught betraying the fighting citizens to the soldiery. But while the insurgents were in complete control of large portions of the city during the whole night, there was not a single case of theft or of wanton destruction. Property was absolutely safe.

The "Prince of Prussia," the oldest brother of the childless king and presumptive heir to the throne—the same prince who as Kaiser William I. was in the course of events to become the most popular monarch of his time—was reported to have given the order to fire on the people, and the popular wrath turned upon him. By order of the king the prince left Berlin under cover of night and hurried to England. Excited crowds gathered in front of his palace on the street "Unter den Linden." There was no military guard to protect the building. A university student put upon its front the inscription "National property," and it was not touched. Immediately after the street battle had ceased the shops were opened again as in ordinary times.

Arms were distributed among the people from the government armories. The king declared, "I have become convinced that the peace and the safety of the city cannot be better maintained than by the citizens themselves." On the 21st of March Frederick William IV. appeared again among the people, on horseback, a black-red-gold scarf around his arm, a black-red-gold flag at his request carried before him, a huge tricolor hoisted at the same moment on the royal palace. The king spoke freely to the citizens. He would "place himself at the head of the movement for a united Germany; in that united Germany Prussia would be merged." He swore that he wanted nothing but a "constitutional and united Germany." At the university building he turned to the assembled students, saying, "I thank you for the glorious spirit you have shown in these days. I am proud that

THE REVOLUTION IN BERLIN, 1848

Germany possesses such sons." It was understood that a new and responsible ministry had been appointed, composed of members of the liberal opposition; that a constituent assembly to be elected by the Prussian people should be convoked to frame a constitution for the kingdom of Prussia; and a national parliament to be elected by the people of all the German states, to meet at Frankfurt for the purpose of uniting all Germany under a new constitutional government. The people of Berlin were in ecstasy.

"The heroes fallen in the glorious struggle for social and political liberty," as the proclamation of the municipal assembly called them, were carried for burial to the Friedrichshain cemetery, accompanied by two hundred thousand citizens, who took the coffins past the royal palace, where the king again stood with uncovered head.

Such were the great tidings the country received from Berlin. Thus the cause of liberty and national union seemed to have achieved a decisive and irreversible victory. The kings and princes themselves, foremost the King of Prussia, had solemnly promised to serve it. The jubilation of the people was without bounds.

Since the French-German war of 1870 and the establishment of the present German Empire it has been the fashion in Germany to scoff at the year 1848, dubbing it the "crazy year," and to ridicule the "thoughtlessness" with which at that time great political programmes were made, comprehensive demands formulated, and far-reaching movements set on foot, to be followed by cruel disappointments and catastrophes. But did the German people of 1848 deserve such ridicule? True, the men of those times did not know how to deal with the existing conditions, nor to carry to the desired end the movement so victoriously and hopefully begun. It is equally true that the popular movement was disjointed and now in retrospect appears in certain lights fantastic. But what reasonable person can wonder at this? The people, although highly developed in science, philosophy, literature and art, had always lived under a severe guardianship in all political matters. They had never been out of leading strings. They had observed only from afar how the other nations exercised their right to govern themselves, and managed their active participation in the functions of the state, and those foreign nations the Germans had learned to admire and perhaps to envy. They had studied the theory of free institutions in books and had watched their workings in current newspaper reports. They had longed for the possession of like institutions and earnestly striven for their introduction in their own country. But with all this observing, learning, and longing, and striving, the larger part of the German people had been excluded by the prevailing rigid paternalism from practical experience in the exercise of political self-government. They had not been permitted to learn the practical meaning of political liberty. They had never received or known the teachings which spring from the feeling of responsibility in free political action. The affairs of government lay outside of the customs and habits of their lives. Free institutions were to them mere abstract conceptions, about which the educated and the seriously thinking men indulged in politico-philosophical speculations, while to the uneducated and the superficial they only furnished political catchwords, in the use of which the general discontent with existing conditions found vent.

Suddenly after a prolonged fermentation, and following an impulse from abroad, the German people rose up in strength. The kings and princes now conceded everything that they had refused before, and the people found themselves all at once in full possession of an unaccustomed power. Is it to be wondered at that these surprising changes brought forth some confused desires and misdirected endeavors? Would it not have been more astonishing if the people had at once clearly defined and wisely limited their desires, and promptly found the right means for the attainment of the right objects? Do we expect that the beggar who suddenly becomes a millionaire will instantly know how to make the best use of his unwonted wealth? And yet, it cannot be said of the large majority of the German people that, however vague their political notions may have been, they asked in the revolutionary movements of the year 1848 in the main for anything that was unreasonable or unattainable. Much of what they at that period sought to accomplish has since been realized. The errors committed by them in 1848 were more in the means employed than in the ends aimed at. And the greatest of these errors sprang from the childlike confidence with which they expected the complete fulfillment of all the promises which the kings and princes, especially the King of Prussia, had made under stress of circumstances. It is idle to indulge in speculations about that which might have been if that which was had been different. But one thing is certain: If the princes had not permitted themselves to be seduced by the machinations of the reactionary parties on the one side, nor to be frightened by occasional popular excesses on the other, but had with unflinching fidelity and with the exertion of all their power done that which in March, 1848, they had given the people reason to expect of them, the essential objects fought for at that period would have proved themselves entirely practicable. It was indeed not prudent on the part of the people in their enthusiastic enjoyment of what they called the "Volkerfrühling"—the People's Springtime—an enjoyment to which they gave themselves with such ingenuous elation, to cherish that credulous confidence, instead of assuring themselves of the necessary guarantees against a reaction bound to come; but this imprudence sprang from no ignoble source. He surely wrongs the German people who lays solely at their and their leaders' doors the responsibility for the failures of the years 1848-49, overlooking the tergiversations of the princes.

But what should make the memory of that " springtime " especially dear to Germans is the enthusiastic spirit of self-sacrifice for the great cause which for a while pervaded almost every class of society with rare unanimity. It is this moral elevation which, even if sometimes it ran into fantastic exaggerations, the German people should prize and honor—of which they should certainly not be ashamed. My heart warms whenever I think of those days. In my immediate surroundings I knew hosts of men who at that time were ready at any moment to abandon and risk all for the liberty of the people and the greatness of the fatherland. We ought to respect him who is willing to throw away all, even life itself, for a good and great idea. And whoever, be it an individual or people, has had in life moments of such self-sacrificing enthusiasm, should hold the memory of them sacred.

Upon the occasion of a crowded public meeting of university men in the " Aula," the great university hall at Bonn, I found myself, quite unintentionally, thrust into a conspicuous position among my fellow-students. I do not remember the special purpose for which the meeting was held. Professor Ritschl, our foremost philologist and, if I recollect rightly, at that time dean of the philosophical faculty, a very highly esteemed and popular man, was in the chair. I stood among the crowd. I had thought much and formed a decided opinion of the subject which was under discussion, but did not attend the meeting with the intention of taking part in the debate. Suddenly I heard some of the speakers say something very repugnant to my feelings, and following a sudden impulse, I found myself the next moment speaking to the assembly. I have never been able to recollect what I said. I only remember that I was in a nervous condition until then entirely unknown to me; that thoughts and words came to me in an uninterrupted flow; that I spoke with vehement rapidity, and that the applause following my speech wakened me out of something like a dream. This was my first public speech. When the meeting had adjourned I met at the exit of the hall Professor Ritschl. As I attended some of his lectures he knew me. He put his hand upon my shoulder and asked:

"How old are you?"

"Nineteen years."

'Too bad; still too young for our new German parliament."

I blushed all over; that I should become a member of any parliament—that was a thought to which my ambition had never soared. I feared the good professor had permitted himself to joke with me.

Before long I was again in the foreground. Like all other orders of society in those days, we university men had our peculiar grievances which in the "new time" were to be redressed. The Prussian Government kept at the universities an official one of whose principal duties it was to watch the political tendencies of professors and students. This office had been created at the time of the "persecution of demagogues," after the notorious ministerial conferences at Carlsbad, and was therefore in bad odor with liberal-minded men. The officer in question was at that time Herr von Bethmann Hollweg.

More on account of his duties than of his personal qualities he was highly unpopular with the students. We thought that such an officer, a product of the period of deepest degradation, did not fit the new order of things and must speedily be abolished. A meeting of students was therefore called at the riding academy, from which, our object having been rumored about, the professors prudently absented themselves. My impromptu speech in the Aula caused my election as president of this meeting. We resolved to present an address to the academic senate, demanding that the officer in question should at once be removed. As chairman of the meeting I was charged with the duty to write the address on the spot. This was done. It was couched in very peremptory language and consisted only of four or five lines. The meeting approved it forthwith, and resolved—as in those days we loved to do things in dramatic style—to proceed in mass to the house of the rector of the university and personally to present the paper to him. So we marched, seven or eight hundred men, in dense column, to the dwelling of the rector and rang the bell. The rector, Herr van Calker, professor of philosophy, an oldish, anxious-looking little man, soon appeared on the doorstep, and I read to him the energetic sentences of our address. For a moment he timidly looked at the crowd of students, and then told us in halting and stammering phrases how rejoiced he was to behold the soaring spirit of German youth and how the students could accomplish in these important days great things, and that he would be happy to submit our address to the academic senate and to the government for speedy consideration and adjustment. We read upon the face of the good little man, toward whom everyone of us felt most kindly, that he contemplated the soaring spirit of German youth with a certain uneasiness, thanked him for his good-will, took our leave politely and

CARL SCHURZ AT NINETEEN

marched back to the market-square. There it was reported to us—whether truly or not—that during our visit to the rector the unpopular officer in question had speedily packed his trunks and already left the town.

While the jubilation over the "Märzerrungenschaften"—the results of the revolutionary movements in March—at first seemed to be general, and even the adherents of absolutism put a good face on a bad business, soon a separation into different party-groups began between those whose principal aim was the restoration of order and authority—the conservatives; those who wished slow and moderate progress—the constitutionalists; and those who aimed at securing the fruits of the revolution in "a constitutional government on the broadest democratic basis"—the democrats. Instinctive impulse as well as logical reasoning led me to the democratic side. There I met Kinkel again, and our friendship soon became very intimate. In the course of our common activity the formal relations between teacher and pupil yielded to a tone of thorough comradeship.

In the beginning the zealous work of agitation absorbed almost all our time and strength. Kinkel, indeed, still delivered his lectures, and I also attended mine with tolerable regularity; but my heart was not in them as before. All the more eagerly I studied modern history, especially the history of the French Revolution, and read a large number of politico-philosophical works and of pamphlets and periodicals of recent date, which treated of the problems of the time. In this way I endeavored to clear my political conceptions and to fill the large gaps in my historical knowledge—a want which I felt all the more seriously as my task as an agitator was to me a sacred duty.

First we organized a democratic club consisting of citizens and students, which found in the so-called Constitutional Club, led by Professor Löbell, a very able man, a most respectable opponent. Then we founded a local organ for the democratic party, the *Bonner Zeitung*, a daily paper, the editorship of which was undertaken by Kinkel, while I, as a regular contributor, had to furnish every day one or more articles. And finally, once or twice a week, in fact as often as we could, we marched out to the neighboring villages to preach to the country people the political gospel of the new time, and also to organize them into democratic clubs. Undoubtedly, the nineteen-year-old journalist and speaker brought forth a great deal of undigested stuff, but he believed sincerely and warmly in his cause and would have been ready at any time to sacrifice himself for it.

My activity in this direction, however, soon after its beginning came very near a sudden stop. Long before the breaking out of the revolution of March, the people of the Duchies of Schleswig and Holstein had made great efforts, while being united with Denmark by a "personal union," to win a politically independent existence. In March, 1848, the people of those Duchies rose in mass to the end of securing this independent position, and of making not only Holstein, but also Schleswig a part of the German Confederation. This uprising awakened in all Germany the liveliest sympathy, and in various places efforts were made to raise volunteer troops for the assistance of the people of the Duchies against the Danes. Especially at the universities these efforts struck a responsive chord, and students in large numbers went to Schleswig-Holstein to join the volunteer organizations. My first impulse was to do likewise. I was already engaged in serious preparations for departure when Kinkel persuaded me to desist, because the liberation of Schleswig-Holstein from the Danish yoke would be recognized by the German Parliament and the German governments as a national cause, and the Prussian and other regular troops would do much better service in the war than the loosely organized and badly drilled bodies of hastily gathered volunteers. Neither did he conceal from me that he was anxious to keep me with him in Bonn, where, as he sought to convince me, I could do the Fatherland much better service in the way of agitation for our cause. As it turned out, the volunteer organizations formed by students fought right bravely in Schleswig-Holstein, but when facing the superior discipline and tactics of the Danish troops, found themselves exposed to all sorts of ugly accidents. The service so rendered was therefore in no proportion to the sacrifices made by their members. The reports brought by several students who, after having served in Schleswig-Holstein for a little time, returned to the universities, consoled me for the restraint I had put upon my warlike ardor.

Several of these Schleswig-Holstein volunteers came to Bonn, and among them Adolph Strodtmann, who at a later period achieved in German literature a respectable place. He became my near personal friend, and will appear as such in this story of my life on various occasions. He was the son of a Protestant clergyman in Hadersleben, a little town in the Duchy of Schleswig. Father and son were enthusiastic adherents of the pro-German national cause, and young Adolph, who shortly before the outbreak of the Schleswig-Holstein uprising had left the gymnasium, joined at once a corps of student-volunteers. He was unfit for military service in a rare degree, for he was not only very nearsighted, but also of imperfect hearing. He told us frequently with great humor of his only martial achievement. One morning the corps of students was surprised in their camp by the Danes and roughly handled. Strodtmann noticed the general tumult and concluded that something extraordinary was the matter. The orders which were given he did not understand; but he joined the crowd of others and soon found himself alone enveloped in powder-smoke. "Then," he added, "I fired my rifle twice, but do not know to this moment whether in the right or wrong direction. I was so nearsighted that I could not distinguish the Danes from our people. I almost fear that I fired in the wrong direction, for suddenly I felt something like a heavy blow in my back; I fell and remained on the ground until the Danes lifted me up and took me away. It was found that a bullet had hit me in the back and had gone straight through me. Of course only a Dane could have shot me in the back, and inasmuch as I always remained in the one spot during the fight, I must have turned my back towards the Danes and fired off my rifle in the direction of our own people." Dangerously wounded, Strodtmann was taken to the "Dronning Maria," the Danish prison-ship, and after a little while exchanged. After a speedy recovery he came to the University of Bonn, to study languages and literature.

His physical infirmities made him a somewhat singular person. His deafness caused all sorts of funny misunderstandings, at which he usually was the first to laugh. He spoke with a very loud voice as if the rest of us had been as deaf as he was himself. In consequence of his wound he had accustomed himself in walking to put one shoulder forward so that he always looked as if he were squeezing himself through an invisible crowd of people, and he was at the same time so inattentive that he ran against all possible objects. But he was a most sincere and honest enthusiast; of almost childlike ingenuousness in his views of men, things, and events; in a high degree capable of self-sacrifice and open to generous and noble impulses. His gifts as well as his inclinations made him devote himself to literature. His verses, which he produced in great profusion and with uncommon facility, excelled less by originality of thought or fancy, than by an abundant and superb flow of poetical expression. It was largely owing to this talent that he subsequently wrote some admirable translations of French, English and Danish poetry and prose. His political instincts were strongly democratic, and he joined the agitation led by Kinkel with great zeal. It was thus that he and I became fast friends.

CHAPTER VI

THE political horizon which after the revolution in March looked so glorious soon began to darken. In South Germany, where the opinion had gained ground that the revolution should not have "stood still before the thrones," a republican uprising took place under the leadership of the brilliant and impetuous Hecker, which, however, was speedily suppressed by force of arms. In the country at large such attempts found at first little sympathy. The bulk of the liberal element did not desire anything beyond the establishment of national unity and a constitutional monarchy "on a broad democratic basis." But the republican sentiment gradually spread and was intensified as the "reaction" assumed a more and more threatening shape.

The national parliament at Frankfurt elected in the spring, which represented the sovereignty of the German people in the large sense and was to give to the united German nation a national government, counted among its members a great many men illustrious in the fields, not of politics, but of science and literature. It soon showed a dangerous tendency of squandering in brilliant, but more or less fruitless, debates much of the time which was sorely needed for prompt and decisive action to secure the legitimate results of the revolution against hostile forces.

But our eyes were turned still more anxiously upon Berlin. Prussia was by far the strongest of the purely German states. The Austrian empire was a conglomeration of different nationalities—German, Magyar, Slavic and Italian. The

German element, to which the dynasty and the political capital belonged, had so far been the predominant one. It was most advanced in civilization and wealth, although inferior in numbers. But the Slavs, the Magyars and the Italians, stimulated by the revolutionary movements of 1848, were striving for national autonomy, and although Austria had held the foremost place in the later periods of the ancient German empire and then after the Napoleonic wars in the German Confederacy, it seemed problematic whether her large non-German interests would permit her to play a leading part now in the political unification of Germany under a constitutional government. In fact, it turned out subsequently that the mutual jealousies of the different races enabled the Austrian central government to subjugate to despotic rule one by the other, in spite of the hopeful beginnings of the revolution, and that the non-German interests of Austria and those of the dynasty were predominant in her policy. But Prussia, excepting a comparatively small Polish district, was a purely German country, and by far the strongest among the German states in point of numbers, of general education, of economic activity and especially of military power. It was, therefore, generally felt that the attitude of Prussia would be decisive in determining the fate of the revolution.

For a while the Prussian king, Frederick William IV., seemed to be pleased with the rôle of a leader in the national movement which the revolution had made him assume. His volatile nature seemed to be warmed by a new enthusiasm. He took walks on the streets and talked freely with the people. He spoke of constitutional principles of government to be introduced as a matter of course. He loudly praised the noble generosity which the people of Berlin had manifested toward him in the hours of stress. He ordered the army to wear the black-red-gold cockade together with the Prussian. On the parade ground at Potsdam he declared to the sulking officers of the guards "that he felt himself perfectly safe, free and happy among the citizens of Berlin; that all the concessions made by him had been made of his own free will and according to his own convictions, and that nobody should dare to question this." But when the Prussian constituent assembly had met in Berlin and began to pass laws, and to design constitutional provisions, and to interfere with the conduct of the government in the spirit of the revolution, the king's mind gradually opened itself to other influences, and those influences gained access to him and surrounded him all the more readily since he removed his residence from Berlin to his palace at Potsdam, a little town preponderantly inhabited by courtiers and soldiers and other dependents of the government. Thus the king's immediate contact with the people ceased, his conferences with the newly appointed liberal ministers were confined to short formal "audiences," and voices appealing to old sympathies, prepossessions and partialities were constantly nearest to his ear.

There was the army, traditionally the pet of the Hohenzollerns, smarting under the "disgrace" of its withdrawal from Berlin after the street battle, and pining for revenge and restoration of its prestige. There was the court nobility, whose business it always had been to exalt and flatter the royal person. There was the landed aristocracy, the "Junker" element, whose feudal privileges were theoretically denied by the revolutionary spirit and practically invaded by the legislative action of the representatives of the people, and who artfully goaded the king's pride. There was the old bureaucracy, the power of which had been broken by the revolution, although its personnel had but little been changed, and which sought to recover its former sway. There was the "old Prussian" spirit which resented any national aspirations that might encroach upon the importance and self-appreciation of specific Prussiandom, and which still had strength in the country immediately surrounding Berlin and in some of the eastern provinces. All these forces, which in a general term were popularly called "the reaction," worked together to divert the king from the course he had ostensibly taken immediately after the revolution of March, with the hope of using him for the largest possible restoration of the old order of things—well knowing that if they controlled him, they would, through him, control the army, and then with it a tremendous, perhaps decisive, force in the conflicts to come. And this "reaction" was greatly strengthened by the cunning exploitation of some street excesses that happened in Berlin—excesses which in a free country like England might, indeed, have brought forth some vigorous measures of repression by the police, but would certainly not have induced anybody to call the practicability of civil freedom or of the constitutional principles of government in question. But these occurrences were used in Prussia with considerable effect to frighten the timid men of the bourgeoisie with the specter of general anarchy, and to persuade the king that after all the restoration of unrestrained royal power was necessary for the maintenance of law and order.

On the other hand, the visible development of the reaction had the effect of producing among many of those who stood earnestly for national unity and constitutional government, a state of mind more open to radical tendencies. The rapid progress of these developments was clearly perceptible in my own surroundings. Our democratic club was composed in almost equal parts of students and citizens, among whom there were many of excellent character, of some fortune and good standing, and of moderate views, while a few others had worked themselves into a state of mind resembling that of the terrorists in the French Revolution. Kinkel was the recognized leader of the club, and I soon became a member of the executive committee. At first the establishment of a constitutional monarchy with universal suffrage and well-secured civil rights would have been quite satisfactory to us. But the reaction, the threatened rise of which we were observing, gradually made many of us believe that there was no safety for popular liberty except in a republic. From this belief there was only one step to the further conclusion, that in a republic, and only in a republic, all evils of the social body could be cured, and the solution of all the political problems would be possible. The idealism which saw in the republican citizen the highest embodiment of human dignity we had imbibed from the study of classic antiquity; and the history of the French Revolution satisfied us that a republic could be created in Germany and could maintain its existence in the European system of states. In that history we found striking examples of the possibility of accomplishing the seemingly impossible, if only the whole energy resting in a great nation were awakened and directed with unflinching boldness. Most of us indeed recoiled from the wild excesses which had stained with streams of innocent blood the national uprising in France during the Reign of Terror. But we hoped to stir up the national energies without such terrorism. At any rate the history of the French Revolution furnished to us models in plenty that mightily excited our imagination. How dangerously seductive such a play of the imagination is, we were of course then unaware.

As usually happens, we tried first to imitate our models in certain external things. To emphasize the principle of equality among the members of our club, we introduced the rule that there should be for all, however different might be their rank in life, only one form of address, namely, "citizen." There was to be no longer a "Herr Professor Kinkel," but only a "Citizen Kinkel," and so on through the list. We did not permit ourselves to be disturbed by the ridicule which this oddity attracted, for we were profoundly in earnest, sincerely believing that by the introduction of this style we could give tone to the developments which would inevitably come. Of the debates in our club my recollection is not distinct enough to say how much reason or how much unreason there was in them. At all events they were carried on sometimes with remarkably eloquent earnestness, because most of the participants spoke from genuine honesty of conviction.

In the course of the summer Kinkel and I were invited to represent the club at a congress of democratic associations in Cologne. This assembly, in which I remained a shy and silent observer, became remarkable to me in bringing me into personal contact with some of the prominent men of that period, among others, the leader of the communists, Karl Marx. He could not have been much more than thirty years old at that time, but he already was the recognized head of the advanced socialistic school. The somewhat thick-set man, with his broad forehead, his very black hair and beard and his dark sparkling eyes, at once attracted general attention. He enjoyed the reputation of having acquired great learning, and as I knew very little of his discoveries and theories, I was all the more eager to gather words of wisdom from the lips of that famous man. This expectation was disappointed in a peculiar way. Marx's utterances were indeed full of meaning, logical and clear, but I have never seen a man whose bearing was so provoking and intolerable. To no opinion, which differed from his, he accorded the honor of even a condescending consideration. Everyone who contradicted him he treated with abject contempt; every argument that he did not like he answered either with biting scorn at the unfathomable ignorance that had prompted it, or with opprobrious aspersions upon the motives of him who had advanced it. I remember most distinctly the cutting disdain with which he pronounced the word "bourgeois"; and as a "bourgeois," that is as a detestable example of the deepest mental and moral degeneracy he denounced everyone that dared to oppose his opinion. Of course the propositions advanced or advocated by Marx in that meeting were voted down, because everyone whose feelings had been hurt by his conduct was inclined to support everything that Marx did not favor. It was very evident that not only he had not won any adherents, but had repelled many who otherwise might have become his followers.

From this meeting I took home with me a very important lesson: that he who would be a leader and teacher of men must treat the opinions of his hearers with respect; that even the most superior mind will lose influence upon others if he seeks to humiliate those others by constant demonstrations of his superiority. That public man will be most successful in enlightening and winning the ignorant who puts himself upon their standpoint, not with condescension, but with sympathy.

On the whole the summer of 1848 was to me a time of work and worry. The newspaper for which I had to write articles, the agitation in clubs and popular meetings, and besides my studies, imposed upon me a very heavy burden of labor, in which—I must confess—my studies fell into a somewhat subordinate place. What troubled me most was the visibly and constantly growing power of the reactionary forces and the frittering away of the opportunities to create something real and durable, by the national parliament in Frankfurt and by the assembly in Berlin. I remember well to have carried with me an oppressive consciousness of my own ignorance in political things, which was the more painful the more urgent appeared the necessity for the people to be prepared for prudent and energetic action in the decisive struggles which impended.

Our activity, however, had also a cheerful side of which my youthful spirits were keenly susceptible. We students enjoyed with the country-people a very great popularity, and even persons who did not sympathize with us politically received us with a kindness which sometimes was so exuberant as to make our presence the occasion of gay festivities.

The most interesting event of those days which I have cherished in my memory was the student-congress in Eisenach, which occurred in September, 1848, and which I attended as one of the chosen representatives of the university men of Bonn. This was the first long journey of my life. I had never before been far enough away from my paternal roof that I might not have returned in a few hours. On a bright September morning I sailed up the Rhine from Bonn to Mainz. I should have enjoyed it with the fullness of youthful spirits had I been able to drive away the disquieting thoughts which were stirred up by confused rumors of a riot and street-battle in Frankfurt. In fact, upon my arrival in that city I found those rumors distressingly verified.

The revolt in Frankfurt was the outcome of the following events. I have already mentioned that the popular uprising in the duchies of Holstein and Schleswig against the Danish rule had been sanctioned as a national cause by the old Diet of the German Confederation, and then by the national parliament and by all the several German governments.

Prussian and other German troops had marched into the duchies and won considerable advantages over the Danish army on the field of battle. Everything promised a speedy and happy termination of the war. It was therefore a painful surprise when the Prussian government, whose head, Frederick William IV., had as usual permitted himself to be intimidated by the other European powers, concluded in the name of the German Confederation a truce with Denmark—the so-called "truce of Malmö"—in which it was agreed that the victorious German troops were to retire from the duchies, that the duchies were to lose their own provisional government, and that a commission composed of two Prussians, two Danes and a fifth member to be elected by them was to govern the disputed country. At the same time all the laws and ordinances that had been issued by the Schleswig-Holstein authorities since the days of March, 1848, were declared invalid. This truce called forth the greatest indignation all over Germany. The representative assembly of Schleswig-Holstein protested. The national parliament in Frankfurt, which saw not only the honor of Germany greviously compromised, but its own authority overruled by these proceedings of the Prussian government, resolved on September 5 to refuse the recognition of the truce of Malmö and to demand the suspension of all the measures stipulated therein. But after several failures to form a new ministry on the basis of this resolution, and not daring to bring the question of authority between itself and the Prussian government to a direct issue, the parliament revoked the resolution of September 5, ten days later, and declared at the same time that the execution of the truce of Malmö could apparently no longer be hindered. This declaration, which seemed to strike the sympathies of the German people full in the face, caused immense excitement, of which the revolutionary leaders in Frankfurt and the surrounding country at once took advantage. On the next day a large mass meeting was held on a meadow near Frankfurt. Inflammatory speeches goaded the passions of the multitude to fury, and the meeting adopted resolutions by which the members of the majority of the national parliament in Frankfurt were branded as traitors to the German nation. Troops of armed democrats poured in from all sides, and an attempt was made to force the parliament to revoke the hateful declaration, or to drive out the traitorous majority. Two prominent conservative members of the parliament, Count Auerswald and Prince Lichnowsky, fell into the hands of the revolutionists and were killed; and then followed a bloody struggle in the streets of Frankfurt, in which the insurgents soon succumbed to the quickly concentrated troops.

When on my way to Eisenach I arrived in Frankfurt, the victorious soldiery still bivouacked on the streets around their burning campfires; the barricades had not yet been removed; the pavement was still stained with blood, and everywhere the heavy tramp of military patrols was heard. With difficulty I made my way to the hotel "Zum Schwan," where I was to meet, according to agreement, some Heidelberg students, in order to continue in their company the journey to Eisenach. With hearts full of gloom we sat together deep into the night, for we all felt that the cause of liberty and of popular sovereignty had received a terrible blow. The royal Prussian government had successfully defied the national parliament, which represented the sovereignty of the German nation. Those who called themselves "the people" had made a hostile attempt upon the embodiment of popular sovereignty which had issued from the revolution, and this embodiment of popular sovereignty had been obliged to call upon the armed forces of the princes for protection against the hatred of "the people." Thus the backbone of the revolution begun in March, 1848, was substantially broken. We young students indeed did not see so far. But we felt that terrible mischief had been done. Our youthful spirits, however, consoled themselves with the hope that what was lost might still be recovered by well-directed and energetic action under more favorable circumstances.

The next day I visited with some of my friends the gallery of St. Paul's Church, in which the national parliament held its sessions. With that profound reverence, the organ of which (to express myself in the language of phrenology) has always been with me very strongly developed, I looked at that historic spot, in which the fate of the revolution of 1848 was already foretold. On "the right" there sat, with a smile of triumph on their lips, men whose principal aim it was to restore the old order of things; in "the center" the advocates of a liberal constitutional monarchy, tormented by anxious doubt as to whether they could control the revolutionary tendencies without making the absolutist reaction all-powerful; on "the left" the democrats and republicans with the oppressive consciousness that the masses of the people, in whom they were to find the source of their power, had grievously compromised them by this wild eruption of passion at Frankfurt and had thus put the most dangerous weapon into the hands of the reactionists.

I remember well the men whom my eyes most eagerly sought. On "the right" Radowitz, whose finely chiseled face, somewhat oriental in its character, looked like a sealed book containing the secret of reactionary politics; in "the center" Heinrich von Gagern, with his imposing stature and heavy eyebrows; on "the left" the Silenus-head of Robert Blum, whom many regarded as the ideal man of the people; and the little shriveled figure of the old poet, Ludwig Uhland, whose songs we had so often sung, and who with such touching fidelity stood by that which he believed to be the good right of his people!

In the evening we traveled on to Eisenach, and soon I found myself in the midst of a company that could not have been more congenial.

The pleasant little town of Eisenach, at the foot of the Wartburg, where Luther translated the Bible into good German and threw his inkstand at the head of the devil, had repeatedly been selected by the old Burschenschaft as the theater of its great demonstrations. The object of the present student-congress consisted mainly in the national organization of German university men with an executive committee to facilitate united action. There were also to be discussed various reforms needed at the universities, of which however, so far as I can remember, nobody could give an entirely clear account. We organized ourselves according to parliamentary rules so that our oratorical performances might begin at once. All the German universities, including those of Austria, having sent delegations to this congress, the meeting was large in numbers and contained many young men of uncommon gifts. Those who attracted the most attention both within and without our assembly were the Viennese, of whom nine or ten had reported themselves. They wore the handsome uniform of the famous "academic legion"—black felt hats with ostrich plumes, blue coats with black shining buttons, tricolored, black-red-gold sashes, bright steel-handled swords, light gray trousers, and silver-gray cloaks lined with scarlet. They looked like a troop of knights of old. When the citizens of Eisenach, who had received up with most cordial kindness, gave a ball in our honor, all competition with the Viennese for the favors of the fair sex was in vain. But it was not their outward appearance alone that distinguished them. They were men of marked ability and already had a history behind them which made them an object of general interest and appealed in a high degree to the imagination.

Nowhere had the university students played so important and prominent a part in the revolutionary movement as in Vienna. To them was largely owing the uprising that drove Prince Metternich from power. The "academic legion," which they organized and which, if I am not mistaken, counted about 6000 men, formed the nucleus of the armed power of the revolution. In the "central committee," which consisted of an equal number of students and members of the citizens' guard, and which stood for the will of the people as against the government, they exercised a preponderant influence. Deputations of citizens and peasants came from all parts of Austria to present their grievances and petitions to the "Aula," the headquarters of the students, which had suddenly risen as an authority omnipotent in the opinion of the multitude. When the imperial ministry was about to promulgate a new press-law, which indeed abolished the censorship but still contained many restrictions, its chief requested the students to express their judgment about that law. And on May 15 the students at the head of the armed people forced the government by their determined attitude to revoke the constitution which the government had framed on its own authority, and to promise the convocation of the constituent assembly. The students successfully maintained their organization against various attempts of the government to dissolve it. They compelled the ministry to agree to the removal of the soldiery from the city of Vienna and to the formation of a committee of public safety, which was to consist principally of the members of the students' organization. So independent and so comprehensive a power was confided to it that in several important respects it stood by the side of the ministry as co-ordinate. Without its consent, for instance, no military force should be employed in the city. Thus it might have been said without much exaggeration that for a certain time the students of Vienna governed Austria.

It was, therefore, not astonishing that the Viennese legionaries, who had already made so much history, were among us regarded as the heroes of the day, and that with eager attention we listened to their reports about the condition of things in their country. Those reports, however, opened a prospect of further serious troubles if not of a tragical end, and of this our Viennese friends were sadly conscious. They knew that the victories of the Austrian Field Marshal Radetzki in Italy over Carlo Alberto, the king of Piedmont, would give Austria's army new prestige and the reactionary court-party new power; that this court-party systematically inflamed and used the Czechs against the Germans in Austria; that the presence in the capital of the constituent assembly, the convocation of which the students themselves had asked for, would greatly impair the power of the revolutionary authorities; that in the civic guards and in the committee of public safety mischievous dissensions had broken out; that the court-party derived from all these things great advantage and would avail itself of the first favorable opportunity to sweep away the fruits of the revolution in general, and to suppress the students' organization in particular, and that the decisive struggle would come soon.

These presentiments sometimes fell like dark shadows upon our otherwise so jovial conviviality, and it required all the elasticity of youthful spirits to console us with the hope that finally all would be well.

While we were still planning various excursions from Eisenach into the surrounding country, our Viennese friends informed us that they had received letters from the "Aula" about the threatening situation of things, which obliged them to return to Vienna without delay. They parted from us with a real "morituri salutamus." "In a few days," they said, "we shall have to fight a battle in Vienna, and then you may look for our names on the list of the dead." I still see one of them before me—he was a young man of rare beauty, by the name of Valentin—who spoke those words. Thus our admired Viennese legionaries took leave of us, and we trembled in appreciating how terribly and how quickly their prediction might come true.

The rest of us also were now obliged to think of journeying home. The only practical object of the student-congress was accomplished. The general organization of the German university men had been resolved upon and the executive authority designated. Subjects for further discussions there were none. The funds of many of us too were beginning to run low. But with every hour our parting appeared harder to bear. We had come to love one another so much and our companionship was so enjoyable that we strained our inventive genius to the utmost to save at least a few days. At last we took an inventory of the money that was still in our pockets in order to form a common purse, out of which, after the means necessary for our respective homeward journey had been reserved, the cost of further convivial pleasures was to be defrayed. In this way we really gained a few days which we enjoyed to our heart's content and at once some festivities were planned, one of which came very near having a bad end.

One evening we marched up to the Wartburg. There a plenteous spread with beer awaited us, having consumed which, we were in the dusk of evening to march down the mountain to the town by the light of torches. As the merry students had become great favorites with the population of Eisenach, a multitude of citizens, and among them a considerable number of soldiers, who were in garrison in Eisenach, accompanied us to take part in our jollification. As was the custom of the time, political speeches were made during the entertainment, and the indignation against the princes, especially the king of Prussia, on account of the truce of Malmö being still very bitter, some of those speeches assumed a decidedly republican tone. Presently the excitement grew hot, and some of the soldiers threw up their caps, cheered for the Republic, and declared that they would put themselves under the order of the students. Meanwhile evening had come and the whole company, preceded and surrounded by burning torches, and singing patriotic songs, marched down the forest road to Eisenach. This spectacle was charming, but the effect produced upon the soldiers by the revolutionary speeches made some of us a little uncomfortable as to results. So far as any of us knew, there was no understanding with other parts of the country which would have insured to a popular uprising in Thuringia any outside support, and to incite harmless people, especially soldiers, to a revolutionary attempt, without plan or purpose, which could have for them only very mischievous consequences, appeared to me for one in a high degree objectionable. If, however, which was probable, nothing came of it beyond what had already happened, there would be no serious harm; and with this comforting hope I went to bed, not knowing what was happening in the meantime. The following morning I heard that a large part of the multitude that had participated in our festival on the Wartburg had gone on to a public resort. There the speechmaking was continued; the number of soldiers among the audience had largely increased, and these had with remarkable unanimity and in a tumultuous way again cheered the Republic, and finally refused obedience to some officers present who had ordered them to go away. During the night the excitement had spread among the soldiers until well-nigh the whole military garrison of Eisenach was in a condition of actual mutiny. The officers had lost all control. Troops of soldiers now came to us with the request that we students should put ourselves at their head. This indeed had not been the purpose of the speechmakers of yesterday, who now had to use every possible effort to prevent further mischief. From Weimar, the capital of the duchy, telegraphic orders arrived forthwith to remove to that city the soldiers garrisoned in Eisenach. But the soldiers stubbornly refused to go; they insisted upon remaining with the students. Now the civic guard of Eisenach was summoned to force the soldiers to depart. But when that civic guard was in line on the market-place, it did not show the least willingness to undertake the task. The guardsmen, rather, amused themselves with cheering the students. The embarrassment grew more and more serious. At last we succeeded in persuading the officers of the troops that all this was only a merry and light-hearted student frolic, and that the soldiers ought not to be held to account for having, amid the general hilarity, and perhaps under the influence of excessive potations, fraternized with the students. The officers at last were induced to take the jocular view of the matter, and we engaged ourselves to bring the soldiers back to their duty, if the authorities promised that nothing would happen to them in consequence of this escapade. The promise came at once and now we succeeded in persuading the soldiers quietly to rally around their colors. Fortunately it was at that time still possible in the small states of Germany to arrange such things in so good-natured a manner. In Prussia an occurrence of this kind would have produced very serious consequences.

After this performance we felt that now it was indeed time for us to depart from Eisenach and to go home. Our financial resources too were very nearly exhausted. On the evening before our departure we had a last great carousal in the Rathskeller. One of us, if I remember rightly a student from Königsberg, who had distinguished himself by wearing a Polish cap and by indulging in extremely revolutionary phraseology, made the motion that before parting we should issue an address to the German people and let them know our opinion about the existing condition of things, and then admonish them closely to watch and with all possible energy to resist the advancing reaction. That such a proclamation, at such a moment, coming from such a lot of young persons, could have an aspect intensely comical, did not occur to us. The motion was discussed with the greatest seriousness and unanimously adopted. The address was drawn up at once. Then, with the signatures of the committee, to which I too had the honor of belonging, it was printed the same night, posted on the walls of the city hall and of various other public buildings, and sent to several newspapers for further publication. This having been done, we sang several patriotic songs and then we parted after tender embraces and vows of eternal friendship. Early the next morning we scattered in all directions.

On the way home an extremely sober feeling came over me. In Frankfurt I still found a "state of siege" and a gloomy atmosphere of anxiety. The day was cloudy, damp and cold when I went down the Rhine on the steamboat. Among the passengers I did not see a single familiar face.

As I sat hour after hour alone and shivering on the deck, disquieting thoughts began to trouble me, not only about the general course of things, but also for the first time about my own personal safety. I remembered the wording of the address which we had published in Eisenach, and which contained several sharp attacks upon the majority of the national parliament and upon the Prussian government. I remembered also to have read in the papers that the parliament in consequence of the September revolt had passed a law which imposed a heavy penalty upon utterances insulting to its members. Had we not actually committed that crime in our published address? Undoubtedly; and thus I began to picture to myself how after my arrival in Bonn I would soon be arrested, and on account of the press-offense against the national parliament and the Prussian government put on trial. Of course I resolved to suffer courageously for my convictions. What troubled me more was the thought that our address probably would have no other effect than this. But my apprehension that I would be arrested and punished proved to be entirely superfluous. If our proclamation had really come to the knowledge of the government, the authorities probably did not think it worth while to take any notice of it; and I drew from this the lesson—a not at all flattering one—that we young people might possibly appear to others much less important than to ourselves. Before long, however, conflicts really serious arrived.

Momentous news from Vienna confirmed the predictions of our Viennese friends in Eisenach. Hungary had in the days of March asserted a high degree of political autonomy under a "personal union" with Austria. It had its own ministry residing in Pesth, without whose counter-signature no order of the Austrian emperor concerning Hungary should be valid.

Without the assent of the Hungarian legislature no Hungarian troops should be employed outside of the boundaries of Hungary, nor should non-Hungarian troops enter within those boundaries. The "Archduke Palatin," an Austrian prince, should as Viceroy of Hungary, have his residence in Pesth. In addition to this, the German and Slavic districts, which so far had been considered as belonging to Hungary, should remain as integral parts of the country subject to the Hungarian government. The to a large extent independent Hungarian government was an object of detestation to the Austrian court-party. That party resorted to various intrigues, which resulted in a direct breach between the Austrian and Hungarian governments, in the killing of an imperial emissary by an excited multitude in Pesth, and in the creation by the Hungarians of a national government-commission in Hungary, followed by a proclamation from the Austrian emperor which virtually amounted to a declaration of war. The Hungarians prepared for the struggle, and when in October Austrian troops were dispatched from Vienna for the subjugation of Hungary, the people of Vienna, the students at their head, rose in revolt against their own government, with the feeling that the attempt to destroy the constitutional rights of the Hungarians was at the same time directed against the rights of the German Austrians, and against all the fruits of the revolution. The minister of war, Count Latour, was hanged to a lamp-post by an infuriated crowd. After a bloody fight the insurrectionists controlled the city. The commander of the garrison, Count Auersperg, found himself obliged to evacuate the town, but he entrenched himself in a strong position outside, and was soon reinforced by large bodies of troops under Prince Windischgrätz. Windischgrätz took command of the army, attacked the city of Vienna on October 23, and after long and bloody struggles he put down the last resistance on the 31st. Vienna was then subjected to the unlimited arbitrariness of military rule, and the revolutionary movement in German Austria had an end. Several of the chivalrous legionaries, with whom we students had enjoyed such sunny days in Eisenach, had fallen in the battle, and the rest were fugitives.

With this catastrophe coincided a marked turn of affairs in Prussia. Since March the Prussian government had moved in constitutional forms, and the ministry, at the head of which stood the liberal General von Pfuel, showed itself willing to fulfill the promises that had been given. But the king and his immediate surroundings had on various occasions manifested a disposition which hardly harmonized with those pledges and called forth grave apprehensions. On October 31 the Prussian Constituent Assembly gave voice to the general sympathy with the struggling people of Vienna and resolved to request his Majesty's government "to take speedy and energetic steps to induce the German central power in Frankfurt to effectually protect the imperiled liberties of the people in the German districts of Austria, and to restore peace." The president of the ministry, General von Pfuel, supported this resolution. The next day he found himself compelled to resign, and the king then appointed a ministry of decidedly reactionary character, at the head of which he put Count Brandenburg, and the leading spirit of which was Herr von Manteuffel. The Constituent Assembly solemnly protested, but in vain. On November 9 the Brandenburg ministry presented itself to the Assembly with a royal message which transferred the meetings of that body to another place and prorogued its sessions until November 27. By a large majority the Assembly denied the right of the royal government to do these things, but the next day the house was surrounded by large bodies of troops under

General Wrangel, who gave the order that nobody should be permitted to enter, but anybody might leave the building. On November 11 the civil guard of Berlin was dissolved and in a few days disarmed. The Assembly moved from one place to another, constantly followed by the soldiery, until finally on November 15, at its last meeting, it refused to vote the supplies, and declared "that this ministry had no right to dispose of the moneys of the state or to levy taxes, so long as the Constituent Assembly could not undisturbed continue its deliberations in Berlin." These events called forth immense excitement all over the country. They seemed to prove that the reactionary court-parties were determined to sweep away by force all the fruits of the revolution.

That the Constituent Assembly in opposing the "coup d'état" was altogether within its right, admitted of no doubt in the minds of the democrats. They blamed it only for not having made the fullest use of its right by calling the people directly to arms, and for having at this moment of great decision limited itself to the weak-kneed policy of "passive resistance." But they thought that this passive resistance by means of a general refusal to pay taxes might finally force the government to yield, assuming that the refusal to pay taxes would become general and be maintained with inflexible steadiness.

The democrats in Bonn, among whom we students played a prominent part, were zealous in demonstrating their determination to support the Constituent Assembly. The declaration that we would refuse the payment of taxes coming from the students looked somewhat like a huge joke, because we had none to pay. The problem we had to solve, therefore, consisted in persuading other people to refuse to pay their taxes. We believed we could strike a demonstrative blow by stopping the levying of octroi duties which were levied at the gates of the city on the food-stuffs brought to the town. We did this in driving the revenue officers from their posts, which pleased the peasants, who were at once ready to bring their products free of duty into the city. This led to conflicts with the police in which, however, we easily had the upper hand.

Now it appeared to us unnecessary to seize upon the general machinery of the tax-department. The next day a committee, of which I was a member, appeared at the city hall to take possession of it. The Burgomaster received us with great politeness and listened quietly to what we had to say to him about the authority of the Constituent Assembly and its power to stop the payment of taxes; but he tried to amuse us with all sorts of evasive talk. At last we became impatient and demanded an immediate and definite answer according to which we would resolve upon further measures. Suddenly we noticed a change in the expression of the Burgomaster's face. He seemed to hearken to something going on outside and then, still politely but with a sort of triumphant smile on his lips, he said: "Gentlemen, your answer you will have to receive from somebody else. Do you hear that?" Now we hearkened too, and heard a still distant, but approaching, sound of a military band playing the Prussian national air. The music sounded nearer and nearer in the street leading up from the Rhine. In a few minutes it reached the market-place and behind it came the heavy tramp of an infantry column which presently filled a large part of the square in front of the city hall. Our conversation with the Burgomaster of course came to a sudden end and we thought it very decent on his part that he permitted us to leave the building undisturbed.

The appearance of the military was easily explained. As soon as we began to refuse the payment of taxes, the authorities in Bonn, which at that time had no garrison, had telegraphed to the nearest fortress for aid, and the call was promptly responded to. This of course put a stop to our doings in the matter of stopping the payment of taxes. The soldiers at once occupied the gates of the city and the octroi duties were levied as before. In the evening we had a meeting of our democratic committee to consider what was next to be done. The first impulse was to attack the soldiers and if possible to drive them out of the town. This would have been a desperate enterprise, but it was taken seriously in view. After mature consideration, however, we all recognized that a fight in Bonn, even a successful one, could have real importance only as a part of a more general uprising. Cologne was naturally regarded as the capital of the Rhineland and as the central focus for all political movements. It was there we had to seek our support, and from there to get our orders. We had already received from Cologne a report that feverish excitement prevailed in that city, and that the signal for a general uprising was to be expected from the democratic leaders. For this we were to prepare quietly and quickly, but we were to avoid everything like an isolated attempt. We sent a messenger to Cologne to inform our friends of what had occurred in Bonn and to get further instructions. In the meantime we made arrangements to collect as many as possible of the muskets of our civic-guard and to make cartridges, which was done with great zeal.

But now disquieting news came about what happened in the vicinity of the gates of the city. Large crowds of peasants from the neighboring villages had assembled outside. They had received information about the coming of the soldiers to Bonn and thought that the democrats and the students must be in great danger. They had now come to help us. Many of them probably imagined the expulsion of the troops from the city to be as easy as had been the driving away of the tax officers from the gates. Some of them were spoiling for a fight. We had indeed reason for apprehending that they would press into the city and involve us in a street-battle with the soldiers under very unfavorable circumstances. It was not an easy task to persuade those impatient people to go home and to keep themselves ready to aid us as soon as the signal for action should come from Cologne. The whole night our committee waited for the return of the messenger we had sent there. About day-break we separated, but only to meet again after a short rest. The preparations for war continued in the meantime. Not one of us slept in his own quarters, so as not to be easily found in case the authorities should try to arrest us. I took refuge in a friend's room that was filled with muskets and cases of cart-ridges which were stored there ready for distribution.

Our messenger did not return from Cologne before even-ing of the next day. He reported that our friends did not feel themselves able to attempt a blow with any prospect of success against the large masses of troops gathered there; that they would confine themselves to the continuation of the "passive resistance," and that they urgently recommended to us to abstain from all violent steps until further orders. Nothing remained to us therefore but to swallow our wrath and to keep our friends in the open country quiet. What happened with us, happened all over the kingdom of Prussia. The Constituent Assembly had yielded to the government a bloodless victory and the resolution to refuse the payment of taxes soon became a dead letter.

But it looked as if the whole affair would come home to the democratic leaders among the students in a disagreeable way. There was a rumor that against three or four of us, against me among others, warrants had been issued, and that we had to expect our arrest any moment. Whether it was really so, I did not know, but it was so believed; and our friends went at once to work to protect us from harm. They spread the impression among the citizens of Bonn that if we were touched by the police, all the students would quit the city. Now, as the prosperity of Bonn depended in a great measure upon the presence of the students, this caused no little alarm among the good burghers. Many of them urgently asked the Burgomaster to use his whole influence to obtain from the higher authorities the promise that nothing should happen to us, and thus to avert the threatening calamity. In fact we were informed by our friends in the course of a few days that such a promise had indeed been given, and that for once we should escape unharmed. We therefore left our hiding places, and I continued to write for our newspaper, to address meetings and to attend lectures, so far as I could find time to do so.

Frederick William IV., after having won his victory over the Constituent Assembly, felt himself strong enough to give to Prussia a constitution of his own exclusive making, without submitting it for assent to the representatives of the people. This constitution of his provided for a Diet consisting of two Chambers. The Chambers were convoked at once and Kinkel stepped forward in Bonn as a candidate for the lower House. He was elected by a large majority, and had to take his seat soon after. Frau Kinkel accompanied him to Berlin. Although they sent me regular contributions for the columns of the *Bonner Zeitung*, the daily duties of the editorship fell upon my shoulders during their absence as a very heavy burden of unaccustomed work.

The *Bonner Zeitung* having only a very small editorial staff, I had not only to furnish political articles, but also many other things which a daily paper must offer to its readers—

among others the reports about the stage. A theater had been established in Bonn which gave respectable performances, and even light opera. To the *Bonner Zeitung* the director of the theater assigned a box for its reporters, the principal reporter having so far been Mme. Kinkel. This box was now at my disposal, and I occupied it, not only when journalistic duties called me to witness the performance of a new play, but sometimes also when I felt the want of a little relaxation from my many labors and cares. Here I must confess that to these labors and cares an affair of the heart had been added.

Until this time no woman outside of my family-circle had played any part in my life, perhaps largely because of my excessive bashfulness. At length inevitable fate laid its hand upon me too. I really fell in love, head over heels, at first sight, with a beautiful young lady. She was the daughter of a little merchant. Her name was Betty. I had never been introduced to her and we had never exchanged a word. I had only seen her sitting at her window, occupied with embroidery; still oftener with a book in her hand, I had frequently passed by this window, and almost always she sat there. Sometimes our eyes met, and I then was conscious of blushing all over. From a friend of hers I heard that she was reading Shakespeare in the English original, which gave me a high idea of her mental gifts and acquirements. The sly manner in which I sometimes turned the conversation with that friend in the direction of Betty, was, of course, self-betraying; and from what he told me in return, I was happy to suspect that Betty too was aware of my existence. I ardently longed to know her and soon found a to me surprisingly favorable opportunity.

One evening while sitting in the theater-box,—Flotow's opera " Martha " was on the stage,—two ladies took seats in the one adjoining mine. A few minutes later I turned and could hardly believe my eyes when, with a violent heart jump, I suddenly became aware that only the low partition between the boxes separated me from Betty. Soon the ladies began to look around for something and I heard them say that they had left their opera-glasses at home. Here was an evident opportunity for me. I held my own opera-glass in my hand. What more natural than to offer it to Betty with a polite word? Indeed, was it not positively impolite not to do so? But—but—the necessary words would not come. I sat completely paralyzed and tongue-tied throughout the whole play. Finally the ladies left the box and with them my long hoped-for opportunity. I rushed from the theater, tormenting myself with self-reproach, and instead of going, as I had intended, to the Franconia, I took a long, lonely walk in the night. But soon this love-dream became more shadowy than ever, for events occurred which tore me altogether out of my surroundings.

Of the larger parliamentary bodies that had issued from the revolution of March, only the national parliament in Frankfurt was still in existence. That existence it had owed to the longing of the German people, or rather the German peoples, for national unity, and it was its natural and universally understood mission to weld the German peoples under a common constitution of national government into one great nation. Immediately after the revolution of March, 1848, the different German governments, and with them also Austria, because of her German possessions, had recognized this object as a legitimate one, and it was with their co-operation that in May the elections for the national parliament had taken place. The large majority of that body, in fact, the German people in general, regarded the Frankfurt parliament as the specific representative of the sovereignty of the German nation. It was to be expected that the princes and those of their adherents, who may be designated as court-parties, would submit to this conception of the powers of the parliament only so long, and only so far, as they found themselves forced to do so. But few of the princes, if any, were sufficiently liberal to accept a limitation of their princely prerogatives with equanimity. Every gain of the people in the matter of political power they felt to be their own loss. Of course they were also opposed to the institution of a strong national government for the reason that this would be conditioned upon the surrender to the national authority of many of the sovereignty-rights of the different states. It was not only a national republic that the individual German sovereigns feared, but they also dreaded a national Kaiser who would be apt to reduce them to the condition of mere vassals. The German princes, with the exception of the one who could hope himself to occupy the imperial throne, were therefore the natural adversaries of German unity, embodied in a strong national government. There may have been some men of national sentiment among them capable of overcoming this reluctance, but certainly there were very few. Austria desired a united Germany in some form, only if it could hope to occupy in it the position of the leading power.

Face to face with the princes and their parties stood the national parliament in Frankfurt, that child of the revolution, which might then have almost been called the orphan of the revolution. It had at its immediate disposal no administrative machinery, no army, no treasury, only its moral authority; all the other things were in the hands of the different German state governments. The only power of the national parliament consisted in the will of the people. And this power was sufficient for the fulfillment of its mission so long as the will of the people proved itself strong enough, even through revolutionary action in case of necessity, to counteract the adverse interests of the princes. The parliament would have been sure of success in creating a constitutional German empire, if it had performed that task quickly and elected and put into office its Kaiser while the revolutionary prestige of the people was still unbroken—that is to say, in the first two or three months after the revolution of March. No German prince would then have declined the imperial crown with a constitution ever so democratic, and not one of them would have dared to refuse the sacrifice of any of his sovereignty-rights to the national power.

But that parliament was laboring under an overabundance of learning and virtue and under a want of that political experience and sagacity which recognizes that the better is often the enemy of the good, and that the true statesman will be careful not to imperil that which is essential by excessive insistence upon things which are of comparatively little consequence. The world has probably never seen a political assembly that contained a larger number of noble, learned, conscientious and patriotic men, and it will be difficult to find a book of the same character richer in profound knowledge and in models of lofty eloquence than its stenographic reports. But it did not possess the genius that promptly discerns opportunity and with quick resolution takes fortune by the forelock; it was not mindful of the fact that in times of great commotion the history of the world does not wait for the theoretical thinker. And thus it failed.

The parliament indeed recognized soon after its opening, that, if it was not to remain a mere constituent assembly, but also, until the constitution should be completed, a temporary government, an executive organ was required; and thus it resolved upon the institution of a " provisional central power," with a sort of lieutenant-emperor at its head. To this office it elected the Archduke Johann of Austria, who enjoyed the reputation of being a liberal. He was authorized by the parliament to appoint an imperial ministry. But, as mentioned before, his minister of foreign affairs had no diplomatic machinery under him; his minister of war had no soldiers except such as were lent to him by some of the several state governments; and his minister of finance no fiscal machinery, no tax-levies, and no money except what the several state governments contributed. All the things which together constitute the substantial force of a government remained after all in the control of the several German states. The real source of its power was therefore after all nothing but the revolutionary strength of the people. At the end of the year 1848 this revolutionary strength did not confront the princes and the court-parties any longer in so imposing a shape as it had done in the spring. A large portion of the people who had been so enthusiastic in March had become more or less tired of the constant excitements, while the princes and their adherents had to a large extent recovered from the terrors of March, had assured themselves of the administrative machinery and of the fidelity of their armies, and had been keeping their aims steadily in view—in point of fact had, at the great political centers, Vienna and Berlin, inflicted very grievous defeats upon the revolutionary spirit. The possibility of new revolutionary action on a large scale had therefore grown very much less. Under these circumstances the national parliament could indeed issue its ordinances and have them proclaimed through the national executive, but the governments of the several German states felt that they need not pay much more attention to them than than they pleased. And yet, the parliament had still its principal task before it: to complete the constitution of the

German empire, to introduce it practically, and thereby to satisfy the great national want of the German people.

It was still engaged in learned and arduous debates about the fundamental right, and liberties the German citizens should possess; it still had to solve doubts as to whether Germany should have a Reichstag to be elected by all the people and whether the head of the national government should be a hereditary or only an elective Kaiser, or a President, or instead of a single head, an executive committee. It had still to determine of what countries and parts of countries the German empire should consist; whether the German-Austrian districts should form a part of it, and which of the two German great powers, Austria or Prussia, should in this event have the hegemony. The parliamentary struggle on these questions lasted long, and only, when the reactionary Austrian minister, Prince Felix Schwarzenberg, demanded that the whole of Austria, organized as a united state with its nearly thirty millions of non-German inhabitants, should form part of the German empire—a demand with which the creation of a really German national union seemed entirely incompatible—only then did the parliament come to a decision. The majority declared itself for a hereditary Kaiser, and on March 28, 1849, elected to that office the King of Prussia.

However unpopular Prussia and the Prussian king were outside the boundaries of that kingdom, especially in South Germany, and however little the democratic party desired the creation of an executive head to the German empire in the shape of a hereditary Kaiser, yet when the work of German unity appeared at last completed, the national enthusiasm was once more kindled into a joyous flame. A committee consisting of thirty-three members of the national parliament, headed by its president, betook itself to Berlin, receiving on the way the most spirited manifestations of popular joy, to offer to the King of Prussia the constitutional headship of the empire.

And now came the bitterest disappointment of all. It was indeed well known that Frederick William IV., full of his absolutist mysticism, had never at heart recognized the sovereign character of the national parliament as a constituent assembly, and that he had claimed for the king of Prussia as well as for the other German princes the right to revise the constitution itself. It was also generally understood that that constitution, as it came from the hands of the national parliament, was too democratic to suit his taste. But when all the German governments, with the exception of those of Bavaria, Saxony and Hanover (Austria was no longer to be considered), had yielded to the pressure of popular sentiment and declared themselves ready to accept the imperial constitution and the Kaiser, and it was certain that even the three opposing kings would offer no serious resistance, the people, still hopeful and confiding, believed that Frederick William IV. could not refuse the great offer. Had he not in March on the streets of Berlin solemnly declared that he would put himself at the head of the national movement, and that Prussia would be merged in a united Germany? How could he possibly reject and desire to destroy the work of national union at the very moment when it required for its completion only his assent and acceptance? But what happened? Frederick William IV. refused the crown. He had indulged himself in all sorts of fantastic dreams about the manner in which Germany might be united, but found that the constitution now presented to him in all essential points diverged seriously from his own conceits. The national parliament he thought had no right to offer to him or anybody else a crown; such an offer could, in his opinion, legitimately be made only by a free resolution of the German princes. Neither would the acceptance of the German imperial crown be compatible with his feelings of friendly obligations to Austria. These and similar reasons for the non-acceptance of the imperial constitution and the Kaisership were uttered by the king, partly in public, partly in private.

It is quite possible that the most serious reason which frightened him lay in the probability that if he accepted the imperial crown, he might have to defend it by force of arms against Austria and Russia; and this apprehension appeared in an almost naïve way in an answer which the king gave to the eloquent words of a member of the Frankfurt parliament, Herr von Beckerath, urging him to accept: "If you could have addressed your appeal to Frederick the Great, he would have been your man; but I am not a great ruler." Indeed, Frederick William IV. from the first day of his government to the pitiable end thereof sufficiently proved that he was not made to be the first Kaiser of the new German empire. His refusal to accept the imperial crown and the constitution of the empire turned the general enthusiasm of the people throughout the country into general dismay and indignation. On April 11 the national parliament declared that it would stand by the constitution it had made. By the 14th the legislative bodies of the governments of twenty-three German states had signified their acceptance of that constitution and of the election of the king of Prussia as Kaiser. But Frederick William IV. persisted in his declination, and the kings of Bavaria, Hanover and Saxony also continued to signify their unwillingness to assent.

On May 4 the national parliament appealed to the "governments, the legislative bodies, the communities in the several states and to the whole German people to stand up for the recognition and the introduction of the national constitution." This appeal sounded very much like a summons to arms, and in various parts of Germany it had already been anticipated. In the Bavarian Palatinate, on the left bank of the Rhine, a detached province of the kingdom of Bavaria, the people had already on April 30 risen up with rare unanimity, and declared in immense mass-meetings that whatever the Bavarian government might do, they would stand and fall with the national constitution. They went even farther. They instituted a provisional government to replace the authorities acting under the king of Bavaria. The revolt rapidly spread to the neighboring grand duchy of Baden, where the whole army of that state, with the exception of a small body of cavalry, joined the revolt and surrendered to it the important fortress of Rastatt. The Grand Duke of Baden took to flight, and a provisional government composed of popular leaders assumed the place of his ministry. In the kingdom of Saxony the people of Dresden, the capital city, attempted to force the king to recognize the national constitution. There too the king found himself obliged to flee after a short struggle between the people and the military, and a provisional government was organized. The king of Saxony applied to the Prussian government for aid. This was willingly granted, and after a bloody fight in the streets of Dresden the revolt was suppressed and the authority of the Saxon king restored by Prussian bayonets.

What were the adherents of the national cause in Prussia to do while their king sent Prussian soldiers to overcome the national movement outside? Uprisings were attempted in Berlin and Breslau, but speedily overcome by force of arms. In the Rhenish provinces the excitement was tremendous. In Cologne a meeting was held of the representatives of the country communes, which almost unanimously demanded the recognition of the national constitution and threatened the defection of the Rhineland from the Prussian monarchy in case of non-compliance. But the Prussian government had long ceased to be frightened by mere mass-meetings or by high-sounding phrases, when there was not a strong revolutionary force behind them.

Clearly, to save the national constitution, quick action was absolutely needed. Again the Rhenish people turned their eyes upon their capital, Cologne; but such masses of troops had been concentrated there that a rising would not have had the slightest prospect of success. In the manufacturing districts on the right bank of the Rhine the revolt really broke out. The immediate occasion was an order issued by the Prussian government to mobilize the army-corps of the Rhine province for the purpose of sending it against the defenders of the national constitution in the Bavarian Palatinate and in Baden, where provisional governments had been set up by the revolutionists. To this end the "Landwehr" (military reserve) in the Rhineland and in Westphalia was called into active service. The members of the Landwehr were at that time, as they are now, men between twenty-five and thirty-five, peasants, tradesmen, artisans, merchants or professional men, many of them fathers of young families. To interrupt their daily work and to leave their wives and children involved to most of them a heavy sacrifice. This sacrifice was all the heavier when they were called upon to help beat down those who in Baden and in the Palatinate had risen for the unity of the fatherland and the liberty of the people, and with whom many, if not a large majority, of the members of the Landwehr warmly sympathized. So it happened that numerous meetings of the Landwehr men were held for the purpose of declaring that they would not obey the summons to arms. There was actual resistance at some of the depots where the Landwehr men were to receive their arms and equipments. In Düsseldorf, Iserlohn and Elberfeld, apparently formidable uprisings took place.

Such uprisings could clearly have had a possibility of success only had they become general throughout the country; and indeed it looked for a moment as if the disaffection of the members of the Landwehr in the Rhineland and Westphalia would spread and become the starting-point of a powerful general movement. But what was to be done had to be done quickly.

In this aspect the question of the moment confronted us in Bonn. Kinkel had returned from Berlin and was on the spot. The Chamber, a member of which he was, had once more urged the king to recognize the national constitution and to accept the imperial crown, and the king thereupon had dissolved it. Kinkel was then in Bonn the recognized democratic leader. Now he had to show his ability to act promptly or to relinquish the leadership to others in the decisive hour. He did not hesitate a moment. But what was to be done? That the Landwehr, at least the largest part thereof, did not wish to take up arms against the defenders of the national constitution, was certain. But in order to maintain this refusal, the Landwehr had to take up arms against the Prussian government. To make this resistance effective, immediate organization on a large scale was necessary. If the members of the Landwehr were ready for that, they could do nothing simpler and better than to take possession of the arms which were stored in the different Landwehr armories, and then under their own leaders make front against the Prussian government. Such an armory was situated at Siegburg, a little town a short distance from Bonn on the right bank of the Rhine. It

KARL MARX

contained muskets and other equipments enough to arm a considerable body of fighters, who then, joined to the insurrectionists in the manufacturing districts, might have formed a respectable power and spread the rising in all directions. This was the thought which occurred with more or less clearness to the democrats in Bonn, and they found also a military head for the execution of the plan in the person of a late artillery lieutenant, Fritz Anneke, who came from Cologne. The Landwehr of the district had been summoned to Siegburg on May 11, to be mustered into service. Thus time was pressing.

On May 10 we had in Bonn a meeting of Landwehr men from the town and the immediate neighborhood. During the morning hours a large multitude assembled in a public hall. The citizen elected to preside admonished the men to refuse obedience to the call of the Prussian government; if arms were to be taken up at all, it must be against those who sought to rob the German people of their liberty and unity. The men received this admonition with many signs of warm assent. The meeting continued during the whole day. The number of Landwehr men coming in increased from hour to hour. Different speakers addressed them, all in the same sense, and, as it appeared, with the same effect. It was agreed that the blow against the armory at Siegburg should be struck the following night. To this end it was essential to hold the men together during the day, so that as large a number as possible might take part in the expedition.

To keep the men together during the whole day was not easy. Some money had been raised to provide for their meals. But that alone was not sufficient. Kinkel, after having delivered his last lecture at the university, spoke to the meeting at four o'clock of the afternoon. With glowing words he inflamed the patriotic sentiments of the audience, admonishing them urgently to stay together, as now the hour of decisive action had come, and promised them at the conclusion of his speech that he would soon be with them again, to share their fate at the moment of danger.

I spent part of the day at the meeting, and part with the executive committee of the democratic club. There we received the current reports from Elberfeld and from the democratic clubs of the neighborhood as to their readiness for action; and the arrangements were made for the march to Siegburg after dark. Specific instructions were given to every member.

There was so much running to and fro during the whole day that many details of what happened are no longer in my memory. But I remember that as often as I appeared on the street, I was stopped by student-friends with the question what was in the wind, and whether they should march along with us; whereupon I told them what I had resolved myself to do in this crisis, and that each one of them would have to shape his conduct upon his own responsibility. Under the feverish excitement of the last days I had come to that desperate state of mind which will do and dare anything. It was evident to me that if the fruits of the revolution were to be saved, we must not shrink from any risk.

I also vividly remember how at dusk of evening I went home to tell my parents what had happened and what I considered it my duty to do, and to bid farewell to my family. Since the breaking out of the revolution my parents had taken the warmest interest in the course of events. They had always been enthusiastic in the cause of a united Germany and of free government. Our political sentiments were therefore in hearty accord. My father was a member of the democratic club, and rejoiced to see me among its most active members and to hear me speak. The noble nature of my mother had always clung with enthusiastic zeal to what she considered to be right and just. Both had watched developments sufficiently to anticipate the approach of a catastrophe. The announcement I made to them did therefore not surprise them. It was not unexpected to them that I had to take part in an enterprise that was so dangerous and for me so full of consequences. At once they recognized my honorable obligation. To be sure, their hopes for the future rested upon me. I was to be the support of the family in the struggle for existence. But without a moment's hesitation and without a word of complaint they gave up all for what they considered a duty of patriotism. Like the Spartan woman or the Roman matron of whom we read, my mother went to the room where my sword hung and gave it to me with the one admonition that I should use it with honor. And nothing could have been further from her mind than the thought that in this act there was something heroic.

Before I left the house I went for a moment to my study. From the window I had a free outlook on the Rhine and the lovely Seven Mountains. How often, gazing upon this charming picture, had I dreamed of a quiet and beautiful life! Now I could in the darkness distinguish only the outline of my beloved hills against the horizon. Here was my room quiet as ever. How often had I peopled it with my imaginings! Here were my books and manuscripts, all testifying of hopes, plans, and endeavors, which now perhaps had to be left behind forever. An instinctive feeling told me that all this was now over.

At the same hour Kinkel took leave of his wife and children, and then returned to the meeting, where he appeared on the platform armed with a musket. With impressive words he announced to his hearers what was to be done to-night and what he himself was resolved to do. He urged nobody to follow him blindly. He concealed from nobody the danger of the enterprise. Only those who in the extreme need of the fatherland felt it to be their duty, he summoned to march with him in the ranks.

I had been instructed to see to it that the ferry across the Rhine should be at our disposal. It was dark when I went to my appointed place on the bank of the river. There I found a fellow-student, Ludwig Meyer, with whom I crossed the river in a rowboat. On the other side we met according to agreement a troop of companions. At once we took possession of the ferry, the so-called flying bridge, ordered the ferryman to swing it over to Bonn, and then to take it back to the right bank of the Rhine, loaded with a crowd of armed men. This was the force that was to march to Siegburg and seize the armory. Kinkel appeared well armed. Two of our friends were on horseback, the rest on foot, most of them provided with weapons of some kind, but not a great many with guns. To me was given a rifle, but without fitting ammunition.

Our commander, Anneke, mustered the crowd and divided it into sections. One of these was put under the command of Josef Gerhardt, who at a later period went to America and did good service as colonel of a Union regiment in the Civil War. Anneke found that his troop did not count over one hundred and twenty men, and could not refrain from giving bitter expression to his disappointment. Many of those who attended the meeting during the day had in the darkness slunk away when the signal was given to march. Patriotic impulses that in the morning were fresh and warm had cooled off in the many hours that elapsed between the first resolution and the moment for action.

Our column being formed in order, Anneke made a short

speech, in which he set forth the need of discipline and obedience, and then the march began. About half an hour after our start one of our horsemen, who had remained behind, came up at a gallop with the report that the dragoons, then garrisoned in Bonn, were at our heels, to attack us. This report should have surprised nobody, for during the day and the evening the preparations for our enterprise had been carried on so openly that it would have been astonishing had the authorities received no knowledge of it, and had they not taken measures to frustrate the expedition. Moreover, we had forgotten to make the ferry behind us unserviceable. Nevertheless the announcement of the approach of the dragoons produced in our ranks considerable consternation. Anneke ordered our horsemen to hasten back and to reconnoiter as to the nearness and strength of our pursuers. Meanwhile our march was accelerated so that we might possibly reach the River Sieg and cross it before the arrival of the dragoons; but in this we failed. Long before we approached the river, we heard not far behind us the trumpet-signal ordering the dragoons to trot their horses. Anneke, who evidently was not very confident of the ability of his men to face regular soldiers in a fight, halted our column and told us that we were evidently not in a condition to offer successful resistance to regular troops; we should therefore disperse, and if we wanted to make ourselves further useful to the cause of the fatherland, we might find our way to Elberfeld or to the Palatinate, where he was ready to go. This signal to disperse was at once obeyed. Most of the men scattered over the surrounding cornfields, while some of us, perhaps twenty, stood still by the side of the road. The dragoons quietly passed us at a trot on their way to Siegburg. There were only some thirty of them, not enough therefore to overcome us or even to force their way through on the road, if those of us who had firearms had offered an orderly resistance.

When the dragoons had passed by and only a handful of our people had again found themselves together, a feeling of profound shame overcame us. Our enterprise had not only come to an unfortunate, but a ridiculous and disgraceful end. Our column had taken to the fields before only a handful of soldiers, scarcely one-third of our number. And this after the big words with which many had pledged themselves to the cause of German liberty and unity. I looked for Kinkel, but I could not find him in the darkness. At last I discerned Ludwig Meyer and others of my nearer friends, who all felt as I did, and we resolved at once to go on to see what might still be done. So we marched after the dragoons and reached the town of Siegburg shortly before daybreak. The democratic club, with which we had been in communication and the leaders of which had been expecting us during the night, had its headquarters in a tavern, and there we went. With them we discussed the question whether, in spite of the miserable failure of the preceding night and the occupation of the armory by the dragoons, we might not after all take that building by assault, and organize a respectable movement in aid of our friends in Düsseldorf and Elberfeld. The democrats of Siegburg could see little to encourage us. I was in a state of feverish excitement, and although extremely tired, could not sleep. In the course of the morning a considerable multitude got together, members of the Landwehr, and their friends from the vicinity. Soon we began to make speeches before large crowds, and the storming of the armory was repeatedly urged. A rumor came that during the day a fight had broken out between citizens and soldiers in Bonn, and I communicated that rumor to the assembled multitude; but further information having arrived, I had to my shame to confess that the tale was not true. I was nervously eager to wash out the disgrace of the night before, and to try the utmost for our cause, even under the most unfavorable circumstances. But it was all in vain. The evening came, the crowds dispersed, and I had at last to make up my mind that the people we had before us could not be moved to do anything desperate. Meyer and I resolved to go where there was fighting in prospect, and set out for Elberfeld. We reached that town the next day.

There we found barricades on the streets, much noise in the taverns, only a small number of armed men, and no discipline nor united leadership. Evidently here was no chance of success. Nothing could come of this, except perhaps a hopeless fight or a speedy capitulation. Meyer and I resolved therefore to go to the Palatinate. Soon we were on board a steamboat running up the Rhine. I wrote home asking my parents to send me some necessary things to our friend Nathan at Sanct Goarshausen, and on the evening of the same day we arrived under his hospitable roof in the shadow of the Loreley-rock.

There I had my first quiet hours after the terrible excitement of the last four days. When I awoke from profound sleep all that had happened appeared to me like a dismal dream, and then again as a clear, more dismal reality. The thought struck me for the first time that now, although safe enough for the time being in Nathan's house, I was a fugitive, running away from the authorities; it was certain that they would not permit an attempt upon one of their armories to pass unpunished. This was a singularly uncomfortable feeling; but a much more hideous thought followed—that I could not be proud of the act to which I owed my outlawry, although its purpose had been patriotic. The outcome had been miserable enough to make impossible my return to my friends, until the shame of it had been wiped out. But my profoundest grief was not with regard to myself. It was the knowledge that all the insurrectionary attempts in Prussia had failed, and that the Prussian government had its hands entirely free to turn against the insurgents in Baden and the Palatinate. I tried indeed to lift myself up to the belief that so great, so just, so sacred a cause as that of German unity and free government could not possibly fail, and that undoubtedly I would still have some opportunity to contribute to its victory, be it ever so little. I have never forgotten the hours which I spent with Meyer and Wessel, one of our friends of the Franconia, who, while not compromised politically, had followed us from friendship, walking up and down discussing these matters under the Loreley-rock, that most dreamy nook of the Rhine valley. My friend Meyer looked at the situation in a somewhat soberer spirit than I could command. After mature consideration, in which probably the thought of his family played an important part, he concluded to return to Bonn and to take the chances of a trial for his participation in the Siegburg affair. I did not try to urge my view of the case upon my dear, brave comrade, and thus we had to part.

The leave-taking from Meyer and Wessel was very hard to me. When I pressed their hands for the last time, I felt as if I had not only to say good-by to them, but also again to my parents and sisters, to my home, to all my dear friends, to my whole past. And now farewell to the beautiful student life and its precious friendships, its ideal endeavors and hopes, its glorious youthful dreams!

The years of apprenticeship were over, the years of wandering began. My friends journeyed down the Rhine to Bonn and I alone up the Rhine to Mainz.

CHAPTER VII

IN Mainz I learned from a member of the democratic club that Kinkel had already passed through on his way to the Palatinate. Mr. Zitz, one of the democratic leaders of Mainz, who had organized a corps of volunteers in the neighborhood, and was to be found at the little city of Kircheimbolander, would probably be able to tell me more. I therefore set out on foot to that place, carrying my baggage in a knapsack on my back. I found Mr. Zitz, a tall, stately man, surrounded by his apparently well-armed and disciplined free corps. (Mr. Zitz, a few years later, was well known in New York as a member of the law firm of Zitz & Kapp.) The camp looked orderly and well-managed. The artillery consisted of three or four little cannon, such as were commonly used to make a noise at popular frolics. Mr. Zitz told me that Kinkel had gone to Kaiserslautern, the revolutionary capital of the Palatinate, to offer his services to the provisional government. I marched on, and found Kinkel and Anneke both in the best of humor. They welcomed me heartily, quartered me in a tavern, and told me that soon they might give me something to do.

The next morning I rose bright and early. With especial curiosity I observed how people under a revolutionary condition look. I found that the guests in the tavern breakfasted as calmly as ever. I was told that the son of mine host would celebrate his wedding in a few days, and that great preparations were going on for the festivity. There was, indeed, a good deal of bustle on the streets—here persons who seemed to be following their daily vocation in the accustomed way;

there troops of young men in their ordinary dress with muskets on their shoulders, who evidently belonged to the "Volkswehr"—volunteer guard—in process of formation; between them, soldiers in the Bavarian uniform who had passed over to the people; and even policemen, in their official uniform with swords at their sides, and engaged in their regular functions as guardians of safety and order. At this I was not a little surprised, but I learned that these policemen had taken the oath of allegiance to the national constitution, that they served the provisional government, and were generally very good fellows. On the whole I found that although the leaders of the revolutionary movement had their busy hours of care and trouble, the population was in a condition of merry contentment, enjoying the charm of the moment without bothering much with thoughts of what the coming day would bring. There was a sort of general Sunday afternoon atmosphere, a real picnic humor—very amiable, but not at all corresponding with the conception which I had formed of the seriousness of a revolutionary situation. I soon learned to understand that this good humor sprung from the generally sunny disposition of the people of the Palatinate.

The Bavarian Palatinate is a country richly blessed by nature; the beauty of the landscape and the wealth of its resources are well apt to nourish in its inhabitants a natural disposition to enjoy life merrily. The Pfaelzers had been known from immemorial times for their light-heartedness. They were an intelligent and excitable folk, good-natured and enthusiastic, self-confident, and perhaps also a little given to contentiousness. There were very few poor among them, at that time at least, except in one small district. It was, therefore, by no means want or distress that made the Pfaelzers discontented and revolutionary. The Vienna Congress, after the Napoleonic wars, had assigned the Palatinate to the king of Bavaria, but as that province was not contiguous to the rest of the kingdom, it had not the feeling of really belonging to it. A Bavarian patriotism would never grow in the Palatinate. When the Bavarian government sent "Old-Bavarian" officers into the Palatinate to help govern its people, the attitude toward one another became still more unfriendly, as the hungry "Old-Bavarians," it was said, were sent to the rich Palatinate to grow fat. Their relations were much like those that existed between the Prussian province on the Rhine and old Prussia. The Pfaelzers were therefore in almost constant opposition to Old-Bavaria, and this opposition would have been sufficient to drive them into the ranks of the liberals had not liberal ways of thinking and feeling been natural to this vivacious and enlightened population. That this liberalism bore a decided German-national character was a matter of course. In fact, one of the most famous national demonstrations at the beginning of the thirties, the celebrated "Hambacher Fest," had taken place in the Palatinate, and among the leaders of the national movement there were always Pfaelzers in the foremost ranks.

When the king of Bavaria refused to recognize the national constitution made by the Frankfurt Parliament, the general indignation in the Palatinate broke out in furious flame. It was a natural sentiment with the Pfaelzers that if the king of Bavaria would not be German, the Palatinate must cease to be Bavarian. On the 2d of May an immense mass-meeting was held at Kaiserslautern in which all the liberal clubs of the Palatinate were represented. This meeting elected a committee for the "defense of the country, which, according to the resolutions adopted, was to take the government of the province into its hands and to organize an armed force. This action accorded with the universal will of the population of the Palatinate, with the exception, perhaps, of a very few civil and military officers.

The terrible confusion which the refusal of the king of Prussia to accept the imperial crown under the national constitution had brought upon all Germany came now to light in an almost grotesque manner. As already mentioned, the national parliament had, on the 4th of May, summoned "the governments, the legislative bodies, the communes of the several German states, the whole German people, to see to it that the constitution of the German Empire be generally recognized and practically introduced." Inasmuch as the king of Bavaria would not recognize the national constitution, the Pfaelzers felt themselves justified in rising against the Bavarian government, for they only obeyed the national parliament, which they regarded as the highest national authority in Germany. The "Committee for the Defense of the Country," therefore, quite logically applied to the national parliament through their representatives in that body, and to the national central power, for recognition, protection, and support. The national central power, at the head of which stood the Austrian Archduke Johann, thereupon sent an imperial commissioner, Dr. Eisenstuck, to the Palatinate with the instruction "to take in the name of the imperial power all measures necessary for the restoration of the laws in that country," and especially to see to it that some of the resolutions adopted by the "Committee for the Defense of the Country" be rescinded. The imperial commissioner, after due investigation, declared those resolutions to be invalid, but he recognized the "Committee for the Defense of the Country" and for the execution of the national constitution as fully competent to organize an armed power and to swear in the members thereof to obey the national constitution, and in case of necessity to defend that constitution by independent action against all attacks by force. With this, of course, Archduke Johann, who had sent him, was not pleased.

That prince had originally become distasteful to the Austrian court by marrying a young woman who did not belong to the nobility, and by uttering now and then a liberal sentiment. This had put him in the odor of liberalism with the great public, and to this circumstance he owed his election to the office of regent of the empire in 1848. It was not unnatural at all that this election created in him the desire to obtain for himself the imperial crown. When the king of Prussia was elected emperor the archduke was greatly disappointed, and he showed his displeasure at once by offering to the national parliament his resignation as regent of the empire. He permitted himself, however, to be pursuaded to withdraw that resignation for the time being, and he did this all the more willingly as he received from the Austrian court the suggestion that he should not abandon so important an office while it existed, because through it he might do very important service to the dynastic interest of Austria. That dynastic interest of Austria was, at the time, to prevent by every means the elevation of the king of Prussia to the dignity of German emperor; and also not to permit any constitution of the German empire which did not comprise the whole of Austria, including its Hungarian and Slavic populations, and in which Austria did not occupy the leading place. The national constitution, which was actually adopted by the Frankfurt parliament, making Prussia the leading power, was therefore to the Austrian court an abomination. The liberalism of the Archduke Johann may originally have been ever so genuine—certain it is that he had the monarchical interest in general, and the

Austrian interest in particular, more at heart than the national constitution and German unity.

Now the following situation of things presented itself; the German national parliament had created an executive authority in the form of the "Provisional Central Power," with the Archduke Johann as regent, in order to enforce respect to its orders and its laws. The most important of the utterances of its will consisted in the national constitution and the election of the king of Prussia as German emperor. The king of Prussia, that is, the emperor-elect, refusing to recognize the national constitution as rightfully existing, and declined to accept his election. The national parliament thereupon summoned not only all German governments, but also all legislative bodies and the communes of the German states, etc., in fact, the whole people, to enforce the national constitution. The people of the Palatinate did exactly what the national parliament had ordered the German people to do. The Pfaelzers had risen for the national constitution, against the king of Bavaria, who refused to recognize that constitution. The imperial commissioner, sent by the regent of the empire into the Palatinate, found himself obliged, by the logic of circumstances as well as by his loyalty to the national parliament, to confirm the "Committee for the Defense of the Country" in the Palatinate, and to recognize it as lawfully empowered to resist all forcible attacks upon the national constitution. And what then did the imperial regent who had been appointed for the purpose of enforcing the will of the national parliament, and especially to secure the recognition and introduction of the national constitution, do? He recalled the imperial commissioner at once, and then went to work to suppress by force of arms the popular movement which had been set on foot in compliance with the summons of the national parliament for the defense and introduction of the national constitution. And for this act of suppression mainly Prussian troops were selected—troops of the same king who in March, 1848, had solemnly promised to put himself at the head of the national movement and to merge Prussia in Germany; who then had been elected German emperor; and who now was to strike down those who insisted that he should become German emperor.

It has been said in defense of this monstrous proceeding that the popular uprising for the national constitution in the Palatinate and in Baden was mixed up with strong republican tendencies; that is, with the desire to subvert the existing political order of things. This is true to a certain extent, but it is also true that if the German princes had loyally done that which in March, 1848, they had given the German people the fullest right to expect that they would do, and if the king of Prussia and his brother-kings had accepted the national constitution, they would have neutralized, disintegrated, and rendered powerless all republican movements in Germany. The German people at large would have been satisfied. They would undoubtedly have consented even to some changes in the monarchical sense in the national constitution. And it is no less true that the manner in which the kings, after so many beautiful promises and pledges, sought to disappoint the hopes of the German people for national unity, was only too certain to destroy all faith in their national sentiment, and to create the opinion that only by means of republicanism a united German nation could be formed. The attitude of the king of Prussia, as well as the kings of Bavaria, Hanover, and Saxony, placed before the German people the clear alternative either to abandon, at least for the time being, all endeavors for German unity and political freedom, or to strive for the realization of these objects by means which are termed by governments revolutionary. The pitiable history of Germany during the next ten years has strikingly demonstrated that those who looked at the situation in the year 1849 in the light of this alternative were entirely right.

Let us now return to the Palatinate and the recall of the imperial commissioner. At first attempts were made to check the revolutionary movement in the Palatinate with small bodies of troops; but this failed, and as also in the meanwhile by the uprising of the people and the defection of the army in Baden the situation of things had become much more serious, the Prussian government began to mobilize some army corps and to prepare for a regular campaign. It was these preparations which had caused the various revolts in the Prussian provinces on the Rhine and in Westphalia. The Palatinate was now, for a little while, left to itself, and the good-natured and sanguine people saw in this temporary quiet a sign that the king of Prussia and his royal associates after all disliked openly to proceed against them with arms in their hands, because other populations in Germany might be as enthusiastic for the cause of German unity and liberty as the people in the Palatinate and Baden. They preferred to believe that the uprising would end as merrily as it had begun; and this explains the fact that the popular light-heartedness in the midst of revolutionary events, which I have designated as a picnic humor, lasted a considerable time. The cooler heads indeed did not indulge in such delusions; they foresaw that this would be a decisive struggle against an anti-national and anti-liberal reaction, in which the princes and court parties would put into the field their large and well organized power, if necessary even to the last reserves, and that against this power the resources of the Palatinate and of Baden looked pitiably inadequate. In the Palatinate a small number of Bavarian soldiers had come out for the popular cause—that is to say, they had left their colors and taken the oath of allegiance to the national constitution and to the provisional government. Aside from these regular soldiers, the provisional government had at its disposition the civic guard of some of the cities, which, however, could be used only for local service, and were indifferently armed. Then they had the little corps under Zitz—some six or seven hundred men—and a small corps under Blenker, and finally the military bodies which were still to be organized on a large scale, but which so far were insignificant as a fighting force. It would probably not have been difficult to raise in the Palatinate an army corps of twenty to twenty-five thousand men had the provisional government had firearms at its disposal. Multitudes of volunteers offered themselves, but as no guns could be put into their hands and they could only be armed with spears, many of them went home again. An attempt to import muskets from Belgium failed, because they were intercepted by Prussian customs officers on their way through Prussian territory. An expedition led by Blenker to surprise the fortress of Landau, situated in the Palatinate, which contained considerable stores of arms and military equipments, also failed. Thus the want of arms remained one of the most pressing cares.

The provisional government consisted of highly honorable, well-meaning, and brave men, who should not be blamed for not having mastered a situation which would have tested the resources of a great organizing genius. Nor did they succeed in finding military men equal to the gigantic task. The chief command of such military organization as they had they gave first to a former leader of the civic guard in Vienna, Fenner von Fenneberg, a man who had developed into a professional revolutionist, and who spent his time mainly in blaming others for not doing what had to be done. He was soon obliged to give up his post, and the command then passed temporarily into the hands of a military commission composed of former Prussian officers, Techow, Beust, Schimmelpfenning, and Anneke. These were well-trained men, but better fitted to take command of bodies of troops already organized and equipped than to create an army in a country the population of which was little accustomed to discipline and ready obedience, and to whom Prussian officers with their systematic ways and abrupt methods were not very sympathetic. Still this commission accomplished all that could have been expected of it. Meanwhile the provisional government had engaged for a considerable sum of money the services of an old Polish general by the name of Sznayde, of whom it was rumored that he was really not a Pole, but a German by the name of Schneider. Men who had served as officers in the great Polish revolutionary wars appeared at that time with a sort of a halo of revolutionary heroism around their heads. The popular legend attributed to them not only extraordinary bravery, but also all possible military talent, and exceptional familiarity with the secrets of the military art. It was as if at the rallying places of the Polish refugees, especially in Paris and Switzerland, a stock of generals was kept in store, to be occasionally disposed of for revolutionary enterprises in any part of the world. Among these Polish officers there were undoubtedly men of very respectable ability, such as Dembinsky, Bem, Mieroslowski, and others; but also much worthless and time-worn material. How the provisional government of the Palatinate hit upon General Sznayde I do not know. It was said that in the Polish-Russian war of 1830-1831 he had been a very brave cavalry officer, but in the year 1849 it would have been difficult to find a general less fit for the command of the volunteer bodies in the Palatinate. He was a very fat and ponderous old gentleman who looked as if he preferred to wield fork and knife rather than the sword, and to whom a good night's rest would be much more welcome than the tumult of battle. Neither could he say the little he had to say in intelligible German. His performance as an organizer of the popular army consisted mainly in hindering the military commission that was to aid him. The consequence was that while the provisional government issued an abundance of appeals and orders, most of them remained unobserved. After a labor of six weeks the Palatinate had not more than seven to eight thousand men, most of whom were very badly armed, and all of whom were indifferently disciplined.

In the neighboring grand duchy of Baden things looked much more favorable; the whole infantry and artillery, as well as the largest part of the cavalry of the state, had come over to the popular side and presented a well-equipped army corps of about fifteen thousand men. Moreover, the fortress of Rastatt had fallen into the hands of the insurrectionists, with all its stores of arms, ammunition and equipments. Newly formed organizations could therefore much more easily be provided with all the necessaries, and thus an army of some forty or fifty thousand men might have been organized in a comparatively short time. To be sure, the officers had mostly remained true to the grand duke, and thus separated themselves from their commands, but their places had been filled with promoted corporals and sergeants, and among these were able men in sufficient numbers to maintain among the troops tolerable discipline. Thus the revolution appeared in Baden in more or less stately armament.

But the political leaders in the Palatinate and Baden

ought to have recognized from the start that the utmost exertion of their strength could not possibly be sufficient to resist the united power of the German princes, or even that of Prussia alone. There was no hope of success unless the popular uprising spread beyond its present boundaries into the rest of Germany. To this end all the available forces that could be mustered should without delay have been thrown across the frontiers in order to draw into the revolutionary movement the population of the neighboring states; in the first place those of Würtemberg and Hessen. A young officer of Baden, Franz Sigel, who had been promoted to major by the provisional government, recognized this clearly enough, and he counseled an advance into Würtemberg. The provisional government permitted him to lead an expedition into the grand duchy of Hessen with a small force, but after an unfortunate engagement he was ordered back. The provisional governments of Baden and of the Palatinate could not screw up their courage to an offensive venture across their boundaries; they did not see that their defeat was inevitable if they waited in a defensive attitude for the attacks of the hostile forces. They continued to cling to the desperate hope that the Prussian government after all at the last moment would recoil from an active assault upon the defenders of the national constitution; or, if not, that the Prussian "Landwehr" would refuse to fight against their brothers who had risen for a common cause. Whatever the Landwehr might have done if the revolutionary army, with bold resolution and victorious courage, had come to meet them on their own ground, and had so appealed to their sympathies, it could hardly be expected of them that they would sacrifice themselves for a cause which was only timidly defended by its champions. But however clear this should have been at the time to the leaders in Baden and the

Palatinate, the provisional governments insisted upon remaining within the boundaries of their own little countries and thus to await the attack.

On the day after my arrival in Kaiserslautern I would have enlisted as a private soldier in one of the volunteer battalions then being organized, had not Anneke not advised me not to be in too much of a hurry, but to permit him to find a fit position for me. He had been made chief of artillery in the Palatinate, and said he could employ me on his staff. Two days afterwards he brought me an appointment as lieutenant, signed by the provisional government, and made me his aide-de-camp. Kinkel found employment as one of the secretaries of the provisional government. The artillery of the Palatinate consisted, at that time, of only the four little guns of the corps commanded by Zitz, of half a dozen small cannon, of which it was said they might be of much use in mountain warfare, and of a battery of six pounders obtained from the provisional government of Baden. The field of activity of the artillery chief and of his staff was therefore a limited one; and I was not displeased when I was told that until the beginning of active hostilities I might also be employed in political affairs.

I was now and then sent to popular meetings which were held to warm the patriotic zeal of the masses; and once I received an order to effect the arrest of a priest who used his influence in his parish—a large village of about three thousand inhabitants—to keep the young men from enlisting in the military organizations then forming. This was regarded as a sort of high treason against the new order of things; and the priest being looked upon as a desperate person who might possibly offer resistance, a little body of fifty men was to accompany me in order to aid me in the execution of my orders. This armed force did, indeed, not look very formidable; the lieutenant who commanded it was in civilian dress, except that he wore a plume on his hat and a tri-colored sash, and a sword. Among the men there was only one military uniform, that of a member of the national guard of Strasburg, whence he had come to enjoy with us the revolutionary frolic in the Palatinate. The rest of the men were in their daily garb. There were only about a dozen muskets among them, mostly with old flint locks. The rest of the armament consisted of spears and scythes fastened straight on poles. As a commissioner of the provisional government, I was distinguished by a tri-colored sash and a sword; I also carried a pistol in my belt, but without cartridges. Thus equipped we marched across the country to the village in which the treasonable priest carried on his mischievous activity. Within sight of the village we halted, and there being nobody among my men who was acquainted with the whereabouts, I sent three of them, without arms, ahead to reconnoiter the location of the parsonage. Two of them should remain there after having discovered it, and the third was to return to serve the expedition as a guide.

When I marched into the village at the head of my armament I found the streets a picture of profound peace. It was a beautiful summer afternoon; the male inhabitants, agriculturists, were working in the fields; only a few old people and little children were to be seen at the doors of the houses or at the windows, looking at the strange procession with stolid astonishment. I must confess that I appeared to myself for the moment somewhat comical, but my official duty left me no choice. The parsonage was promptly surrounded by part of my force, so that my culprit should not slip away through a back door; the main body was drawn up in front of the house on the street. I knocked at the door and found myself soon in a plain but very comfortably furnished room with the priest before me. He was a young man, perhaps thirty-five years old; a robust figure and a well-formed head, with lively penetrating eyes. I tried to assume a severe martial attitude, and acquainted him at once, in short words, with my charge, put my hand upon his shoulder, as was customary in making an arrest, and called him my prisoner. To my astonishment he broke out in a merry laugh, which seemed quite genuine.

"You want to arrest me," he exclaimed; "that is nice. You are evidently a university student. I have been the same, and understand this sort of thing; the whole story is only a joke. Drink a bottle of wine with me." Thereupon he opened the door of the room and called to a servant to bring wine.

I did not like to be at once discovered as a university student, and resented that my mien of official authority should not impress him. So I said in as severe a tone as possible, "Reverend sir, this is not a joke. You have hindered in your parish the organization of the army; such treasonable conduct cannot be permitted by the provisional government. In the name of that provisional government I have arrested you. You must follow me; do not hesitate to obey. Your house is surrounded by soldiers; do not oblige me to use force!"

"Force! We will see about that!" he exclaimed, and in his eyes there gleamed something like anger and defiance, but he controlled himself, and continued in a serious but quiet tone: "There cannot be so much hurry about this that you may not listen to a word from me. Here is the girl with the wine, and if I must follow you, permit me at least to drink a glass with you, to your health. It is true I have warned my poor peasant boys not to enter the army and to expose themselves to be shot for nothing. You yourself do not think that this insane revolt can succeed; in a few days the Prussians will chase your provisional government across the Rhine. Wherefore then this nonsense which may cost many people their lives?" With this he pulled the cork out of the bottle and filled two glasses. I had no time to consider whether, thirsty as I was, I should drink with my prisoner, when I heard the bell on the church steeple near by give a violent signal of alarm. This could be nothing else than a tocsin; it seemed that the peasants had somehow or other been informed of the danger threatening their priest, and as if this church bell summoned them to his protection. The priest seemed to understand the situation clearly; a sly smile flew across his face.

"How many men have you outside?" he asked.

"Enough," I answered.

I opened the window and saw crowds of peasants hurrying on from all sides with flails and pitch-forks and bludgeons. My men were still standing in line on the street; some of them seemed to look around with anxiety at the villagers rushing upon the scene. I ordered the lieutenant to post my men with their backs against the house and to let nobody in; in case of an attack he should defend the door to the utmost of his ability. I directed him to give the same orders to the men who watched the back door of the parsonage. The multitudes in front of the house grew larger and larger. Threatening exclamations were heard; evidently the situation was becoming complicated. Whether the handful of my volunteers could resist that big crowd of fanatic peasants appeared very questionable.

The priest still smiled. "My parishioners will defend me with their lives. It looks to me as if your armed force were in their power."

Then a happy thought shot across my mind.

"In any case, you, Herr Pastor, are in my power," I answered, drawing my pistol from my belt and cocking it. The priest would have continued to smile if he had known that the pistol was not loaded. He evidently thought it was a dangerous weapon, and his smile disappeared suddenly.

"What do you want?" he asked.

"I want you," I said with a show of coolness which, however, I did not really feel; "I want you to step at once to this window and to admonish your peasants to return to their homes without delay. You will add that you have affairs with the provisional government in the interest of your parishioners; that you will go to the city in the company of your friend here—that means me—to transact that business, and that these armed volunteers have come to protect you on the way against all danger and annoyance. While you make this speech to your peasants I stand with this pistol behind you. Do your business well, my friend; the provisional government will remember it." The priest looked at me for a moment with an expression of surprise, and smiled again, but it was an embarrassed smile; the pistol in my hand evidently did not please him. Then he rose, stepped to the window and was received by the peasants with loud exclamations. He commanded silence, and said exactly what I had prescribed to him. He did his business finely. The peasants obeyed without hesitation, and quiet reigned again in the streets. The priest and I then emptied our bottle of wine with all comfort. At dusk we left the house by the back door and wandered together toward the city like two old friends in merry conversation, my armed escort a hundred paces behind us. On the way I toyed with my pistol, throwing it into the air and catching it again with my hand.

"Take care," said the priest, "the pistol might go off."

"Impossible, Herr Pastor," I answered; "it is not loaded."

"What!" he exclaimed, "not loaded?"

We looked at one another and broke out into loud laughter.

I reported to the provisional government how the priest had helped me and my people out of a very precarious situation, and he was very kindly treated and allowed to return home forthwith. The provisional government had indeed much more important things to think of.

The attack which the merry Pfaelzers—at least many of them—had so long deemed improbable now really came. On the 12th of June a body of Prussian troops crossed the frontier. If the curses which those otherwise so good-natured people hurled against those Prussians had all been cannon balls, the Prussian troops could hardly have stood up against them; but the real fighting force at the disposal of the provisional government was so insignificant and so ill-equipped and undisciplined that an effective defense of the country was not possible. It was therefore necessary to avoid an encounter with the Prussians, and so it happened that the first military operation in which I participated consisted in a retreat. A few days before this my chief, Lieutenant Colonel Anneke, had instructed me to be ready to march at any moment, which I did not find difficult, because my baggage was extremely scant. I was given a horse, a fine bay, and as I had never learned to ride, my commander sent me to a riding school, where the master ordered me to mount the animal, explaining to me in a few words what I was to do with my legs and my hands to guide my mount; whereupon he struck him with a smart cut of his whip, and I had to keep my seat as well as I could on my prancing steed. After this had gone on for an

CARL SCHURZ AS A STUDENT

hour or so the master dismissed me, saying: "The next lesson you will get on the march." He was right; the constant exercise in active service gave me a pretty firm seat.

The sudden necessity of retreating considerably increased the general confusion. There was no end of orders and revocations of orders until we finally got started. I think it was in the night from the 13th to the 14th of June. With our artillery we had, indeed, no great difficulty, inasmuch as it consisted of very few pieces. At two o'clock in the night we mounted our horses and were off. A night march is almost always a miserable affair, especially a night march in retreat. Yet I must confess that the dull rumble of the wheels on the road, the rustle of the marching columns, the low snorting of the horses, and the rattling of the sabers and scabbards in the darkness, affected me as something especially romantic. In the appreciation of this I found sympathetic response with the wife of my chief, Mathilda Franciska Anneke, a young woman of noble character, beauty, vivacity, and fiery patriotism, who accompanied her husband on this march. I remember well our common pleasure, when in that night we passed by a tavern on the roadside, where some of the men, bearded fellows with black hats covered with plumes, and fantastically ornamented blouses, their rifles hung over their shoulders, in the feeble flicker of a lamp crowded around the woman of the hostelry, who poured wine for them. The picture might have been a scene of Schiller's "Robbers." The majority of our men not being uniformed, every soldier dressed more or less according to his fancy, and this gave tempting scope to individual taste. Many of the men evidently endeavored to look very wild and terrible, which they would have done had their faces not been so strikingly good-natured.

About sunrise after this first night's march we found ourselves in a deep gorge between precipitous ledges, near a place called Frankenstein, where we took a defensive position across the road to Neustadt. A cold morning brings, under such circumstances, a feeling of truly unromantic sober-mindedness with it, and I then learned that a hot cup of coffee, ever so thin, and a piece of dry bread, belong to the great benefactions of life. The Prussians, however, did not press us, and we remained undisturbed in our bivouac near Frankenstein during the entire day. On the 15th and 16th of June the troops of the Palatinate were drawn together near Neustadt-an-der-Hardt.

In this rich country the population of the villages manifested their friendly sentiments toward us by putting large pails filled with wine in the doors of their houses, so that the passing troops might refresh themselves. There I saw for the first time the leader of a considerable corps, Colonel Blenker, who twelve years later, during the Civil War in the United States, attracted much attention as a brigade commander. He was an excellent horseman, and as he appeared splendidly accoutered at the head of his staff, he presented a stately and imposing figure. The spectacle of several well-armed battalions revived, to some extent, the courage of our troops, which had been somewhat dampened by the retreat, and here and there arose the cry that now the confounded Prussians might come on; but the retreat was continued and the Palatinate abandoned without the striking of a blow. About the 19th of June, 1849, some seven or eight thousand strong, we crossed the Rhine into Baden territory and marched toward Karlsruhe, the capital of the grand duchy.

Our entry into that neat little city created among the inhabitants a sensation which was by no means flattering to the troops of the Palatinate. The Karlsruhe burghers, who had been accustomed to the trim appearance of the grand duke's soldiers, did not seem to relish the picturesque and romantic appearance of our Palatinate fighters for liberty, but were rather inclined to close their doors and shutters as though feeling the necessity of protecting themselves against the inroad of a band of robbers. At any rate, the faces of many of the people who stood on the streets watching our entering columns bore the unmistakable expression of anxious expectancy. We consoled ourselves with the thought, and gave that thought very vigorous utterance, that the population of this little capital consisted mainly of courtiers, high and low, and of government officials, and that at the bottom of their hearts they hated the revolution and wished the grand duke to return, although many of them had, since his flight, talked like republicans. The wish of the people of Karlsruhe to get rid of their neighbors from the Palatinate, was so great that our troops were not even given sufficient opportunity to prove to those timid souls what honest and peace-loving beings were concealed under those wild beards, those red plumes, and those belts stocked full of daggers and dirks. On the same day a camp was assigned to us outside of the city, and on the 20th of June we marched northward to the aid of the revolutionary army of Baden, which in the meantime had got into a critical situation.

The army of Baden had defended the northern frontier of the grand duchy against General Peuker, commander of a corps formed of regular Würtemberg and Hessen troops. Just at the time when the hostilities broke out, the Badish army also received its Pole, General Mieroslawski, as commander-in-chief. He was still a young man, and had shown much ability as well as bravery in the last Polish uprising, but he possessed no knowledge of local conditions, and was ignorant of the German language. However, he was vastly preferable to old Sznayde. On the 20th of June the Prussian corps passed the Rhine from the Palatinate near Philipsburg, and so got into the rear of the Badish army. With a rapid movement Mieroslawski turned against these Prussians, checked them by a bold attack near Waghaeusel, and then executed a clever flank march by which he passed between the Prussian troops and those of General Peuker, and opened communication with the corps of the Palatinate and thc reserves which approached from the south of Baden. The engagement at Waghaeusel was by no means discreditable to the Badish troops. We could hear the roar of the guns as we marched northward by way of Bruchsal, and soon rumors began to circulate among us of a great victory won by our people over the Prussians. But then later news came that Mieroslawski was retreating along the Würtemberg frontier and that we had to cover his flank. This did not much disturb our belief that the battle of Waghaeusel had really been a victory, the fruits of which, however, as was said, were lost through the treachery of the colonel of the dragoons, who was ordered to pursue the beaten enemy. On the 23d of June we advanced to Ubstadt and there we received the report that the next morning we would have to meet the Prussian vanguard. The orders which I received from my chief kept me busy on horseback until night, and it was late when I reached my quarters in the tavern at Ubstadt. My chief had already gone to rest. Upon all sides I heard the snoring of sleepers. Only the daughter of our host, a buxom young maiden of resolute expression of face, seemed to be at work. I asked her for a bed and something to eat, and both requests were granted by her with a robust outbreak of her feelings against the "accursed Prussians," who had nothing to do in the Badish land, and whom we should send home on the morrow with a sound thrashing. Now I expected within myself the solemn "emotions on the eve of battle" of which here and there I had read. But no emotions came; I fell asleep as soon as I had stretched myself out.

Neither did those emotions come the next morning, "on the morning of the battle." It almost appeared to me as if overmuch had been imagined about such emotions. In later life I have gathered the experience that indeed they will occur, but only on exceptional occasions. Ordinarily the thoughts of the soldier on the morning before the battle turn to things of a very practical nature, among which breakfast occupies an important place. So it happened to me on that morning at Ubstadt. At an early hour we were in the saddle, and soon we saw at a little distance in our front some cavalrymen who approached at a moderate pace. This signified that the Prussians had deployed one or more squadrons of uhlans as skirmishers who would be followed by infantry and artillery to make an attack. The uhlans disappeared after having fired a few shots from their carbines, and then began a lively rattle of infantry fire. Soon cannon were posted on both sides and the balls flew to and fro with their peculiar rushing sound, without, however, doing much damage. At first my attention was occupied entirely by orders which I had to transmit or to execute, but after our artillery had been placed, and we sat quietly on our horses in the immediate neighborhood of the battery, I had leisure to become conscious of my thoughts and feelings. Then I experienced another disappointment. For the first time I was "under fire." I cannot say that I was entirely calm; my nerves were in an unaccustomed stir: but that stir was not fear, nor was it the heroic joy of battle, of which I had read so much, for I was obliged to stand still. As the Prussian guns directed their fire upon our artillery position, their balls flew one after another immediately over our heads. At first I felt a strong inclination when I heard the noise right above me, to duck; but it occurred to me that this was unbecoming an officer, and then I remained straight upright in my saddle. I also forced myself not to quiver when a musket bullet whizzed close by my ear. The wounded men who were carried past excited my warm sympathy; but the thought that the same might happen to me the next moment did not occur to me at all. When my chief afterwards sent me again with orders hither and thither, all the reflections ceased and I thought of nothing but the things I had to do, and of the course of the action as I could observe it. In short, I felt little or nothing of those stormy, irrepressible agitations which I had imagined to be inseparable from a battle, but the experience convinced me that under similar circumstances I should always be likely to retain my presence of mind.

The engagement at Ubstadt was a comparatively small affair, with no purpose on our side but to retard the advance of the enemy until the Badish army could have reformed in our rear, and then slowly to fall back upon its position. At Ubstadt this instruction was carried out in a comparatively orderly manner. That such things cannot be done as perfectly with hastily organized and indifferently disciplined volunteers as with well-schooled regular troops is a matter of course. The next day we had a more considerable engagement with the Prussian vanguard near Bruchsal, which again ended in a retreat on our part. As frequently happens in popular uprisings, excited people are apt to ascribe the failure of their enterprise to the treachery of this or that leader; and on this occasion the cry was raised against poor General Sznayde.

On the retreat he was suddenly surrounded by a band of mutineers and dragged from his horse. He then disappeared from the scene of action, and the troops of the Palatinate were put under the immediate orders of the Badish commander.

On the line of the Murg River, the left wing leaning on the fortress of Rastatt, the united corps of the revolutionists of Baden and of the Palatinate fought their last defensive fight on the 28th, 29th and 30th of June, 1849, in part very gallantly, although without success. On the evening of June 30 Lieutenant Colonel Anneke sent me with an instruction concerning artillery ammunition into the fortress of Rastatt, where I was to wait for him in a certain fortification from which we could observe a large part of the battlefield. There he would call for me, he said. I discharged my order and then went to the place indicated by my chief, tied my horse to a gun carriage and sat down on the rampart, where after having watched the fight outside for a little while I fell asleep from sheer fatigue in spite of the roaring of the cannon. When I awoke the sun was about to set. I inquired among the artillerymen standing around for Colonel Anneke, but nobody had seen him. I became restless and mounted my horse to look for my chief outside of the town. When I arrived at the gate the officer on duty informed me that I could not get out; that our army was pressed back toward the south, and that the fortress was completely surrounded by the Prussians. I galloped to the headquarters of the commander of the fortress and received there the confirmation of what I had heard. The prospect of remaining in the city with Prussians all around, and this not in obedience to orders, but by mere accident, struck me as exceedingly undesirable. I could not resign myself to it, and inquired again and again whether there was no way out, until at last an officer standing near the gate said: "I feel just as you do. I do not belong here and have tried all possible points where I thought I might slip through, but all in vain. We have to submit and remain." Of Anneke I found no trace. He had either left the city or perhaps had not been in it all.

Having given up all hope of escape, I reported myself to the Governor of the fortress, Colonel Tiedemann. He was a tall, slender man, with fine, regular features, and a bold, resolute expression of face. As the son of a privy counselor, a far-famed professor of medicine in Heidelberg, he had received a good education. In early youth his inclination led him into the army, and he followed to Athens the Bavarian Prince Otto, who became the first king of Greece. The revolution in Baden found him at home, and the provisional government entrusted to him the command of the fortress of Rastatt. He received me kindly, listened to my report, and attached me to his staff. As to my duties, I was to report to him the next morning. I received quarters in the house of a confectioner by the name of Nusser. My host and his wife, very kind and well-mannered people, welcomed me heartily and put at my disposal a pleasant room and a seat at their table. Also my servant, Adam, a young soldier from the Palatinate, who fortunately had followed me into the fortress, found shelter in the house.

All this looked cheerful enough. But when my host and Adam had left me alone and I could, in the silence of my chamber, think over the new situation, my heart became heavy. That our cause, unless a miracle happened, was lost, I could no longer conceal from myself; and what kind of a miracle it might be, my hopeful imagination failed to guess. Could it be the passing over of the Prussian Landwehr to the revolutionary army? That would have been possible at the

HENSEL

FREDERICH TIEDEMANN

beginning of the campaign, if at all. Now, after a series of defeats that possibility had disappeared. Could it be a great victory of our troops in the highlands of Baden? Not to be thought of, as the retreat of our forces from the Murg River must have weakened them more by the inevitable demoralization than they could have been strengthened by reinforcements from other parts of the country. Could it be a great victory of the Hungarians in the East? But the Hungarians were far away and the Russians were marching upon them. Could it be a new uprising of the people in Germany? But the revolutionary impulse was evidently exhausted. Here we were shut up in a fortress surrounded by the Prussians. A stubborn defense of the fortress could serve our cause, only in so much as it might prove that a popular army could also possess courage and maintain its military honor. But under all circumstances the fortress could resist only a very limited time. And then? Capitulation. And then? We would fall into the hands of the Prussians. The supreme commander of the Prussian troops in Baden was "The Prince of Prussia," in whom, at that time, nobody would have recognized the afterwards so popular Kaiser Wilhelm I. At that period the prince was regarded as the worst enemy of all movements for freedom. The generally credited rumor that it was he who on the 18th of March, 1848, in Berlin, had given the order to fire upon the people had earned for him, with the people, the title of the "Grapeshot Prince." The excitement of the masses against him during those days of March was in fact so violent that the king thought it best to send him away to England for some time, and this journey was carried out in a manner which looked very much like flight. That in the year 1849 when the imperial crown was offered to his brother, Frederick William IV., he belonged to those who advised a favorable consideration of that offer, and that if he instead of his brother had been king of Prussia, the crisis might have taken a turn much more propitious to the realization of German unity, was at that time not yet known; nor would it have found much belief, for the prince of Prussia was then generally thought to be an honest and inflexible absolutist, who candidly and firmly believed that kings were ordained by God and had to render account only to God; that the people must have nothing to do with the business of the government; that resistance to the kingly power was equivalent to a direct offense against God Himself, and that it was an important duty of those in power to impose upon such a crime the heaviest possible penalty. So in the minds of the people the prince appeared as a fanatical soldier to whom the Prussian army was a very idol; who saw in it the "sword of God," the bulwark of the order of the universe; in whose eyes the Prussian subject that fought against the Prussian army committed an unpardonable crime not less accursed than patricide itself, and from whom such a criminal could expect no grace. We natives of Prussia, therefore, if we fell into the hands of that prince, had the best possible prospects of being condemned to death by a drumhead court-martial and of being shot. With these dismal thoughts I went to bed. Nevertheless I slept soundly and awoke long after sunrise.

The duties assigned to me by the governor were not onerous. I had to spend certain hours on the highest gallery of the tower of the castle, armed with a telescope, to observe the enemy and to make report of what I might see. Then I had, periodically, to visit certain bastions and gates, and to inspect certain watches, and in addition to do such other things as the governor might see proper to entrust to me. To fit me for that duty I donned the uniform of a regular infantry lieutenant of the Badish army, which transformed me into a respectable-looking officer and gave me a sort of military consciousness which until then I had not possessed.

Colonel Tiedemann succeeded in maintaining among the garrison—which was composed partly of regular Badish soldiers and partly of volunteers—pretty good discipline. Only once, as far as I can remember, I witnessed a serious breach of order. Some soldiers thought they had detected a spy, and soon a furious crowd rushed after the poor fellow, who tried to save himself by flight, but who succumbed after a few steps to the saber thrusts and stones hurled at him. It was all the work of a moment. The officers who accidentally were near, among them myself, succeeded, after a while, in quieting the soldier mob, but we were unable to save the victim. We had also other excitements.

One morning, shortly after break of day, I was awakened by a violent explosion on the street immediately under my window. As I jumped out of bed the thought struck me that the Prussians might, during the night, have penetrated into the city, and that there was now a street fight going on. A second explosion, immediately above the house, and the rattling noise of heavy objects falling upon the roof, taught me that the fortress was being bombarded, and that a shell had knocked down the chimney of my house. One explosion came after another, and the guns of our fortress boomed in response. I hurried as quickly as possible to headquarter in the castle and there I beheld a heartrending spectacle. The court of the castle was crowded with citizens, among them many women and children who had fled out of their houses and instinctively sought in the vicinity of the commander, protection against the threatening catastrophe. Most of the grown-up people, and even some of the children, carried beds or boxes and all other house belongings on their heads or under their arms. As often as a shell rushed over the castle yard or exploded in the vicinity, the poor people, overcome by terror, threw down all they were carrying and ran toward shelter, screaming and wringing their hands. Then a moment of silence would intervene and they picked up their goods and chattels from the ground; but as soon as another shell came along the same scene repeated itself. We staff officers had our hands full in trying to quiet the people, and as far as possible to place them in safety in the bomb-proof casemates of the fortress. Meantime the church-bells began to peal and a multitude—women with their children, and not a few men—ran across the market-place to the church, where, with loud lamentations, they prayed God to save them.

The bombardment, however, was not very serious. It lasted only a few hours, and did very little damage. A few fires caused by it were speedily extinguished. The Prussians probably intended only to let us know that the surrender of the fortress must not be too long delayed, if we would avoid greater discomfort. Thus we were bombarded only with field pieces and a few mortars. The heavy siege guns were to be brought on if it should be necessary to compel surrender by extreme means. The governor preferred, however, for the time being, to continue defense, and the next day a sortie was undertaken to drive away the battery that had annoyed us. The officer who commanded that sortie afterwards reported that the mortars had been taken and spiked by our men.

Beyond this nothing of great importance happened. With the higher officers of the garrison I came into contact as a member of the staff, but as I was still a very young man our intercourse was not intimate. The principal figures that I remember were Colonel Biedenfeld, a stiff old soldier who had been an officer in the regular army of Baden; Colonel Böhning, a white-haired, venerable-looking free corps commander; Major Heilig, the chief of artillery, about six and a half feet in height, a kindly and very popular officer; Lieutenant Colonel Otto von Corvin, a strikingly handsome young soldier, who had been a lieutenant in the Prussian army, and who, if I remember rightly, like myself, had remained in the fortress accidentally; and Major Mahler, a former lieutenant in the regular army of Baden, a young, gay infantry officer who, many years afterwards, fought for the Union under my command as a Colonel of the Seventy-fifth Pennsylvania, and who was killed at Gettysburg.

The duty which most interested me was that of the lookout, from the height of the castle tower. From there I had a magnificent view—toward the east the mountains in which Baden-Baden is nestled; toward the north the smiling Rhine valley with its rich fields and vineyards, its shady forests and the church steeples of many villages hidden among the fruit trees; toward the south the Black Forest; to the west Alsatia on the opposite side of the Rhine, with far-away blue mountain lines. How beautiful was all this! How benevolent Nature in her rich, lavish goodness! And over there, in these apparently peaceful surroundings, lay "The Enemy," who had us firmly in his grasp. There I saw the outposts regularly relieved, and the patrols of horsemen busily moving to and fro, keeping a sharp eye upon us so that not a soul of us should escape them. There I saw the batteries of the enemy ready to hurl destruction and death at us. There I saw their camps teeming with human beings, many of whom, aye, perhaps a large majority, thought as we thought and desired what we desired—possibly among them children of neighbors in my native village—and yet, all prepared at the command of their superiors, to fire the deadly bullet into our breasts. And over all this there streamed down in those summer days the beautiful sunlight of heaven, so warm and so peaceably radiant, as if there were nothing but harmony and happiness in the world. All this so cruelly unnatural, and yet so cruelly true!

A strange life that was in the besieged fortress. With the exception of one sortie, there being no further fighting excitement, we soldiers did our routine service day after day with mechanical precision, and the burghers pursued what occupation there still remained to them, all in a state of strained expectation, waiting for the fate that could not be averted. The world outside lay far, far away from us in unmeasurable distance. There we sat within our ramparts, excluded from all humanity, as if we did not belong to it. Not a sound of it penetrated to us except a distant rolling of the drum or the trumpet signals of the enemy besieging us. From time to time mysterious rumors arose, of which nobody knew whence they came. Our troops, it was once said, had won a great victory in the upper country and driven the Prussians before them. Then a fresh revolution had broken out in France, and all Germany was in new commotion. Then the Hungarians had disastrously defeated the united Austrians and Russians, and were ready to send their victorious legions to the aid of the German revolutionists. Once the higher officers of the garrison rushed up to me on the observation tower because somebody had actually heard, in the direction of the upper country, a long continuing thunder of cannon, constantly approaching; and now they had come to see the clouds of dust raised by the columns advancing to our relief. But the imagined thunder of artillery was inaudible to us; all remained still, and we sank back into our dull hopelessness.

Sometimes we tried to amuse ourselves with frolics in the wine houses—for the town was still well provided with wine. Then there was occasionally an effort at gayety, but it was little more than an effort, for everybody knew that behind his chair stood the dark specter of the inevitable catastrophe.

Suddenly one day—it was in the third week of the siege—a Prussian officer, under a flag of truce, came into the fortress with a summons to surrender, bringing the news that the revolutionary army had crossed the Swiss frontier, and had therefore ceased to exist; that not a single armed insurgent remained on German soil, and that the Prussian commander would consent to permit any man whom the garrison of Rastatt would entrust with such a mission, to convince himself of these facts with his own eyes, and to this end they would give him safe conduct wherever he might wish to go. This caused tremendous excitement. At once the governor called a general council of war, which, if I remember rightly, consisted of all officers of the garrison from captain upward. The council met promptly in the great hall of the castle. After a stormy discussion it was resolved that the offer of the Prussian commander should be accepted, and Lieutenant Colonel Corvin received the commission to explore the condition of things outside; and in case he found it to be as the Prussian flag of truce had represented, to negotiate for a capitulation on conditions as favorable as could be obtained.

The hall in the castle in which that council of war was held, had been, during the siege, always accessible to me, and one of the big lounges, upholstered with yellow silk damask, had been my accustomed resting place when I returned from my observations on the castle tower, or from my rounds through the fortress. I had selected this sofa because from it

I had an especially good view of a fresco on the ceiling which had a peculiar charm for me. It was an allegorical group, in which probably some ancestor of the grand ducal family of Baden was portrayed in the shape of Jupiter, or Mars, or Apollo. The subject of the picture did not attract me. But I found therein the face of some goddess which reminded me vividly of Betty, and when I looked up from my sofa the eyes of Betty looked kindly down upon me. No wonder, therefore, that I loved to rest upon this spot and that I indulged myself in all sorts of waking dreams, forgetting my dismal situation, until my eyes closed in sleep.

On the second morning after Corvin's departure, in the gray dawn I lay down upon the sofa for a short rest. Soon I was awakened by the noise of heavy steps, rattling sabers and a confusion of voices. From what I saw and heard I concluded that Corvin had returned from his mission and that the great council of war was reassembling. The governor entered, demanded silence and asked Corvin, who stood at his side, to make his report orally to the whole assembly. Corvin then told us that, accompanied by a Prussian officer, he had traveled down to the Swiss frontier and had convinced himself on the spot that no revolutionary force was left in Baden, the revolutionary army having crossed into Switzerland, surrendered its arms, and dissolved. He had also satisfied himself from the newspapers, that in the rest of Germany there was not the slightest vestige of a revolutionary movement. Everywhere submission and quiet. The Hungarians, too, had suffered decisive defeats in consequence of the Russian intervention and would undoubtedly soon succumb. In short, the garrison of Rastatt was entirely forsaken, and could not hope for any relief; and finally, Corvin added, he had been informed at Prussian headquarters that the com-

"A PRUSSIAN OFFICER, UNDER A FLAG OF TRUCE . . . WITH A SUMMONS TO SURRENDER"

mander of the besieging army would insist upon a surrender of the fortress at discretion, without conditions of any kind.

Deep silence followed this speech. Every one of the hearers felt that Corvin had told the truth. Finally, somebody—I do not remember who—asked to be allowed to put some questions. Then there was a confusion of voices in which some hotheads talked of "dying to the last man"; whereupon the governor gave the floor to a former Prussian soldier, who had become an officer in the forces of the Palatinate. This officer said that he was as ready as anyone to sacrifice to our cause his last drop of blood, and that those of us who were Prussians, when they fell into the hands of the besieging army, would have to die in any case. Nevertheless he advised the immediate surrender of the fortress. If we did not surrender to-day, we would be obliged to do it to-morrow. We ought not to expose the citizens of the town, with their wives and children, to famine, or to another bombardment, and all in vain. It was time to make an end, whatever might happen to us personally. A murmur swept through the hall approving this advice, and then it was resolved that Corvin should try once more to secure, at the Prussian headquarters, for the officers and men of our garrison as favorable conditions as possible. But if after a reasonable effort he saw the impossibility of obtaining such conditions, he should agree with the Prussian headquarters upon the necessary arrangements for a surrender at discretion. When we left the hall most of us undoubtedly felt that nothing else could be hoped for.

That afternoon I mounted once more my tower of observation upon which I had spent so many watchful and dreamy hours. The magnificent landscape lay before me in the beautiful sunshine. It appeared to me even more beautiful than ever. I felt as if I must take a last leave of it.

"We Prussians will probably have to die in any case." These words echoed in my ear, and I was convinced of their truth. To these Prussians I belonged. I remember vividly the thoughts which then on that tower of observation went through my head. One recollection forced itself again and again upon my mind, how a few years before my father had, with me, visited Professor Pütz in Cologne; how the professor had put his hand upon my shoulder and smilingly said to my father, "A hopeful boy"; and how proudly then my father had nodded his head and looked at me. "Of that hopeful boy there is now an end," I said to myself. Many of the bold dreams of a great and fruitful activity which I had formerly cherished recurred to me, and it seemed hard, very hard, to depart from the world before I had been permitted to render it any worthy service. A sensation of profound sorrow came over me, not on account of myself alone, but also on account of my parents who had expected so much of me, to whom I was to be the support of old age, and who now saw all their hopes shattered and destroyed forever. Finally, nothing remained to me but the determination if I was so to end, to look my fate in the eyes with courage and dignity.

I remained on the gallery of the observation tower until the sun was down. Then I descended and reported myself to the governor, whether he still had orders for the night. "To-night," he said, "every one of my officers ought to be on the ramparts. I apprehend that the men know that we shall surrender to-morrow, and will leave their posts. That should not be." I was glad to have something to do that would occupy my thoughts. In the fortifications and in the town there was now a great deal of noise and confusion. Many of the men regarded it as superfluous to take further care of the service; it would be all over anyhow the next day. There was also much hubbub in the wine houses, when the soldiers would have have their last cup together. But the admonitions addressed by the officers to the men who were running about or drinking did not find any vicious resistance. The number of those who still continued to do their duty was sufficient to maintain tolerable order.

Toward daybreak I stretched myself once more on my accustomed sofa, and after several hours of profound sleep woke up with the thought, "To-day you will be taken by the Prussians, to be shot dead." Then I went to headquarters, where I learned that Corvin had not succeeded in negotiating any conditions, and that the surrender at discretion was a certain thing. At twelve o'clock noon the troops were to march through the gates to lay down their arms between two lines of Prussians outside on the glacis of the fortress. The orders had already been issued. I went to my quarters to write a last letter to my parents. I thanked them for all the love and care they had devoted to me, and asked them to forgive me if I had disappointed their hopes. I told them that following my honest convictions I had taken up arms for a cause that I believed to be right, for the liberty and unity of the German people, and if it should be my lot to die for that cause, it would be an honorable death of which they would never have reason to be ashamed. This letter I put into the hands of good Mr. Nusser, my host, who, with tears in his eyes, promised to put it into the mail as soon as communications should be opened again. In the meanwhile the hour of noon approached. Already I heard the signals calling the troops on the ramparts and in the barracks to the rally, and I prepared myself to go up to headquarters. Then a new idea suddenly flashed through my head. I remembered that only a few days previously my attention had been attracted to a subterranean sewer for the waters of the street gutters which, near the Steinmauerner gate, led from the interior of the city, under the fortifications, into an open field outside. This sewer was probably a part of an uncompleted drainage system. The entrance to it in the interior of the city was situated in a trench near a garden hedge. Outside it emptied into a ditch overgrown with shrubbery, which bordered a corn field. When these circumstances had first come to my knowledge, it had occurred to me that if the opening as well as the exit of that sewer were not well watched, spies might easily pass through it from the outside into the town. I had reported the matter to the governor, but immediately afterwards came the negotiations with the enemy, the mission of Corvin, and the excitement about the impending capitulation, which drove the affair of the sewer out of my mind.

Now at the last moment before the surrender the remembrance came back to me like a ray of light. Would it not be possible for me to escape through that sewer? Would it not, if I thus gained the open in this way, be possible in some manner to reach the Rhine, there to procure a boat and to cross the river to the French side? My resolution was promptly taken—I would at least try.

I called my servant, who had prepared my belongings for the surrender. "Adam," I said, "you are a Palatinate man, a volunteer. I believe if you surrender to the Prussians you will soon be sent home. I am a Prussian, and us Prussians they will probably shoot dead. I will therefore try to escape, and I know a way. Let us therefore say good-bye."

"No, Herr Lieutenant," Adam exclaimed, "I shall not

leave you. Where you go, I go." The eyes of the good boy sparkled with pleasure.

"But," said I, "you have nothing to gain, and we shall probably have to incur great dangers."

"Danger or no danger," replied Adam, with decision, "I remain with you."

At this moment I saw an artillery officer of the name of Neustädter, whom I knew well, pass by my window. He, like myself, was born in Rhenish Prussia, and had formerly served in the Prussian artillery.

"Where are you going, Neustädter?" I called to him through the window.

"To join my battery," he answered. "We are to surrender in half an hour."

"The Prussians will shoot you dead," I replied; "go with me and let us try to escape."

He stopped, came into the house and listened to my plan, which I explained to him in a few words.

"Good," he said; "I will go with you."

There was now no time to be lost. Adam was sent out to purchase a loaf of bread, two bottles of wine and some sausages. Then we put our pistols under our clothes, and rolled up our cloaks. In mine, a large dark cape lined with scarlet, received recently from our stores, I wrapped up a short carbine which I possessed. The bottles and the eatables which Adam had bought were packed up as well as we knew how. In the meantime the garrison began to march in close columns across the market-place. We followed the last column a short distance, and then turning into a side lane soon reached the inner mouth of our sewer. Without hesitation we slipped into it. It was between one and two o'clock in the afternoon of the 23d of July.

The sewer was a tube of brick masonry, sufficiently high and wide for us to move through it with bent knees and curved backs, half walking, half crawling. The water running through the sewer covered our feet and ankles. As we penetrated into the interior we found, here and there, narrow manholes covered on top with iron gratings, through which air and, during the day, some light came down. At such places we rested a moment and stretched ourselves out so as to get our spines into shape again. According to our calculation we should have reached about the middle of the sewer, when I happened to strike my foot against a piece of board lying in the water, which was just long enough to be squeezed between the walls of the sewer so that it served us as a sort of bench to sit upon. Upon this bench, which made our condition a little more comfortable, we huddled together for a longer rest.

Until then the constant movement to which we had been compelled had hardly permitted us to survey our situation. Now, sitting on the bench, we had leisure enough to collect our thoughts and to hold council as to what was further to be done. During the siege I had had frequent opportunity to observe the immediate surroundings of the fortress, and I therefore pretty well knew the ground on which the sewer emptied outside. I proposed to my companions that we should remain on the bench until about midnight, then leave the sewer, and seek cover in a field planted with corn, which I knew to be in the neighborhood. From there we could, if the sky was tolerably clear, overlook a little part of the road to Steinmauern, a village distant about an hour's walk from Rastatt, on the bank of the Rhine, and assure ourselves whether we might leave the protection of the cornfield without danger. And so, seeking cover from time to time in order to reconnoiter the road ahead of us, we might hope before daybreak to reach Steinmauern and there to find a boat that might carry us to the French side of the river. This plan was approved by my companions.

While we were thus engaged in taking counsel, we heard above us a dull, rumbling noise as from the wheels of vehicles and the heavy tread of great masses of men, from which we concluded that the Prussians were now entering the fortress and occupying the gates and the ramparts. We also heard the striking of a church clock which gave the hour, our bench being near one of the manholes, so that the sounds of the upper world reached us without much difficulty. About nine o'clock in the evening it began to rain so heavily that we could clearly hear the splashing of the water as it poured down. At first it seemed to us that the bad weather would be favorable to our plan of escape. But before long the matter appeared in a different light. We felt that the water was rising in our sewer, and soon it began to shoot through it with great vehemence like a mountain stream. After a while it flooded the bench upon which we were sitting and reached up to our chests. We also perceived living creatures which suddenly, with great activity, rushed and crawled around us. They were undoubtedly rats. "We have to get out," I said to my companions, "or we shall be drowned." We left our bench and pushed forward. I had hardly advanced a few steps when in the darkness I ran my head against a hard object. I touched it with my hands and discovered that the obstacle was an iron railing. At once the thought came to me that this railing had been put there for the purpose of cutting off, in time of siege, communication through the sewer between the interior of the town and the outside. This thought, which I communicated at once to my companions, brought us almost to despair. But when I grasped the railing with both hands, as a prisoner may sometimes shake the iron rods of his dungeon window, I noticed that it could be moved a little, and a further examination proved that it did not reach quite down to the bottom, but left a free space of about two feet. It was probably so arranged that it could be pulled up or let down, so that the sewer might be opened for purposes of cleaning and then shut again. Fortunately, nobody had, during the seige, known anything of this railing, and thus the possibility of escape still remained open to us.

Now, in order to slip through the low aperture under it we were obliged to crawl with our whole bodies through the water; but that circumstance, although disagreeable, did not disturb us. We pushed vigorously on, and when we believed ourselves to be near the outward opening of the sewer, we stopped a minute to gather strength and presence of mind for the dangerous moment of our issuing forth from our concealment.

Then a terrible sound struck our ears. Close ahead of us, distant only a few paces, we heard a voice call, "Who goes there?" and at once another voice answered, "Good friend." We stood still as if struck by lightning. In a short time we heard the same calls repeat themselves at a somewhat greater distance, and again and again. It was clear that we were close to the opening of the sewer, that outside there was a dense chain of Prussian guard posts, and that just then a patrol or round had been passing along that chain. Softly I ventured a step or two further on. Really, there was the mouth of the sewer overgrown with brush so thick that I stood in darkness almost as dense as was that in the interior of the canal. But when I raised myself up a little I could distinctly perceive the dark figures of a Prussian double sentinel immediately before me, as well as some camp fires at a short distance. Had we been able to get into the open without being noticed, which seemed almost impossible, still the road to Steinmauern was evidently closed to us.

Softly as we had come we crawled back into our sewer and sought safety there, at least for the moment. Fortunately the rain had ceased. The water was, indeed, still high, but it did not rise any more. "Back to our bench," I whispered to my companions. We crawled again under the railing and found our bit of plank. There we sat close together. Our next council of war had a certain solemnity about it. There were few words, but a good deal of thinking. It was clear, we could not venture into the open. To remain a longer time in the sewer was not to be thought of, because there was the danger that if it rained again we might be drowned. There was therefore nothing to be done but to go back into the town. But how could we go back into the town without falling into the hands of the Prussians? After we had exchanged these thoughts in a whisper, a long pause followed. At last I interrupted the silence, saying, "Let us eat and drink a little; good counsel may come then." Adam unpacked our provisions, and as we had eaten nothing since breakfast time of the preceding day—midnight was now long past—hunger and thirst were keen. Our bread was, indeed, quite wet, but it tasted good; also the sausages. We remembered, in time, that we must not consume our whole store, for we did not know when and where we should get the next meal. Moreover, we were more troubled by thirst than by hunger, as is always the case under such circumstances. For nearly twelve hours our feet had been in the water, and were therefore as cold as ice. This had driven the blood to our heads. Adam now opened one of the two bottles which he had bought for us, and we discovered that they contained rum instead of wine. Although rum had always been repugnant to me, still I drank like my companions, in eager draughts, and my brain remained entirely clear in spite of it.

After we had finished our meal Adam took the floor. "I have a widowed cousin in the town," he said. "Her house is not far from the entrance to the sewer. To reach it we have only to go through a kitchen garden or two. We might hide ourselves there in the barn until we find something better."

This proposition had our approval, and we resolved to make the attempt. At the same moment something occurred to me that was depressing in the extreme. I remembered that during the siege our garrison had a sentinel close to the entrance of the sewer. If this post was occupied by the Prussians too, then we sat in the sewer between two Prussian guards. I communicated my apprehension to my companions. But what was to be done? Possibly the Prussians had not occupied that post. Perhaps we might slip by. In any case, nothing else remained to us than to make the attempt.

When we left our bench to begin our retreat, we heard the church clock outside strike three. I went ahead and soon reached the last manhole. I availed myself of the opportunity to stretch myself out a little, when something happened that at the first moment appeared very unfortunate. I had used my short carbine in moving through the canal in a bent position, as a sort of crutch. When I lifted myself up the carbine fell from my arm into the water and caused a loud splash. "Hello!" cried a voice just above me. "Hello! There is something in this hole; come here." At the same moment a bayonet descended like a probe through the grating which covered the manhole. I heard it strike against the iron rods in time to duck myself and thus avoid being touched by it. "Now out quickly!" I whispered to my companions, "or we are lost." With a few hasty paces we reached the end of the sewer.

Without looking around we jumped over a hedge into the nearest kitchen garden, and gained, with a rapid run, a second hedge, which we cleared in the same way. Then we halted, breathless under cover of some shrubs, to listen whether anybody was following us. We heard nothing. It is probable that the falling of my carbine into the water attracted the attention of the guard post in the immediate vicinity, and diverted it from the mouth of the sewer. Thus our escape may have been facilitated by the accident, which at first seemed so unfortunate.

When Adam looked around from our halting place he found that we were close by the house of his cousin. We leaped another hedge which separated us from the kitchen garden belonging to that house, but there we were greeted by the loud barking of a dog. To pacify the animal we sacrificed the last remnant of our sausages. Finding the door of the barn open, we entered it, stretched ourselves out on a pile of hay, and soon fell into a profound sleep.

But this rest was not to last long. I awoke suddenly and heard the church clock strike six. Adam had already risen and said he would now go into the house to ask his cousin what she could do for us. After a few minutes he returned and the cousin with him. I still see her before me—a woman of about thirty years, with a pale face and wide-open, anxious eyes. "For God's sake," she said, "what are you doing here? You cannot remain. This morning some Prussian cavalrymen will be quartered here, and they will surely look in the barn for litter for their horses. Then they will find you and we shall all be lost."

"But be reasonable, cousin," said Adam; "where can we go now? You certainly will not deliver us up."

But the poor woman was beside herself with fear. "If

you do not go," she replied, with decision, "I must tell the soldiers that you are here. You cannot expect me to sacrifice myself and my children for you."

There was more talk, but all in vain. We had no choice; we must leave the barn. But where to go? The woman showed us through the open door a ditch covered with high and thick shrubbery on the other side of the little yard, in which we might hide ourselves. Our situation became desperate. There we stood, all three in the military uniform of Baden, easily recognizable as the soldiers of the revolutionary army. Now we were to have no other refuge but some shrubbery covering a ditch in the midst of a town teeming with hostile troops! Of course, we hesitated to leave the barn, although it was a dangerous resting place for us, but at any rate it offered us a roof over our heads, and perhaps it might be possible to find in it some hiding corner. We still hoped that Adam's cousin would yield to our prayers. She went to the house, as she had to expect every moment the arrival of the cavalrymen. After about half an hour she came back and said the cavalrymen were there and were just sitting at their breakfast. Now was the moment for us to pass through the yard without being seen by them. She insisted on this with such determination that we had to submit. Then we ran across the yard to the ditch, which on the opposite side was separated from the street by a tall board fence. It again rained hard, and in the immediate vicinity nobody seemed to be stirring. Thus we could, with some assurance, explore our new refuge. We found that at the end of the ditch cord wood was heaped up in the form of a hollow square, open on the side toward us. We could slip through the brush into the square and were in that close space pretty well protected from the eyes of the passerby. There we sat down on blocks of wood.

But what was to become of us now? The discomfort of our miserable situation, as well as our sitting there wet to the skin, we might easily have borne had we had the slightest prospect of escape. My faithful Adam, otherwise so good-natured, was much wrought up over the conduct of his cousin. Neustädter regarded our situation as hopeless, and asked whether it was not better to put an end to our distress by a voluntary surrender to the soldiers in the house. I must confess that my sanguine temperament, too, was severely tested. Still I gathered up courage, and we then resolved to trust to luck. So we sat there hour after hour waiting for something to turn up, with the heavy rain mercilessly streaming down on us, pictures of misery. About noon we heard steps in the garden near our place of concealment. Cautiously I looked out from the open side of our cord wood square, and perceived coming from the house a man with a saw in his hand. According to his looks and the tool he carried I concluded he must be a laborer, and as the laboring men throughout were in favor of the revolutionary cause, I did not hesitate to confide myself to him. I threw a little chip of wood at the man, which hit him on the arm, and as he stood still I attracted his attention by a low cough. He saw me and came to us. With as few words as possible I explained to him our situation, and begged him to find us a place of safety, and also to procure for us something to eat, as our last morsel was gone. My confidence was not misplaced. He promised to do what was possible. Then he left, but returned in half an hour, and showed us near by a large open shed. At the end of that shed there was a little closed compartment in which the laborers probably deposited their tools, and on top of this, under the roof of the shed, a small loft enclosed in boards. "I will break loose one of these boards," said our man. "You can then climb over the cord wood and slip under the roof of the loft and lie down there. I will soon come back and bring you something to eat."

We followed his advice, and succeeded in slipping into the little loft without being observed. The space we occupied was just large enough to permit us to lie side by side on our backs. We lay in a white dust, inches thick, which was, in view of the wet condition of our clothing, extremely disagreeable. But at least we felt secure for the time being. It was about one o'clock of the afternoon when we crawled into our new asylum. We waited quietly for our friend to bring us the necessary food, and would then consult with him about a plan of escape. But we heard the church clock strike two, three, and four, and our man did not return. Shortly after four o'clock a lively noise arose in the shed below. From the talk and the shouting and the rumbling we heard we concluded that a troop of cavalrymen must have arrived, and that they were now occupied in putting the shed in order for their horses. The horses came soon, and on all sides soldiers swarmed around us. Through the chinks of the wooden wall of our loft we could easily see them. Our situation became extremely critical. If it had occurred to one of those soldiers to investigate the compartment and to look into the loft, it would have been all over with us. Any kind of noise, a cough or a sneeze, would have betrayed us. We took the utmost pains to breathe softly, and longed for the night. The night came and we were still undiscovered, but the man on whose assistance we had counted had not yet shown himself.

We began to be very hungry and thirsty, and had neither a bit of bread nor a drop of water. What was left of our rum had been lost on the hasty run from the sewer to the house. Now we lay still like corpses. Gradually it became more quiet in the shed; soon we heard heavy snoring, and from time to time somebody moving around, probably to look after the horses. We were afraid to sleep ourselves, although very much exhausted. But at last we came to a whispered agreement alternately to sleep and to lie awake, and to shake the temporary sleeper if he breathed heavily. So the night passed over and morning came, but not the friend whom we so longingly expected. Noon, afternoon, evening, the whole second day, passed, but of our friend no sign. There we lay, still and stiff, surrounded by hostile soldiers, and the prospect of succor growing less every moment. Thirst began to torture us. Fortunately the next night it rained again. Above my head there was a broken tile in the roof, and through the hole, although it was small, some of the rain trickled down. I caught it in the hollow of my hand, and so enjoyed a refreshing draught. My companions followed my example. Again morning came, and our hope for the return of our friend sank lower and lower. The church clock struck one hour after another, and no aid. My limbs began to ache from the rigid stiffness of our position, and yet we hardly dared to move. Three days and two nights we had been without nourishment, and an unwonted feeling of weakness set in. So the third night arrived. All hope of the coming of our friend was gone. We recognized the necessity of making a new attempt at escape before our strength had entirely vanished. We thought and thought, without saying a word, except, perhaps, "He will not come any more."

At last I had an idea. When, during the third night, we heard the soldiers below snoring vigorously, I whispered to my neighbor, Neustädter, holding my mouth close to his ear, "Did you not, as we clambered over the cord wood, notice a little house about fifty paces from here?"

"Yes," said Neustädter.

"There must be a poor man living there," I continued,

"probably a laborer. One of us must go to him and see whether he cannot help us. I should be glad to go myself, but I would have to clamber over you [Neustädter lay nearest to the opening in the board wall], and that might make a noise. You are, anyhow, the lightest of us. Will you try?"

"Yes."

I had a little money, for immediately before the capitulation we had received our soldiers' pay.

"Take my purse," I whispered, "and give to the man who lives in the little house ten florins, or as much as he asks. Tell him to bring us some bread and wine, or water, and to inform himself as soon as possible whether or not the Prussian guard posts are still standing outside of the fortress. If those posts have been drawn in, we can try to-morrow night again to get through the sewer. Now go and bring us a piece of bread if you can."

"Good," said Neustädter.

In a minute, lightly and softly like a cat, he had slipped through the hole in the board wall. My heart beat fast while he was gone. A false step, an accidental noise, would betray him. But in less than half an hour he came back just as lightly and softly as before, and lay down by my side.

"It is all right," he whispered; "here is a piece of bread, all he had in the house, and also an apple that in passing by I picked from a tree, but I am afraid it is still green."

The bread and the apple were soon divided among us, and devoured with avidity; and then Neustädter reported with his mouth to my ear, that he found in the little house a man and his wife. The man, to whom he had given the ten gulden, had promised to bring us some food, and also the desired information about the condition of things outside of the fortress.

This refreshed our spirits, and, much relieved, we slept alternately until high morning. Now we expected with every moment our rescuer, but one hour after another passed and he did not come. Were we again to be disappointed? At last, about noon, we heard somebody in the compartment immediately below us noisily moving things from one place to another; then a low cough. The next moment a head appeared in the opening of our board wall, and a man climbed up to us. It was our new friend. He brought a basket apparently filled with tools, but out of the depth of which he took two bottles of wine, a couple of sausages and a large loaf of bread.

"This is something for hunger and thirst," our friend whispered. "I have been also all around the city. The Prussian guard posts are no longer outside. I shall be glad to help you; only tell me what I am to do."

I now asked him to go to Steinmauern and look for a boat which in the coming night might take us across the Rhine. Then, about midnight, to be in the cornfield near the Steinmauern gate, outside of the fortress, and wait for us. He would hear the signal of a whistle; this he should answer, and then join us in order to take us to the boat. He should ask his wife to have something for us to eat at about eleven o'clock of the night.

I gave him a little more money, and he promised to do all I had asked, and disappeared again as he had come. Now we held a royal feast, during which our good humor made it very difficult for us to preserve the necessary silence. All the longer appeared to us the ensuing hours that were so full of hope and at the same time of anxiety. About two o'clock we heard the rattling of musketry at a distance.

"What is that?" whispered Neustädter. "There, they are killing somebody."

So it seemed to me. We took it as an indication of the lot that would be ours if we were captured. In fact, however, as we learned subsequently, the executions began only a few days later. What we had heard was probably some shots fired in cleaning guns.

Toward three o'clock a great ado began in the shed below. The cavalrymen were evidently preparing for departure; but they had hardly gone when another troop took possession of the premises. We concluded from the conversations overheard that it was a troop of Hussars. Toward evening a large crowd of people seemed to gather below, and we distinguished among them also women's voices. Then the trumpeters began to play waltzes and the merry company to dance. This was by no means disagreeable to us, for we expected that after such a frolic, which could scarcely pass off without some drink, our Hussars would sleep all the better. But before nine o'clock the crowd dispersed, and all would have been quiet had not one of the Hussars held back on the spot a Rastatt maiden. The couple stood or sat immediately under our hiding place, and we could understand every word they exchanged. The conversation was of a very sentimental character. He assured her that she was charming; that she had inflamed his heart when she first looked at him, and that he loved her tenderly. She answered he should not trouble her with his bad jests. But he may have observed that she really did not want to be left untroubled, and so he continued to vary the theme in all sorts of bold and flowery figures of speech. At last she seemed to be really inclined to believe all he told her. We should certainly have laughed had we dared. But when this otherwise interesting conversation would not come to an end, I began to be a little anxious lest it last until midnight, and so this Hussar love might interfere seriously with our plans. I felt, therefore, very much relieved when finally, after ten o'clock, the wooing vows died away in the distance.

Now we counted the minutes as the decisive moment approached. When it struck eleven Neustädter slipped out of the opening in the plank wall, stepped upon the pile of wood, and jumped lightly to the ground. I followed him. My legs had become very stiff in consequence of my lying for days and nights immovable on my back, and as I put my foot upon the wood several sticks fell down with a great noise. A moment later I heard not far away the tread of a patrol. I only had time to whisper back to my faithful Adam that he should remain until the patrol should have passed, and then follow me. I succeeded in reaching the little house before the patrol turned the corner of the lane. Neustädter was already there, and Adam came a few minutes later.

"The patrol passed quietly by," said he, "and they snored so loud in the shed that any other noise would hardly have been heard."

The wife of our friend in the little house had prepared a precious repast of beef broth, with rice, for us. After this and a dish of boiled meat and roast potatoes had refreshed our strength, we set out through the garden for the sewer. The moon was shining brightly, and we kept cautiously in the shadows of the hedges. But when we arrived at the ditch close by the mouth of the sewer a new fright awaited us. A sentinel was pacing to and fro just beyond the sewer, hardly thirty feet away from it. We halted and stooped under the hedge. There was but one thing to do. As the man turned his back upon us and walked to the other side, one of us was to slip cautiously into the sewer. The two others had to do the same. In a few minutes we were reassembled in the darkness of our refuge. We crawled ahead and found our old bench again, where we rested a while. Then pursuing our way we found the railing in its old place, dipped under it, and soon perceived a gleam of light through a mass of dark leaves, which suggested that the opening was immediately before us. We stood still once more to make our pistols ready for action. Whether after having been so wet, they would have gone off is very questionable. After all we had suffered, we were now determined to do our utmost. But the field was clear, the chain of guards had disappeared. The cornfield lay immediately before us. A low whistle on our part was promptly answered, and our man joined us a moment later.

He reported that the road was free. We marched vigorously on and in less than an hour we reached the village of Steinmauern. Our friend conducted us to the bank of the Rhine and showed us a boat in which a man lay fast asleep. He was quickly roused, and our friend announced to him that we were the men he was to take across the Rhine. "That will cost five florins," growled the boatman, who, upon my question as to what countryman he was, told me he came from Coblenz. I gave him the reward asked for, and offered also some more money to our kind friend. "You have given me already enough," he said; "what you still have you will be very much in need of. My name is Augustin Loeffler. Perhaps we may meet again in this world. God protect you."

Then we shook hands most cordially and parted. We fugitives stepped into the boat, and our friend wandered back to Rastatt. Many years later, when I was Secretary of the Interior in the government of the United States, I received one day a letter from Augustin Loeffler. It was dated at a little place in Canada. He wrote me that he had left Germany a short time after the revolutionary period, and was doing very well in his new home. He had read in the newspapers that I was one of the three young men who in that July night, 1849, had been conducted by him from Rastatt to the Rhine. In answer I expressed my joy at the receipt of his letter, and requested him to write again, but I have heard nothing from him since.

In an unexpectedly short time the boatman put us ashore in a dense growth of willows. It was between two and three o'clock in the morning, and as the surroundings seemed to be rather uninviting, we resolved to sit down upon old stumps of trees and there to await the light of day. At daybreak we arose to look for the nearest Alsatian village; but soon we discovered that we were on an island. A little house which stood in the middle of the island seemed to be the abode of a frontier guard of the grand duchy of Baden. So it looked as if we were still in the enemy's country, and as if the boatman from Coblenz had deceived us. The shutters and the doors of the little house were closed. We listened, but heard no sounds inside. A rapid run over the island convinced us that, excepting us three, there was no human being on it. We went to the water's edge opposite Alsatia, and in the rising sunlight saw on the other side two men whom we soon recognized to be French customs officers. We called out to them across the water that we were fugitives and desired to be taken over. One of the men came over to us in a little skiff and took us across to Alsatian soil. We gave up our arms to him and assured him and his comrade, amid great laughter, that we had brought with us from Rastatt nothing else subject to tariff duty. When I felt myself now really in freedom and security, my first impulse was, after a silence of four days, to shout as loudly as I could. My companions had the same feeling, and so we burst forth to our hearts' content, watched with great astonishment by the French officers, who may have taken us for madmen. We had landed near a little village called Münchhausen. The officers told us that in the town of Selz, near by, there were many German fugitives, and to Selz therefore we went. On the way we gazed at one another in the clear sunlight, and discovered that we looked like savages. For days and nights we had waded or squatted in wet clothes in water, mud and dust. Our hair was matted and our faces were streaked with dirt. A near rivulet furnished us the indescribable luxury of a washing, and thus retsored to human shape, we soon reached the inn at Selz.

The refugees there from Baden, none of whom had been in Rastatt, welcomed us heartily, and asked us at once for the story of our adventures. But our first wish was for a hot bath, a breakfast, and a bed. All this we obtained. I slept twenty-four hours with slight interruptions. Then I acquainted the company of refugees in the inn with the circumstances of our escape from Rastatt. From them I learned also for the first time that Kinkel had been captured by the Prussians in a fight near the fortress, before the beginning of the siege. When we left the Palatinate and he could no longer make himself useful in the offices of the provisional government, he had joined a battalion of volunteers and shouldered his musket as a private soldier. Thus he would share the lot of the revolutionary army. In the fight on the line of the Murg River he was wounded in the head and fell into the hands of the attacking Prussians. He was then incarcerated in one of the casemates at Rastatt, together with the captured garrison, in order to have him tried by court-martial, which would, no doubt, order him to be shot. This news threw a black veil over my joy at my own recovered freedom.

On the day after our arrival in Selz a police officer appeared at the inn, by the authority of the mayor, to learn our names, and also whether we expected to remain, or, if not, where we intended to go. "We want to go to Strasburg," I answered haphazard. The mayor gave us thereupon a sort of passport, with the instruction that we should report ourselves at once in Strasburg to the prefect. The depressing seriousness came over me that I was now really a homeless man, a fugitive, and under police surveillance. After having written to my parents and described to them my escape, we started for Strasburg without further delay. The real goal, however, of my journey was Switzerland, where, as I learned, Anneke and many others of my friends might be found.

If I had remained only a few days longer in Selz I should have seen my father in the same inn in which I had slept my first night in freedom. The mischance happened in this wise: The letter I had written to my parents on the day of the surrender at Rastatt, in the expectation that I would be taken prisoner together with the rest of the garrison, struck them like a clap of thunder, and at once my father set out to look for his son. Arrived in Rastatt, he reported himself at the office of the Prussian commander, to learn something about my fate. The commander received him kindly, but on inquiry could not give him any further information than that my name was not on the list of the captives. This surprised my father very much, and he requested permission to visit the casemates in which the prisoners were kept. This permission he received, and an officer accompanied him on this anxious search. From casemate to casemate they went three days long, and of one man after another they inquired about me, but all in vain. Many of those they saw knew me, but nobody knew what had become of me. Nobody had seen me on the occasion of the surrender. My father found Kinkel among the crowd. "What," Kinkel cried, "is Carl here, too? Alas, I believed him to be secure in Switzerland!"

In speechless grief the two men pressed each other's hand.

When my father had thus many days looked for me in vain, a ray of hope dawned upon him that after all I might have escaped. From citizens in Rastatt he learned that there were several refugees from Baden on the other side of the Rhine in Selz. Possibly one of these might be able to give him tidings about me. A few hours later my father appeared at the inn in Selz, and there he inscribed his name. Then he learned the whole story of my flight, and how only a few days before I had been in Selz and was now gone to Strasburg, with the intention of traveling further, nobody knew where, probably to Switzerland. My father burst into tears of joy, and exclaimed again and again, "That boy! That boy! Now I must quickly go home to tell his mother." As he could hardly hope still to find me in Strasburg, and expected to hear from me before long, he returned without delay to Bonn. One of the refugees from Baden, who had seen my father in the inn at Selz, and who had given him the happy news about me, told me all this a month later in Switzerland, and he could hardly master his emotion when he described to me my father's joy.

CHAPTER VIII

FROM Selz to Strasburg we wandered on foot. It was a beautiful Sunday afternoon. For a time we could see from our road the steeples of Rastatt. This distant view of the prison from which he had escaped would have been more joyful had it not reminded us of the unfortunate friends who in this dungeon awaited a sad fate. As we were still wearing uniforms, having no other clothes, we were easily recognized as fugitive revolutionary soldiers, and not seldom the village folk stopped us and wished to know how we had escaped. Then we were invited to rest, and were entertained with wine, refreshments and merry conversation until late in the evening, when we reached Strasburg. There we stopped at the hotel, the "Rebstöckl," the host of which was well known for his warm German sympathies. He gave us a hearty welcome and took especial care of us after he had heard our story. The next day we were obliged to report ourselves to the prefect. This officer informed us that the French government had resolved to send the German refugees into the interior; we could therefore stay neither in Strasburg nor in any other place near the frontier. Neither could he give us passports to Switzerland. But as it was our special desire to go to Switzerland, we resolved to continue our journey secretly without the assent of the authorities.

Meantime the news had come that those of the private soldiers of Baden and the volunteers of the Palatinate, who had done nothing but simply serve in the revolutionary army, were to be sent home without punishment. Only the officers and other noted transgressors were held back. Nothing therefore stood in the way of Adam's return home, and I urged him to avail himself of this opportunity. Adam once more gave expression of his warm attachment to me, of the sincerity of which I certainly had no reason to doubt. But he recognized that my advice was good, and resolved without delay to return to his family in the Palatinate. I divided the money I had with him, and thus we parted with the sincerest emotion and with the promise occasionally to write to one another. Only when Adam was gone it occurred to me that I had never known his family name, so that my efforts to find him out remained unsuccessful. I could not write to him; and thus it happened, that, as he did not write to me, I have never heard from him again since that day of parting.

After having spent some hours in visiting the Strasburg Cathedral, Neustädter and I prepared for departure. We purchased alpaca dusters to conceal our military uniforms, and then took a railway train for Basel, which, however, we left at a way-station shortly before reaching the Swiss frontier. It was near evening. We went into a village near by and found a little tavern, through the open door of which we saw a woman busy at the cooking stove. We entered and asked for something to eat. In her Alsatian idiom, hard for us to understand, she promised us some ham and eggs. While she was preparing our meal a man entered, whom we took to be her husband and the landlord of the inn. As his face inspired confidence, I thought it best to acquaint him frankly with our situation, as well as with our wish to cross the frontier into Switzerland without meeting any official person who might demand a passport. Our host seemed to be highly interested, and showed a surprising familiarity with the bypaths and trails used by the smuggling fraternity on the Swiss frontier. We suspected directly that he was of that fraternity himself. After dark he accompanied us part of the way, and then instructed us how we could avoid contact with all the customs officers and reach the Swiss village of Schönebühl, where we would find, at a certain minutely described spot, a barn which would probably be open, and where we would have a good night's rest on the stored hay. We followed the advice, and about midnight we reached the barn and stretched ourselves out to sleep.

Soon after sunrise we were on our feet again and inquired of some peasants, who seemed to be going to their work, the road to Bern—for I had heard in Strasburg that Anneke and the other friends whom I wished to join were in that city. The road led us first through fertile valleys. The fields teemed with men and women busy gathering their crops. I remember well the emotion experienced on that march. It was a joyful picture I beheld, but again and again the thought arose in me, "How much happier those toilers are than I! When they have done their hard work they return to their homes. They have a home, and I have none." I could not get rid of those somber reflections until we reached the Münsterthal, that magnificent cleft in the Jura Mountains. After a short rest I could not restrain the desire to take a look directly at the high Alps. So we climbed up the Monto, which rises to an elevation of about 4000 feet, and there we beheld for the first time in the distance the marvelous sublimity of the snowy mountain heads. It was a strange, invigorating and inspiring sight.

In a deep valley, on the other side of the Monto, we stopped at a wayside tavern, in which we found an intelligent-looking man, and a boy, who were refreshing themselves with wine and bread and cheese. The man, when we asked for the road and the distances from place to place, informed us kindly that he lived at Bern, and was just enjoying a little excursion with his son. Pushing our inquiries further, we learned that he knew several of the German refugees, among others my friends, and that these had indeed spent some time in Bern, but about a week ago had left that city to go to Dornachbruck, near Basel, where he was sure I could now find them. This was disagreeable news to me. In order to join them I had to retrace my steps the way we had come. I resolved at once to do so. But Neustädter, who did not know my friends, and who hoped to find some occupation in Bern, preferred to continue his journey in that direction. Thus we parted in the little tavern, and did not meet again until eighteen years later, in St. Louis, on the Mississippi River, where he occupied a modest but respected position, and where we then pleasantly rehearsed the common adventures of our youthful days.

My arrival at Dornachbruck brought me a new disappointment. In the village inn I learned that Anneke and others of my friends had indeed been there a few days before, but after a short stop had left for Zürich. I would gladly have traveled after them at once had I been sure that those whom I sought had not left Zürich again. My purse, too, was nearly empty, and, moreover, I felt physically very much exhausted. So I concluded it would be best, for the time being, to remain in Dornachbruck. I took a room in the inn, wrote home for some money and the clothes I had left behind, and went to bed. The great excitements and fatigues of the past days began to tell on me. I was thoroughly tired out, and felt myself lonely and forsaken. Sleep refreshed me but little. In very low spirits I wandered about in the village and surrounding country, and spent many an hour in the crumbling tower of a castle ruin, lying in the grass or sitting on moss-covered masonry. My melancholy grew deeper and darker. The future lay like a black cloud before me. I imagined myself at last seriously ill, and then spent the larger part of the day lying on my bed in a drowsy condition. It may have been on my tenth day in Dornachbruck when, one morning, I heard a remarkably loud voice downstairs calling my name. " That must be old Strodtmann," I exclaimed, and jumped from my bed. Indeed it was he, my Schleswig-Holstein friend. He had come from Bonn, to bring me a letter from my parents and dozens of them from my university friends. Also a purse bursting with gold, and whatever else I stood in need of. My escape from Rastatt had created in Bonn a most joyful sensation, which in the letters brought by Strodtmann found lively expression, and of which Strodtmann could not tell me enough. My melancholy was gone at once. Suddenly I felt perfectly well, and after having celebrated our reunion with the best dinner that the inn in Dornachbruck could furnish, we resolved to set out on the next day for Zürich, where Strodtmann promised to remain with me for a while.

Thus we marched forth, student-fashion, frequently stopping by the way, and then resuming our journey with constantly increasing gayety. On the River Aar, in view of the ruins of Hapsburg, not far from the spot where centuries ago the Emperor Albrecht had been killed by his nephew, Johann von Schwaben, we lay down in the grass, lost ourselves in historic contemplations and poetic outbursts, and fell asleep. It was evening when a Swiss policeman woke us. We found good quarters in an inn near by, and the next day secured seats on top of the mail coach for Zürich. When we arrived at Zürich, whom should I see? There, at the halting-place of the mail, stood my friends: Anneke, Techow, Schimmelpfennig and Beust, the very friends that I had been pursuing on my journey hither and thither—there they stood, just as if they had expected me. Their surprise was no less than mine. When I jumped down among them, as if I had dropped from the clouds, they hardly trusted their eyes. They had heard nothing of my escape from Rastatt. Neither had they found my name in the newspapers that gave an account of the revolutionary officers imprisoned in the casemates. Nobody had been able to tell them about me. Thus they had come to believe that I had been lost, perhaps in one of the last engagements, perhaps in an attempt to pass the Prussian lines. As they now saw me before them, alive and well, there was no end to their exclamations of astonishment.

Before evening I was lodged in the house of a baker's widow, in the Dorf Enge, a suburb of Zürich. Strodtmann found quarters in a neighboring inn. My other friends lived near by in the house of the schoolmaster. All this was very convenient and comfortable, although extremely simple. While Strodtmann was with me my thoughts moved in the atmosphere of the old conditions and surroundings, and my sojourn in Zürich appeared almost like part of a student's jaunt. But ten days later my dear good friend returned to Bonn, and what now began for me was the life of a refugee in its true reality. I had not become quite conscious of it all when the illness, which had threatened in Dornachbruck and had then been interrupted by the happy meeting with Strodtmann, developed into a violent fever, which kept me in bed two weeks. The village physician, as well as the baker's widow and her daughter, took care of me, and after a time I fully recovered. But when I rose from my bed I found myself in a strange world. It came over me that I had absolutely nothing to do. My first impulse was to look for a regular occupation. But soon I convinced myself that a young man like myself, who might have given lessons in Latin, Greek or music, had little to hope for in a population which, although it had hospitably received a great mass of fugitives, did, after all, not like them much. The other refugees were in the same condition, but many of them looked down upon such endeavors with a certain contempt, so long, at least, as their pecuniary resources were not exhausted. They firmly believed that a new upheaval would occur in the old Fatherland before long. Nobody cultivates the art of deceiving himself with the windiest illusions more cleverly, more systematically and more untiringly than the political refugee. We succeeded easily in finding in newspapers some news that clearly indicated to us the inevitable and fast-approaching outbreak of a new revolution. We were certain that we would soon return triumphantly to Germany, there to be the heroes of the day, the true champions of a victorious cause. Why should we therefore trouble ourselves with cares for the future? It appeared to us much more important and appropriate to discuss and determine the part each should play in the coming action. With the profoundest seriousness we debated the question who should be a member of the provisional government, or minister, or military leader.

We gravely sat in judgment over each other's character, capabilities, and especially fidelity to revolutionary principles, and but few forgot in this respect the positions to which they believed themselves entitled. In short, we disposed of the glorious future as if we had actually held the power over it in our own hands. Such delusions were well apt to develop among us a light-hearted and idle tavern existence, to which many of our companions gave themselves without restraint. I heard some of my refugee friends say, with a sort of lofty condescension, that the Fatherland looked to us as its great helpers and leaders; that we had to devote our lives solely to this exalted duty, and that therefore we should not fritter away our time and our strength in commonplace philistine occupations.

I must admit that in a simple-hearted, naïve way I shared this illusion—I was still only twenty years old—as to the imminence of a new revolutionary uprising. But the tavern had no charm for me whatever, and soon the life of a refugee began to yawn at me like a horrible void. A restless craving for systematic mental activity seized upon me. First I thought of the tasks which, as a young man, I would have to perform in the anticipated new struggles in Germany. With my nearest friends, who had all been officers in the Prussian army, and were excellent teachers, I reviewed and studied the military operations in Baden on a map specially drawn by us for that purpose. Then followed a series of military studies, of tactics and strategy, for which my friends furnished me the necessary material and instruction, and which I carried on with great zeal. Who could have thought that the knowledge thus gathered would be of use to me on a field of operations far away from Germany, and that one of my teachers, Schimmelpfennig, would then be a brigadier in my command!

This work, however, did not altogether satisfy me. My old love for historical studies was as strong as ever, and as I succeeded in gaining access to a good library, in which I found the works of the historian Ranke and many other books of value, I was soon again profoundly immersed in the history of the Reformation.

When winter came my lodgings in the house of the of the good baker's widow became uncomfortable on account of the cold. Then I took, with a companion in the Palatinate revolution, an old Prussian head forester by the name of Emmermann, two cosy rooms in the house of a merchant on the

Schanzengraben. My chum had the typical face of an old forester, weather-beaten, illumined by keen eyes, furrowed with a network of deep wrinkles, and ornamented with a gigantic gray mustache. He was an old bachelor, an amiable, benevolent soul, and we lived together in cheerful peace and friendship. He told me often that his forest-house had been situated in the neighborhood of a place called Tronegg, which had been in the immemorial past the seat of the gloomy hero of the Nibelungen Lied, Hagen von Tronje.

Thus I lived in agreeable domestic conditions and continued diligently my military and historical studies. Although I avoided the tavern as much as possible, I did not keep entirely aloof from intercourse with a larger circle of refugees. We had a political club that met once a week, and in the transactions of which I took an interested part. This club was in correspondence with democratic friends in the Fatherland, informed itself about the state of the public mind and about everything that could be considered symptomatic of the coming new revolution, and endeavored to put in its own work here and there—an activity of which I learned only some time later how utterly illusory it was. From time to time it occurred to me that the revolution might delay its coming much longer than we believed, and I began to make plans for my own future. There was a rumor that the federal government of Switzerland intended to found a great university at Zürich. I thought if the new German revolution kept us waiting all too long, I might establish myself at the university as a "Privat-Docent" of history, and then win for myself by-and-by a regular professorship. For the time being I gladly accepted the proposition of my friend, Dr. Hermann Becker, dubbed the "red Becker" at the university, to write articles for the newspaper edited by him in Cologne, the remuneration for which was sufficient to keep me above water until something better could be found. Thus I believed to perceive some bright spots in the fogs of the future.

My most remarkable acquaintance of those days was Richard Wagner, who, in consequence of his participation in the revolutionary uprising in Dresden, had been obliged to leave Germany, and now lived as one of the refugees in Zürich. He had then already written some of his most important creations, but his greatness was appreciated only by a very small circle of friends. Among the refugees at Zürich he was by no means popular. He passed for an extremely arrogant, domineering character, with whom nobody could long associate, and who treated his wife, the first one—a stately, good-natured, but mentally not highly gifted woman—very neglectfully. If anyone among us had then prophesied his magnificent career he would have found little credence. As an insignificant and reticent young man, of course, I did not come close to him. Although I met him and spoke with him occasionally, he probably never noticed me sufficiently to remember me.

In the course of time I should probably have succeeded in obtaining some position as teacher, if not at the university, at least at some other minor institution, had not my life of quiet study had been interrupted by an event that was destined to turn it into very different channels. The unhappy lot of my friend, Professor Kinkel, was constantly in my mind, all the more as it had taken an unexpected and particularly shocking turn. After having been wounded in the head and taken prisoner by the Prussians, Kinkel was carried first to Karlsruhe, and then after the surrender of Rastatt, to that fortress, where he was to be tried by a court-martial. On the 4th of August Kinkel appeared before that tribunal, which was composed of Prussian officers. Sentences

GOTTFRIED KINKEL IN CHAINS

of death were at that time the order of the day. And there is no doubt that, at army headquarters as well as at the seat of the Prussian government, Kinkel's condemnation to death was desired and expected. But Kinkel conducted his defense himself, and even the warriors composing the court-martial, men educated in the strictest allegiance to royal absolutism, could not resist the charm of his wonderful eloquence. Instead of condemning him to death, they sentenced him to confinement for life in a fortress.

To Kinkel's friends, to the admirers of the poet, I may say, to a large majority of the German people, this sentence appeared cruel enough. But the Prussian government at once manifested its dissatisfaction with it, for the reason that it was too mild. A rumor arose that the verdict would be set aside on account of some neglected formalities, and that Kinkel was to be put before a new court-martial. For weeks the poor prisoner, with alternate hope and fear, looked forward to the confirmation or rejection of the sentence, until at last, on the 30th of September, the following public announcement appeared:

"Warning. The late professor and member of a free corps, Johann Gottfried Kinkel of Bonn, having fought among the insurgents in Baden with arms in his hands against Prussian troops, has been sentenced by the court-martial instituted at Rastatt to lose the Prussian cockade and instead of the penalty of death only to confinement for life in a fortress. For examination of the legality of this sentence, it was submitted by me to the royal auditor-general, and by him to his Majesty, the king, for rejection on account of illegality. His majesty has graciously deigned to affirm the sentence, with the qualification that Kinkel shall undergo imprisonment in a civil penitentiary. According to this most high order, I affirm the verdict of the court-martial, to the effect that Kinkel is to be punished on account of treason with the loss of the Prussian cockade and with imprisonment for life, and that in execution of this sentence he shall be taken to a house of penal servitude; all of which is herewith brought to public knowledge.

"Headquarters, Freiburg, 30 September, 1849.

"The Commanding General von Hirschfeld."

This monstrous proceeding called forth, even from many of those who did not share Kinkel's political opinions and who disapproved of his acts, expressions of the profoundest indignation. The sentence pronounced by a regular court-martial was called illegal simply because it was not a sentence of death. It was called an "act of grace," that the king, nominally accepting that so-called illegal sentence of the court-martial, changed the confinement in a fortress into imprisonment in a penitentiary. What was confinement in a fortress? It was imprisonment in a fortified place under military surveillance, which permitted the prisoner to retain all the signs of his civil identity, his name, his clothes, his character as a man, and had treatment on the part of his guards not unworthy of that character—a kind of imprisonment in which he could continue his accustomed mental occupations—imprisonment, to be sure, but not disgrace, not degradation to the level of the common felon. And what was confinement in a house of penal servitude? Imprisonment in an institution intended for the ordinary criminal, where the prisoner was on the same level with the thief, the forger, the highwayman; where his head was shorn, his ordinary dress exchanged for the striped jacket, where he lost his name and received in its stead a number, where, in case of a breach of disciplinary rules, he was punished with flogging, where he had to abandon his whole mental life to do menial labor of the lowest kind. And this was called an act of grace! It was not to mitigate a sentence of death, because there was no such sentence, but to change the sentence of confinement in a fortress, such as I have described, into something infinitely more cruel, something loaded with debasement and infamy—a sentence of penal servitude—and this to Kinkel, the art-historian, who had opened the realms of the beautiful to so many a youthful mind; the poet, who had cheered and lifted up so many a German heart; the genial, refined, amiable, warm-hearted gentleman, whom only enthusiasm for liberty and fatherland had made to do what they called his crime! Even if he had, according to the law, deserved punishment after fighting in a lost cause, the sound sense and the human sympathy of many of his opponents revolted at the brutal arbitrariness which, overriding the obvious sense of a court-martial verdict, would not only punish, but degrade him and bury him amid the dregs of the human kind. Even death, which would have left to him his dignity as a man, would have seemed less inhuman than such an "act of grace."

Kinkel was first taken to the prison at Bruchsal in Baden, and soon afterwards to the penitentiary at Naugard in Pomerania. It was evidently intended to remove him as far as possible from the Rhineland, where sympathy for him was warmest. With shorn head, clothed in a gray prison jacket, he spent his days in spinning wool. On Sundays he had to sweep his cell. He was denied, so far as possible, all mental activity. His diet was that of the criminal in the penitentiary. From the day of his arrival in Naugard, October 8, 1849, until April, 1850, he received altogether only one pound of meat. But he moved the heart of the director of the penitentiary, and his treatment assumed gradually a more considerate character, a few small favors being granted to him. He was permitted more frequent correspondence with his wife, his letters being opened and read, however, by the officers; and he was relieved of the task of cleaning his cell. A little gift of sweetmeats, which his family sent at Christmas-time, was delivered to him. But he was still obliged to spin wool; and when our good Strodtmann, at that time a student in Bonn, appealed to the popular heart in Kinkel's behalf, in a poem called the "Spinning Song," the young poet was promptly dismissed from the university.

In the meantime the preparations for the trial of those who had taken part in the attack upon the Siegburg armory in May, 1849, went on in Cologne, and early in the year 1850 there was a rumor that the government intended to transport Kinkel from Naugard to Cologne in the spring, for the purpose of having him also tried for that revolutionary attack.

In February, 1850, I received a letter from Kinkel's wife. In burning colors she described to me the terrible situation of her husband and the distress of the family. But this high-spirited and energetic woman did not speak to me in the tone of that impotent despair which pusillanimously submits to an overpowering fate. The thought that it must be possible to find ways and means for the liberation of her husband gave her no rest day and night. For months she had been corresponding with friends in whose character she had confidence and whose energy she hoped to excite. Some of them had discussed with her plans for the rescue of her husband, and others had put sums of money at her disposal. But, so she wrote, nobody had shown himself ready to undertake the dangerous enterprise himself. What was needed, she said, was a friend who had sufficient tenacity of purpose, and who would devote his whole strength to the work until it should have succeeded. She herself would make the attempt did she not fear that her appearance in the vicinity of her husband's prison would at once excite suspicion and stimulate the watchfulness of his keepers. But it was necessary to act promptly, before the gnawing tortures of prison life should have completely destroyed Kinkel's mental and bodily strength. Then she informed me that Kinkel, according to rumor, would be taken to Cologne for trial on account of the Siegburg affair, and that there might then possibly be a favorable opportunity for his deliverance. She asked now for my advice, as she confided in my friendship as well as in my knowledge of the situation.

The night after the arrival of this letter I slept but little. Between the lines I could read the question whether I would not be the one to undertake the venture. It was this question that kept me awake. The spectacle of Kinkel in his prison jacket at the spinning-wheel was constantly before my eyes, and I could hardly endure the sight. I loved Kinkel dearly. I believed also that with his great gifts, his enthusiasm and his rare eloquence, he might still do great service to the cause of the German people. The desire to restore him if I could to Germany and to his family became irresistible. I resolved that night to try and make the attempt.

The next morning I began to consider the matter in detail. I remember that morning very clearly. Two doubts troubled me much. The one was whether I would be capable of carrying so difficult an undertaking to a happy end. I said to myself that Frau Kinkel, who after all had most to win and most to lose, seemed to believe me capable, and that it was not becoming in me to put my ability in doubt in the face of her confidence. But would those whose coöperation in so dangerous a risk was necessary give their confidence to so young a man as I was? I might perhaps gain it by a bold attitude. I cheered myself with the thought that as a young, insignificant and little known person I might better succeed in remaining unnoticed than would an older and more widely known man, and that therefore I might trust myself with less danger in the jaws of the lion. Finally, would older, more experienced, and more careful men be willing to do and dare all that might be required for the purpose of the task? Perhaps not. In short, this was, all things considered, a piece of work for a young man, and my youth appeared to me at last rather in the light of an advantage than of a hindrance.

My second doubt touched my parents. Could I with regard to them take the responsibility, after having just escaped from a terrible catastrophe, to put my life and freedom again in such jeopardy? Would they approve? One thing was clear: I must not in this case ask my parents for their permission, for I would then have to correspond with them about my project, and such a correspondence, subject to all possible chances of detection, might thwart the whole plan. No; in order to succeed, the undertaking must remain a profound secret, of which only those engaged in it were to have knowledge, and even then, if possible, only in part. To my family I could not confide it, for a conversation among them, accidentally overheard by others, might betray it. Therefore the question as to the approval of my parents I must answer myself, and I answered it quickly. They were among Kinkel's warmest admirers and devoted to him in loyal friendship. They were also good patriots. My mother, I thought, who the year before had given my sword to me with her own hands, would say: "Go and save our friend." And thus all my doubts were overcome.

On the same day I wrote to Frau Kinkel that in my opinion she would probably only aggravate the lot of her husband if she permitted an attempt to liberate him in Cologne on the occasion of the Seigburg trial, because then the authorities would doubtless take the most comprehensive precautions. She should hold her pecuniary means together without thinking of anything to be undertaken soon, and wait patiently and silently until she heard again from her friend. My letter was so worded that she could understand it, while it would not betray my intentions if it fell into wrong hands. As she also was familiar with my handwriting, I signed with a different name and directed the address to a third person whom she had mentioned to me. I conceived at once the plan to get secretly to Bonn for the purpose of talking over with her further steps, instead of risking such communications to paper.

Without delay I began my preparations. I wrote to my cousin, Heribert Jüssen, in Lind, near Cologne, whose outward appearance corresponded in all essential points with mine, asking him to procure from the police a traveling passport in his name and to send it to me. A few days afterwards the passport was in my hands, and now I could like an ordinary unsuspected mortal travel without difficulty wherever I was not personally known. Then I gave the officers of our club to understand that I was ready as an emissary to visit various places in Germany for the purpose of organizing branch clubs and to put them into communication with our committee in Switzerland. This offer was received with great favor, and I obtained, together with minute instructions, a long list of persons in Germany who could be depended upon. Of course of my real plans I did not give the slightest intimation. All was ready for my departure, and as I went on a secret expedition as an emissary, my friends found it quite natural that about the middle of March I should suddenly and entirely unnoticed disappear from Zürich.

CHAPTER IX

ON my errand I had to pass through the grand duchy of Baden, and saw from the window of my railroad carriage the castle tower of Rastatt, on which I had spent so many an hour. My first stopping place was Frankfurt-on-the-Main, where I was to find several persons who had been designated to me by the directors of my club at Zürich as worthy of confidence. From them I obtained various information about the condition of things in the western and middle part of Germany, and reported back what I learned to my friends in Switzerland. In general I faithfully carried out the instructions which I had received from them, and succeeded in keeping up the impression with regard to the object of my journey so completely that not one of my Zürich friends suspected me in the least of ulterior designs. Next I visited a number of cities, Wiesbaden, Kreuznach, Birkenfeld, Trier, where I found friends of our cause and established new communications. There were still among them people who hoped to bring on new revolutionary upheavals by means of secret conspiracies. This is one of the usual afterthroes of miscarried revolutionary movements. I traveled down the Moselle to Coblenz, where I passed a quiet day, intending to take the night mail coach to Bonn. In this I succeeded without trouble. As I approached my home, however, the journey became more precarious. At about two o'clock in the morning I arrived in Godesberg, where I decided to leave the coach. The remainder of the way to Bonn I did on foot. The house of my parents was outside of the city on the Coblenzer Strasse, and I reached it by three o'clock in the morning. By a fortunate accident I still possessed the latchkey which I had used as a student, and it opened the back door. In this way I got into the house and soon stood in the bedroom of my parents. Both were sleeping profoundly. After having sat for a while quietly on a chair until the light of dawn crept in through the windows I woke them up. Their surprise was indescribable. For some moments they could not persuade themselves that I was really there. Then their astonishment passed into the liveliest joy. My mother thought that I looked indeed a little fatigued, but otherwise very well. At once she would see to the breakfast. After I had given them the most necessary explanations about my sudden appearance, my father, who was beyond measure proud of me, wanted to know whom I desired to see in the course of the day. I had hard work to convince him that above all things my presence must be kept absolutely secret, and that therefore I did not wish to come into contact with anybody except the most trustworthy intimates.

Very fortunately it so happened that Frau Johanna Kinkel visited my parents that same morning, and I had opportunity for a confidential talk with her. I told her that I was ready to devote myself to the liberation of her husband if she would put the enterprise entirely into my hands, speak to nobody about it, and not ask me for more information than I might voluntarily give her. With touching enthusiasm she thanked me for my friendship and promised everything. After having agreed upon what was at the time to be done or to be left undone, I gave her a receipt for a magic ink which I had obtained in Zürich. With that ink our correspondence was to be carried on. It was simply a chemical solution, which, when used as ink, made no mark on the paper. A letter containing indifferent subject-matter was to be written over this in ordinary ink; the person receiving the letter then was to cover the paper, by means of a brush or sponge, with another chemical solution, which made what had been written in ordinary ink disappear. Thereupon the paper was to be warmed near a stove or a lamp to make the communication written with the magic ink become legible. Kinkel's eldest son, Gottfried, at that time a little boy, told me later that he had often looked on while his mother washed sheets of paper and then dried them near the stove.

When I had seen Frau Kinkel my most important business in Bonn was finished and I could give myself for some days, or so long as I could hope to remain undiscovered, to the joy of living once more with my family. With some of my oldest student friends I came together in the rooms of one of them, and there I met also a young student of medicine, Abraham Jacobi. Jacobi was a zealous democrat who afterwards won in America a great name for himself as a physician and scientist—so great, indeed, that many years later, when he had become one of the most prominent physicians of America, this revolutionary exile was distinguished by the university of Berlin with a call to a professorship. His invaluable friendship I have enjoyed down to this moment, and hope to enjoy it to the last.

In the darkness of night I went out to take my accustomed walks once more; and on one of those nightly expeditions I could not refrain from passing Betty's window in order, perhaps, to catch a gleam of light which might issue through the shutters; but all was dark. The next morning, however, I received more than an accidental gleam of light. One of my best friends, who also knew Betty, came to the house of my parents bringing a bouquet of flowers. "This bouquet," he said to me, "is sent to you by a girl whom I could safely tell that you are here." I blushed over and over in accepting the flowers and expressed my thanks. I put no further questions, for I did not doubt who the girl must be.

Before many days the number of my friends who had been informed of my presence was so large, and the danger that I might be betrayed by some accidental conversation between them became so great, that I thought it necessary to disappear. In response to my request my cousin, Heribert Jüssen, whose passport and name I bore, came to Bonn with his vehicle to take me during the night to Cologne. The parting from my parents and sisters was very sad, but after all they let me go in a comparatively cheerful state of mind. I left with them the same impression I had left with my friends in Switzerland—that I was exclusively engaged in business entrusted to me in Zürich. But we often talked about Kinkel's dreadful lot, and my parents repeatedly and emphatically expressed the hope that someone might be found to make an attempt to rescue him. Although they probably did not have me in mind when saying this, still it was sufficient to convince me that they would approve of my being that one. When I left Bonn nobody knew of my purpose except Frau Kinkel.

In Cologne I found quarters in the upper story of a restaurant which was kept by a zealous democrat. My friend the "Red Becker," the democratic editor, was there my special protector and confidant. I had made his acquaintance at the university. He was indeed at that time no longer a student. His examinations he had passed long before, but he was fond of visiting his Burschenschaft, the Allemania, in the old way; and nobody possessed a merrier humor and a more inexhaustible sitting power at the convivial meetings than he. Everybody knew and loved him. His nickname, the "Red Becker," he owed to a peculiarity of appearance. He had thin gold-red hair and a thin gold-red beard; he also suffered from a chronic inflammation of his eyelids so that his eyes seemed to have been framed in red. Not only his amiable disposition and his bubbling wit, but also his keen, critical mind and his comprehensive knowledge made him a most agreeable and much-desired companion. Nobody would have anticipated at that time that this jolly comrade who found so much enjoyment in continuing his university life beyond the ordinary measure of years, and who had already, in a high degree, acquired the oddities of an incorrigible student loiterer, would later distinguish himself as a most excellent public administrator, as a popular burgomaster of Cologne, and as a member of the Prussian House of Lords.

We had become close friends in consequence of our common political sympathies. He was not only at that time the editor of a democratic paper, but also the leader of the democratic club in Cologne, and I could safely count upon it that if anybody cherished a purpose to liberate Kinkel during the impending trial for the Siegburg affair, he would certainly know it all. Becker told me with the utmost frankness what had been planned and that all the world talked about "something that must be done." It became clear to me at once that if all the world talked about it, an attempt could not possibly succeed, and I was rejoiced to hear Becker himself share this conviction. Thus I was satisfied that nothing would be done in Cologne that might be apt to render later attempts more difficult of success.

The secret of my presence in Cologne was communicated to my nearest friends and to many others with such unconcern that I thought it was time to leave. Therefore I took a night train by way of Brussels to Paris. My intentions with regard to Kinkel I had confided to nobody in Cologne. Becker knew no more than that I had gone to Paris for the purpose of putting myself into communication with the German refugees living there, to write some letters about the situation of things in the French capital for his newspaper, and that I perhaps would spend some time in historical studies. In fact, all I had in view was to sit still in a secure place until the trial of the Siegburg affair, with all its excitements, was over, and Kinkel had been transported back to Naugard or to some other penitentiary, so that I might find him fixed at a certain place, and there begin my venturesome work.

Some impressions I received on the day of my arrival in Paris will always remain indelible in my mind. I was well versed in the recent history of France with its world-moving revolutionary events. Since the days of March, 1848, I had studied them with especial interest, hoping thus to learn more clearly to judge what was passing in my own surroundings, and now I had arrived at the theater of these great revolutionary actions in which the elementary forces of society in wild explosions had demolished the old and opened the way to the new order of things. From the railway station I went to the nearest little hotel, and soon, map in hand, I set out to explore the city. Eagerly I read the names of the streets on the corners. Here they were, then, those battlefields of the new era, which my excited imagination peopled at once with historic figures—here the Square of the Bastile, where the people won their first victory—there the Temple, where the royal family had been imprisoned; there the Faubourg Saint-Antoine, which on the days of great decision had sent the masses of the Blousemen upon the barricades into the bloody conflict; there the Carré Saint-Martin, where the first barricades of the February rising had been raised; there the Hôtel de Ville, where the commune had sat and where Robespierre with a bloody head had lain upon the table; there the Palais Royal where Camille Desmoulins, standing upon a chair, had fulminated his fiery speech and stuck a green leaf as a cockade on his hat; there the Place de la Concorde, where on the 10th of August the royal power of Louis XVI. fell into the dust.

Thus I wandered about for several hours as if entranced, when at a shop window I heard two men speaking German together. This woke me out of my reverie, and it occurred to me that it was time to look up the German refugees whose addresses I possessed. I therefore accosted the German-speaking men and asked them where I could find a certain street. I received a polite response and found myself soon in the room of a friend whose acquaintance I had made in the Palatinate—the Saxon refugee Zychlinski. He procured for me a furnished room in the neighborhood of the Church Saint-Eustache and instructed me quickly in the art of living in Paris on little money.

My sojourn in the French capital lasted about four weeks. My first care was to practice myself in the language of the country. I had appreciated already in Brussels that the instruction in French which I had received at the gymnasium hardly enabled me to order a breakfast. Now I began at once with a pocket dictionary in hand to read newspapers, including the advertisements, and then to avail myself of every opportunity to put the words and phrases I had thus learned to use in conversation with the concièrge of my house or the waiter at the restaurant or with anybody who would listen to me. After a few days I found that I could get along measurably well as to the everyday requirements of life. I did not make any important acquaintances in Paris at that time. Indeed I saw the leading men of the legislative bodies, but only from the distance of the gallery. Fellow-refugees brought me into contact with some Frenchmen who belonged to the extreme revolutionary class. From them I heard little more than the ordinary tirades against Louis Napoleon, who at that time was still president of the republic, but who gave significant indications of ulterior ambitions. In the circles in which I moved it was regarded as certain that this "Napoleonic business" could not possibly last long and that the new revolution doing away with the president would inevitably spread over the larger part of Europe. Although I took all possible pains to form a sober and impartial judgment of the condition of things in France, reading attentively to this end the journals of all parties, my conclusions did not escape from the influence of my wishes and illusions. If I should now in the light of historical events see again the letters which then I wrote in good faith as correspondent of Becker's newspaper, the reading would not be welcome. The errors of judgment which I then committed and which in less than two years I learned correctly to estimate, have been to me a lasting and salutary lesson. A large part of my time I spent in studying the treasures of art collected in Paris, which opened to me a world of charming vistas.

I remember an occurrence which, although unimportant in itself, has frequently in later times risen up in my mind and set me to thinking. I was in the habit of meeting Zychlinski and some other Germans in a certain Quartier Latin café. One evening I failed to find my friend there. This was especially disagreeable to me, for I had wished to ask Zychlinski to lend me some money. A remittance due me from Becker had not come, and all the change in my pocket consisted of a few sous, which were sufficient only for a cup of coffee and the tip to the waiter. I sat down and ordered my cup as usual, with the confident expectation that either one or the other of my friends would soon appear. I drank my coffee as slowly as possible, but when I had emptied the cup not one of my expected friends was there. I put the remainder of my sugar into a glass of water, and prepared my "eau-sucré" in the manner of the thrifty guests of the French cafés. I read one journal after another, sipping my sugar-water with painful slowness, but nobody came. I may have sat there more than two hours and it began to be very late. The "dame du comptoir," to whom payment was made, yawned, and even Monsieur Louis, the attendant of the billiard table, who for more than an hour had been unoccupied, became sleepy. I still see the amiable Monsieur Louis before me, from time to time rolling the ivory balls on the billiard table with his finger from one spot to another and then looking at me. I felt as if both had become annoyed at the long time that I devoted to my cup of coffee. So I resolved to pay with my last sous and to go home. But when I got up from my chair an accident happened. By an awkward movement I pushed the coffee cup off the little table upon the marble floor, and it broke into many pieces. I thought that as a matter of course I must pay for the broken cup. I had money enough for the coffee, but not for the broken cup. The dame du comptoir exchanged glances with Monsieur Louis. Those glances darted into the depth of my guilty conscience. What should I do? At this moment several new guests came in, French students, of whom two or three began to joke with the dame du comptoir. Could I now step into this group and in my clumsy French make to the Dame du Comptoir a confession of my embarrassment? Would I not expose myself to the laughter of the whole company? In the excitement of the moment I recklessly resolved to order another cup of coffee, taking a last chance of my friends still turning up. I waited long, but not in vain. Zychlinski really came. The terrible burden fell from my soul. I had to restrain myself not to cry out for delight. I told him my story, and we laughed heartily about it, but with all this I did not feel at ease. Zychlinski lent me the needed money, but when I got up to leave and asked the dame du comptoir how much I owed for the broken cup, she replied with a gracious condescending smile that in this café no payment was ever accepted for accidentally broken crockery. My anguish had therefore been altogether superfluous. When I returned to my quarters I found a letter from Becker containing the delayed check.

This little adventure has in later life frequently come to my mind again. As a result of my ruminations I give to those who read this story the serious advice not to follow my example under similar circumstances and never to add to one obligation an unnecessary new one, trusting to a happy chance for payment. It was a cause of that false pride which has led so many men, originally honest, down the inclined plane of mischief. Many a man has gone to destruction for not having the moral courage to face embarrassing situations or on occasion frankly to confess: "I have not money enough to do that which others do."

While I was in Paris the trial of the participants in the Siegburg affair took place in Cologne. At an early hour on the 10th day of April, Kinkel left the penitentiary at Naugard accompanied by three police officers and arrived in Cologne on the 13th. On the journey, which was made in great secrecy, he was permitted to wear an ordinary overcoat and a little black hat, but as soon as he arrived in the penitentiary in Cologne he had to don the penitentiary garb again. A few days later Frau Kinkel was permitted to see her husband in the prison, but only in the presence of the turnkeys. She took with her her six-year-old Gottfried, who did not recognize his father with his closely clipped hair, his drawn features, and his convict dress, until he heard his voice.

The public trial before a jury of burghers opened on the 29th of April. Ten persons were accused "of an attempt to upset the present constitution of the kingdom, to excite the citizens or inhabitants of the state to sedition, to arm themselves against the royal authority, and to bring about a civil war by arming the citizens or inhabitants of the state against one another, or by inciting them so to arm themselves." Of the defendants, four were present, six having fled the kingdom, of whom I was one.

The population of Cologne was in feverish excitement. The court house was surrounded by an immense multitude eager to see Kinkel and to manifest their sympathy for him, the captive defender of liberty, the poet condemned to the penitentiary. The authorities had taken the most extensive measures to prevent any possibility of his being liberated. The carriage in which Kinkel rode from the prison to the court house was surrounded by a strong force of cavalry with drawn sabers. The streets he passed through, as well as all the approaches to the court house, were bristling with bayonets. On the court house square stood two cannon with an ammunition wagon, and the artillerymen ready for action. When Kinkel appeared he was, in spite of all this, received by the assembled multitude with thundering cheers. He had again been put into ordinary citizen's dress. On the way he appeared stolid and impassive. The aspect and the acclaim of the people revived him. Boldly and proudly he lifted up his closely clipped head as he strode from the carriage between lines of soldiers into the hall of justice. There his wife had, early in the morning, secured a place which she continued to occupy every day throughout the trial. The public prosecutor moved in Kinkel's case the penalty of death. The testimony of the various witnesses brought out the facts of the case as they were generally known; the public prosecutor, as well as the attorneys of the defendants, pleaded their causes with coolness and skill. My friend and fellow-student, Ludwig Meyer, made a manly speech in his own defense, and at last, on the 2d of May, Kinkel himself asked to be heard.

The assembled audience, aye, the whole nation, were in a state of anxious expectancy. People asked one another: "What will he say? Will he humiliate himself, and bow his head like a penitent sinner? Will he present the picture of a broken and thenceforth harmless man in order to purchase grace? Or will he defy those in power by maintaining all his former professions, by standing by what he has said and done, and thereby forfeit the last claim to a mitigation of his awful lot?" The grievously suffering man would probably have been forgiven by public opinion had he by a yielding attitude sought an alleviation of his misery.

Kinkel's speech in his own defense was a full answer to all these questions, in the highest degree imposing, and touching at the same time. He began with a concise description of the public situation in Germany after the revolution in March, 1848. "The people," he said, "had then won their sovereignty. This sovereignty of the people had been embodied in the constituent assemblies elected by universal suffrage—in the Prussian assembly in Berlin, as well as in the national parliament in Frankfurt. It had so been understood by all the world. The national parliament had proceeded with signal moderation; it had created a magna charta of popular rights in a constitution for the empire, and it had elected as the head of the empire and the protector of that magna charta the king of Prussia, the same king who on the 18th of March had put himself at the head of the movement for German unity and freedom. The realization of this idea had been the great hope of the nation. But the king of Prussia had refused to complete the work of national unity by declining the imperial crown. He had dissolved the Prussian constituent assembly, which had urged him to accept the charge, and thereby annihilated the possibility of an agreement with the people, and with it also all hope of the accomplishment of social reforms. Then nothing had remained but an appeal to arms. He too, the accused, had taken up his musket, and he declared now in the presence of his judges his belief that he had done right. He stood to-day by the acts he had committed in the preceding May. What he had done, he had done as a patriot and a man of honor." He went still farther in his avowal. He called himself a socialist—although in the now-accepted party sense Kinkel had really never been that. He had never been an adherent of any of those systems which contemplate a complete subversion of the traditional institutions of society. When he called himself a socialist he meant only that, as he said, "his heart was always with the poor and oppressed of the people, and not with the rich and powerful of this world." He expressed, therefore, only those sympathies which had taken possession of so many hearts, and in order to designate them he chose the name of socialist because it was nearest at hand. "And because I am a socialist," Kinkel continued, "therefore I am a democrat, for I believe that only the people themselves can feel their own deep wounds and cleanse and heal them. But because I am a democrat, because I consider the democratic state as the only and certain possibility to banish misery from the world, therefore I also believe that when a people have once won democratic institutions they have not only the right, but also the duty to defend those institutions to the last with all means within their reach, even with musket and pointed steel. In this sense I profess to accept the principle of revolution for which my own blood has flowed, and even to-day, wholly in the power of my adversaries, I confess with the pale lips of the prisoner that this principle is mine. And therefore I also believe that together with the friends at my side I was right when I took up the battle and offered to my principles the highest sacrifice. A high aim was before our eyes. Had we conquered we would have saved to our people peace within itself; the unity of the Fatherland, this fundamental idea of the German revolution, and with it the key to all future developments of prosperity and greatness. Gentlemen, we have not conquered. The people have not carried this struggle through, but have abandoned us, us who advanced in the lead. The consequences fall upon our heads."

Now he declared how in this struggle he had not hesitated to associate himself with persons without education and even of doubtful repute. "For," he said, "no great idea had ever been disgraced because the populace and the publicans accepted it." Then he explained how the penal provisions of the Code Napoleon, which was still the law in the Rhineland, could not be applied to the public conditions of 1848; that this code had been designed for an absolute military monarchy; that after the revolution the Germans were entitled to arm themselves as a people with free choice of their leaders—and this for the purpose of enabling the people to protect their rights against encroachments. "We are told that we attempted to subvert the existing constitution of the kingdom. What constitution is meant? The new Prussian? Who ever thought of that? Or the Frankfurt national constitution? To protect this we took up arms. Upon your conscience, gentlemen, are we the men that made attempts upon that constitution? But we are charged to have incited civil war. Who dares to assert this? Who will deny that in the face of the uprising of the whole people in arms, a grand solemn uprising, the crown would have been urged upon the path of progress, without civil war? Yes, if all were true that is asserted in the indictment, if we had really conspired to oppose force to force, if we had armed ourselves to storm an armory, if we had put arms into the hands of citizens for such an enterprise, even then, yes, even then, we would, after a defeat, be only unfortunates, but not punishable culprits. We would have done it, not to destroy a constitution, but to support one that was attacked; we would have done it not to incite civil war, but to prevent civil war, that horrible civil war, which drove the Landwehr of Iserlohn into the deadly fire of the German riflemen on the tower of Durlach, that condemned, in consequence, Dortu to be shot and Corvin to penal labor. What has become of the Fatherland now that we have not conquered? That you know. But if we had conquered in this struggle, before God, gentlemen, instead of the guillotine with which the prosecuting attorney threatens us, according to the law of the French tyrant, we would receive from you to-day the civic crown." This part of his speech was heard by all those assembled in the hall with astonishment and by many with admiration. The presiding officer found it difficult to suppress the storm of applause which at times would break out, but everybody felt that this accused man who faced so boldly and proudly those in power, even if he escaped a new sentence, had now forfeited all hope for a mitigation of the punishment already imposed upon him. But what now followed overwhelmed the audience to an unexpected degree. In a few sentences Kinkel pointed out the contradictions and weak points in the testimony of the witnesses, and then he continued:

"The only thing that remains is that I have incited citizens to take up arms. I will tell you how this incitement came about. I am glad to tell you, because in my action there is only one thing that might appear ambiguous, and that is, that I endeavored rather to dissuade others from the enterprise which I myself undertook. With perfect clearness that 10th of May still stands before my mind, for that day on which I, a happy man, took leave of all the happiness of my life, has etched itself into my soul with burning needles of pain. The strain and stress of that time tore piece after piece from my heart; but at five o'clock in the afternoon I had not yet formed a final resolution. I went to the university. I delivered my lecture with quiet composure. It was my last. At six o'clock arrived the tidings from Elberfeld and Düsseldorf. They struck hot fire into my breast. I felt that the hour had come for me when honor commanded to act. From the meeting of citizens I went to my dwelling to say farewell. I took leave of the peace of my house; of the office which for twelve years had made me happy, and which I believe I had faithfully administered; leave of my wife, for whose possession I had already once risked my life; leave of my sleeping children, who did not dream that in this hour they lost their father. But when I crossed my threshold and stepped into the darkening street, then I said to myself, 'You have taken this resolution prepared for whatever may follow; for you know what the consequences may be. You will always have the consolation of the ideas and convictions you cherish. You have no right to persuade another husband, another father, to the same terrible decision.' In this state of mind I mounted the platform of the citizens' meeting; and I warned every one of my hearers whose heart was not firm like mine—and out of this speech the public prosecutor makes an incitement to revolt! Do not think, gentlemen, that I wish to appeal to your emotions and to awaken your pity. Yes, I know it, and the 'acts of grace' of the year 1849 have taught me that your verdict of guilty means a sentence of death; but in spite of this, I do not want your compassion; not for my fellow-defendants, for to them you owe not pity, but satisfaction for the long and undeserved imprisonment; not for me, for however inestimable your sympathy as citizens and men may be to me, your compassion for me would have no value. The sufferings I have to bear are so terrible that your verdict can have no added terrors for me. Beyond the measure of the punishment at first imposed upon me, the authorities have increased mine by the horrible solitude of the isolated cell, the desolate stillness, in which no trumpet call of the struggling outside world will penetrate, and no loving look of faithful friends. They have condemned a German poet and teacher who in more than one breast has lighted the flame of knowledge and beauty, they have condemned a heart full of sympathy slowly to die in soulless mechanical labor, in denial of all mental atmosphere. The murderer, the lowest, most hideous criminal, is permitted as soon as the word of grace and pardon has descended upon him to breathe the air of his Rhenish home, to drink the water of his beloved river. The fourteen days I have been here have taught me how much consolation there is in the air and light of the homeland. But I am kept in the far-away gloomy north, and not even behind the iron bars of my prison I am allowed to see the tears of my wife, to look into the bright eyes of my children. I do not ask for your commiseration, for however bloody this law may be you cannot make my lot more terrible than it is. The man whom the public prosecutor has insinuatingly dared to accuse of cowardice has in this last year looked death in its various forms into the eyes so often, so nearly, so calmly, that even the prospect of the guillotine can no longer shake him. I do not want your compassion, but I insist upon my right. My right I put upon your consciences, and because I know that you citizens, jurymen, will not deny this right to your Rhenish compatriot. Therefore I expect with quiet confidence from your lips the verdict of not guilty. I have spoken; now it is for you to judge!"

The impression produced by these words has been described to me by eyewitnesses. At first the audience listened in breathless silence, but before long the judges upon the bench, the jurors, the densely crowded citizens in the hall, the prosecuting attorney who had conducted the case, the police officers who watched the accused, the soldiers whose bayonets gleamed about the door, burst out in sobs and tears. It took several minutes after Kinkel concluded his speech before the presiding judge found his voice again. At last the case was given to the jury. The jury instantly returned a verdict of "Not guilty." Then a thundering cheer broke forth in the hall, which was taken up by the multitude outside and resounded in the streets far into the city. Frau Kinkel pressed through the crowd to her husband. A police officer ordered his subordinates who surrounded Kinkel to hold her back, but Kinkel, rising to his full height, cried out with a commanding voice, "Come, Johanna! Give your husband a kiss. Nobody shall forbid you." As if yielding to a higher power the police officers stepped back and made way for the wife, who threw herself into her husband's arms.

The other defendants were now free to go home; only Kinkel, still under the former sentence imposed upon him by the court-martial in Baden, was again quickly surrounded by his guards, taken to the carriage amid the resounding acclamations of the people and the rolling of the drums of the soldiers, and carried back to the jail.

As was to be expected, the authorities had taken every possible measure to prevent an attempt to liberate Kinkel in Cologne. The government had meanwhile also resolved not to take him back to the penitentiary at Naugard, but to imprison him in Spandau, probably because in Naugard warm sympathies with the sufferer had manifested themselves. To mislead Kinkel's friends and to avoid all difficulties on the way, he was not, as generally expected by the public, transported by rail, but in a coach, accompanied by two police officers. The departure took place on the day after the trial in all secrecy, but just these arrangements had made possible an attempt at escape which Kinkel undertook of his own motion and without help from the outside, and which he narrated to me later as follows:

One evening the police officers stopped the coach at a wayside tavern of a Westphalian village where they intended to take supper. Kinkel was placed in a room in the upper story, where one officer remained with him, while the other went down to make some arrangements. Kinkel noticed that the door of the room was left ajar and that the key was in the lock outside. The idea to take advantage of this circumstance occurred to him instantly. Standing near the window he directed the attention of the police officer who guarded him, sitting near the door, to a noise outside on the street. As soon as the police officer stepped to the window, Kinkel sprang with a rapid jump through the door and turned the key in the lock outside. Then he ran as fast as he could down the stairs through the back door into the yard, into the kitchen garden, and in the direction that was open to him, into the fields. Soon the fugitive heard voices behind him and turning saw lights in the distance moving to and fro. He ran with furious speed, spurred on by the pursuit, which was evidently at his heels. Suddenly he struck his forehead against a hard object and fell down stunned.

The pursuers also had their difficulties. The police officer who had been in the room with Kinkel jumped for the door, and finding it locked, he hurried back to the window, which in the excitement of the moment he did not succeed in opening quickly. He smashed it with his fist and shouted into the street that the "rogue" had escaped. The whole house was promptly alarmed; the police officers told the servants that the fugitive was one of the most dangerous criminals of the Rhineland, and offered a reward of at least a hundred thalers for his capture. Of course, the village folk believed all they were told. The postilion who had driven the coach, not suspecting that his passenger was Kinkel, showed himself especially active. At once lanterns were brought to look for the tracks of the fugitive. The postilion soon discovered them, but Kinkel had gained considerable headway by these delays, and only his running against a pile of wood, a projecting log of which struck his forehead, had neutralized this advantage. In less than a quarter of an hour he was in his benumbed condition discovered by the postilion, who really believed that he had before him an escaped highwayman, and soon the police officers, hurrying on, again laid their hands upon him. These now redoubled their watchfulness until finally the door of the penitentiary of Spandau closed upon the unfortunate man.

When the excitement caused by the trial in Cologne had subsided, and Kinkel, sitting quietly in the Spandau penitentiary, had temporarily ceased to occupy public attention in an extraordinary degree, I left Paris for Germany. I had in the meantime received new instructions from the Zürich committee which I faithfully carried out. To this end I visited several places in the Rhineland and in Westphalia, and even attended a meeting of democratic leaders which took place in July in Braunschweig, where I hoped to establish useful connections. There I made the acquaintance of the Mecklenburg deputy, Moritz Wiggers, with whom soon I was to have very interesting transactions.

At the beginning of August I returned to Cologne, where I had another meeting with Frau Kinkel. She reported that the sum collected for the liberation of her husband had grown considerably, and I was rejoiced to hear that it was sufficient to justify the beginning of active work. We agreed that the money should be sent to a confidential person in Berlin from whom I might receive it according to my requirements. Frau Kinkel also told me that she had found a method to convey to Kinkel information in a manner not likely to excite suspicion, if anything were undertaken in his behalf. She had written to him about her musical studies and put into her letters long explanations about the word "fuge." Kinkel had made her understand by words which were unintelligible to the officers who reviewed his letters, that he appreciated the significance of the word "fuge," Latin, "fuga," English, "flight," and that he was anxious to correspond more with her upon that subject. Frau Kinkel promised me to be very circumspect with her letters and not to cause him any unnecessary excitement, also not to become impatient herself if she should hear from me but seldom. So we parted and I started for the field of my operations.

At the railroad station I found my friend Jacobi, who was on his way to Schleswig-Holstein, to offer his services as a physician to our struggling brethren. A part of the way we could journey together. This was an agreeable surprise, but a much less agreeable surprise was it when in the coupé in which we took seats we found ourselves directly opposite to Professor Lassen of the University of Bonn, who knew me. We were greatly startled. Professor Lassen looked at me with evident astonishment, but as Jacobi and I began to chat and laugh as other young men would have done with apparent unconcern, the good orientalist probably thought that he was mistaken and that I could not possibly be the malefactor whom I resembled in appearance. On the 11th of August I arrived at Berlin. My passport, bearing the name of my cousin, Heribert Jüssen, and fitting me admirably in the personal description, was in excellent order, as the passports of political offenders venturing upon dangerous ground usually are, and thus I had no difficulty in entering Berlin, the gates and railroad stations of which were supposed to be closely watched by an omniscient police bent upon arresting or turning away all suspicious characters. Without delay I looked up some student friends who had been with me members of the Burschenschaft Franconia at the university of Bonn, and they gave me a hearty welcome, although they were not a little astonished to see me suddenly turn up in Berlin. They were discreet enough not to ask me for what purpose I had come, and thus made it easy for me to keep my own secret. Two of them, who occupied a small apartment on the Markgrafen Strasse, invited me to share their quarters; and as I went out and in with my friends the police officers on that beat no doubt regarded me as one of the university students, a good many of whom lived in that neighborhood.

It was at that period customary in Berlin, and perhaps it is now, that the tenants of apartment houses were not furnished with latchkeys for the street doors, but that such keys were entrusted to the night-watchman patrolling the street, and that a tenant wishing to enter his house during the night had to apply to the watchman to open the door for him. Having been seen by our watchman once or twice coming home with my friends, I was regarded by him as legitimately belonging to the regular inhabitants of the street; and as it happened several times that, returning late in the night alone from my expeditions to Spandau, where I was preparing for the deliverance of a man sentenced to imprisonment for life, I called upon this same police officer to open for me—for me, who was then virtually an outlaw—the door of my abode, which he always did without the slightest suspicion. This afforded me and my friends much amusement, and, indeed, considering the great reputation of the Berlin police for efficiency, the situation was comical enough. It is, therefore, not surprising that I became a little reckless and did not resist the temptation to see the famous French actress, Rachel, who at that period, with a company of her own, was presenting the principal part of her repertoire to the Berlin public.

Rachel had then reached the zenith of her fame. Her history was again and again rehearsed in the newspapers: how that child of poor Alsatian Jews, born in 1820 in a small inn of the canton of Aargau in Switzerland, had accompanied her parents on their peddling tours through France; how she had earned pennies by singing with one of her sisters in the streets of Paris; how her voice attracted attention; how she was taken into the Conservatoire; how she soon turned from singing to elocution and acting, and how her phenomenal genius, suddenly blazing forth, at once placed her far ahead of the most renowned of living histrionic artists. We revolutionary youths remembered with especial interest, the tales that had come from Paris after those February days of 1848, when King Louis

Philippe was driven away and the republic proclaimed, describing Rachel as she recited the " Marseillaise " on the stage, half singing, half declaiming, and throwing her hearers into paroxysms of patriotic frenzy.

Some of my student friends having witnessed Rachel's first performance in Berlin, gave me extravagantly enthusiastic reports. My desire to see her became very great. Indeed, the attempt would not be without risk. In thus venturing into a public place I might fall into the hands of the police and go from there straightway to prison. But my friends told me that the government detectives would hardly look for state criminals in a theater, and that I would be safe enough in the large crowd of Rachel enthusiasts. I could put myself into some dark corner of the parterre without danger of meeting a detective for one night at least. Finally, with the light-heartedness of youth, I resolved to take the risk.

So I saw Rachel. It was one of the most overpowering impressions of my life. The play was Racine's " Phèdre." I had read most of the tragedies of Corneille, Racine and Voltaire, and was well enough acquainted with them to follow the dialogue. But I had never liked them much. The stilted artificiality of the diction in the tedious monotony of the rhymed Alexandrine verse had repelled me, and I had always wondered how such plays could be made interesting on the stage. That I was to learn. When Rachel stepped upon the scene, not with the customary stage stride, but with a dignity and majestic grace all her own, there was first a spell of intense astonishment and then a burst of applause. She stood still for a moment, in the folds of her classic robe like an antique statue fresh from the hand of Phidias. The mere sight sent a thrill through the audience: her face a long oval, her forehead, shadowed by black wavy hair, not remarkably high, but broad and strong; under her dark arched eyebrows a pair of wondrous eyes that glowed and blazed in their deep sockets like two black suns; a finely chiseled nose with open, quivering nostrils; above an energetic chin a mouth severe in its lines, with slightly lowered corners, such as we may imagine the mouth of the tragic Muse. Her stature, sometimes seeming tall, sometimes little, very slender, but the attitude betraying elastic strength; a hand with fine tapering fingers of rare beauty; the whole apparition exciting in the beholder a sensation of astonishment and intense expectancy.

The applause ceasing, she began to speak. In deep tones the first sentences came forth, in tones so deep that they sounded as if rising from the innermost cavities of the chest, aye, from the very bowels of the earth. Was that the voice of a woman? Of this you felt certain—such a voice you had never heard, never a tone so hollow and yet so full and resonant, so phantomlike and yet so real. But this first surprise soon yielded to new and greater wonders. As her speech went on that voice, at first so deep and cavernous, began, in the changing play of feelings or passions, to rise and roll and bound and fly up and down the scale for an octave or two without the slightest effort or artificiality, like the notes of a musical instrument of apparently unlimited compass and endless variety of tone color. Where was now the stiffness of the Alexandrine verse? Where the tedious monotony of the forced rhymes? That marvelous voice and the effects it created on the listener can hardly be described without a seemingly extravagant resort to metaphor.

Now her speech would flow on with the placid purl of a pebbly meadow brook. Then it poured forth with the dashing vivacity of a mountain stream rushing and tumbling from rock to rock. But her passion aroused, how that voice heaved and

RACHEL

From the Painting by Edouard Dubufe

surged like the swelling tide of the sea with the rising tempest behind it, and how then the thunderstorm burst, booming and pealing, and crashing, as when the lightning strikes close, making you start with terror! All the elementary forces of nature and all the feelings and agitations of the human soul seemed to have found their most powerful and thrilling language in the intonations of that voice and to subjugate the hearer with superlative energy. It uttered an accent of tender emotion, and instantly the tears shot into your eyes; a playful or cajolling turn of expression came, and a happy smile lightened every face in the audience. Its notes of grief or despair would make every heart sink and tremble with agony. And when one of those terrific explosions of wrath and fury broke forth you instinctively clutched the nearest object to save yourself from being swept away by the hurricane. The marvelous modulations of that voice alone sufficed to carry the soul of the listener through all the sensations of joy, sadness, pain, love, hatred, despair, jealousy, contempt, wrath, and rage, even if he did not understand the language, or if he had closed his eyes so as not to observe anything of the happenings on the stage.

But who can describe the witcheries of her gestures and the changeful play of her eyes and features? They in their turn seemed to make the spoken word almost superfluous. There was, of course, nothing of that aimless swinging of arms and sawing of the air and the other perfunctory doings of which Hamlet speaks. Rachel's action was sparing and simple. When that beautiful hand with its slender, almost translucent, fingers, moved, it spoke a language every utterance of which was a revelation to the beholder. When those hands spread out with open palms and remained for a moment in explanatory attitude—an attitude than which the richest fancy of the artist could not have imagined anything more beautifully expressive—they made everything intelligible and clear; at once you understood it all and were in accord with her. When those hands stretched themselves out to the friend or the lover, accompanied by one of those smiles which were rare in Rachel's acting, but which, whenever they appeared, would irradiate all surroundings like friendly sunbeams breaking through a clouded sky—a tremor of happiness ran all over the house. When she lifted up her noble head with the majestic pride of authority, as if born to rule the world, everyone felt like bowing before her. Who would have dared to disobey when, the power of empire on her front, she raised her hand in a gesture of command? And who could have stood up against the stony glare of contempt in her eye and the haughty toss of her chin, and the disdainful wave of her arm, which seemed to sweep the wretch before her into utter nothingness?

It was in the portrayal of the evil passions and the fiercest emotions that her powers rose to the most tremendous effects. Nothing more terrible can be conceived than was her aspect in her great climaxes. Clouds of sinister darkness gathered upon her brow; her eyes, naturally deep-set, began to protrude and to flash and scintillate with a truly hellish fire. Her nostrils fluttered in wild agitation as if breathing flame. Her body shot up to unnatural height. Her face transformed itself into a very Gorgon head, making you feel as if you saw the serpents wriggling in her locks. Her forefinger darted out like a poisoned dagger against the object of her execration; or her fist clenched as though it would shatter the universe at a blow; or her fingers bent like the veriest tiger's claws to lacerate the victim of her fury—a spectacle so terrific that the beholder, shuddering with horror, would feel his blood run cold, and gasp for breath, and moan, "God help us all."

This may sound like wild exaggeration, like an extravagant picture produced by the overheated imagination of a young man charmed by a stage-goddess. I must confess that I was at first somewhat suspicious of my own sensations. I, therefore, at that as well as at later periods, repeatedly asked persons of ripe years who had seen Rachel, about the impressions they had received, and I found that theirs hardly ever materially differed from mine. Indeed, I have often heard gray-haired men and women, persons of cultivated artistic judgment, speak of Rachel with the same sort of bewildered enthusiasm that I had experienced myself. I am sure, there was in my admiration of Rachel nothing of the infatuation of an ingenuous youth for an actress which we sometimes hear or read of. If anybody had offered to introduce me personally to Rachel, nothing would have made me accept the invitation. Rachel was to me a demon, a supernatural entity, a mysterious force of nature, anything rather than a woman with whom one might dine, or speak about every-day things, or take a drive in a park. My enchantment was of an entirely spiritual kind, but so strong that in spite of the perils of my situation in Berlin I could not withstand it. So I visited the theater to see Rachel as often as the business I had in hand, which then required occasional night drives to Spandau, permitted such a luxury. Of course, I was not altogether unmindful of the danger to which I was exposing myself. I always managed to have a seat in the parterre near the entrance. While the curtain was up, I was sure that all eyes would be riveted on the scene. Between the acts, when people in front of me would turn around to look at the audience, I kept my face well covered with an opera glass examining the boxes. And as soon as the curtain fell after the last act, I hurried away in order to avoid the crowd.

But one night, when the closing scene enchained me in an

unusual degree, my exit was not quick enough. I found myself wedged in among the multitude pressing for the street, and suddenly in the swaying throng, a face turned toward me which I knew but too well for my comfort. It was that of a man who two years before had been a student at the university at Bonn, who had been a member of our democratic club, and who, by some exceedingly questionable transaction, had become suspected of acting for the police as a spy. I had heard of his presence in Berlin, and there, also, he was talked of among my friends as one whom it would be well to avoid. Now he looked at me in a manner clearly indicating that he recognized me, but as if he were astonished to see me there. I returned his gaze, as if I resented the impertinence of a stranger looking at me so inquisitively. So we stood face to face for a few moments, both unable to move. When the pressure of the crowd relaxed, I made the greatest possible haste to disappear among the passersby on the street. That was my last Rachel night in Berlin.

But I saw her again later in Paris, and still later in America. In fact, I have seen her in all her great characters, in not a few of them several times, and the impression was always identically the same, even during her American tour when her fatal ailment had already seized upon her, and her powers were said to be on the wane. Endeavoring to account more clearly for those impressions. I sometimes asked myself, "But is this really the mirror held up to nature? Did ever a woman in natural life speak in such tones? Have such women as Rachel portrays ever lived?" The answer I uniformly arrived at was that such questions were idle; if Phèdre, Roxane, Virginia ever lived, so they must have been as Rachel showed them; or, rather, Rachel in her acting *was* happiness, misery, love, jealousy, hatred, revenge, anger, rage—all these things in an ideal grandeur, in their highest poetic potency, in gigantic reality. This may not be a very satisfactory definition, but it is as precise as I can make it. It was to see, to hear, and to be carried away, magically, irresistibly. The waves of delight or of anguish or of horror with which Rachel flooded the souls of her audiences baffled all critical analysis. Criticism floundered about in helpless embarrassment trying to classify her performances, or to measure them by any customary standard. She stood quite alone. To compare her with other actors or actresses seemed futile, for there was between them not a mere difference of degree, but a difference of kind. Various actresses of the time sought to imitate her; but whoever had seen the original simply shrugged his shoulders at the copies. It was the mechanism without the divine breath. I have subsequently seen only three actresses—Ristori, Wolter, and Sarah Bernhardt—who now and then, by some inspired gesture or intonation of voice, reminded me of Rachel; but only at passing moments. On the whole, the difference between them was very great. It was the difference between unique genius which irresistibly overpowers and subdues us and to which we involuntarily bow, and extraordinary talent which we simply admire. Rachel has therefore remained with me an overshadowing memory, and when in later years in my familiar circle we discussed the merits of contemporaneous stage performances, and someone among us grew enthusiastic about this or that living actor or actress, I could seldom repress the remark —in fact, I fear I made it often enough to become tiresome—"All this is very fine, but, ah!—you should have seen Rachel."

A few days after the meeting with the spy a real misfortune befell me. I went with my friends Rhodes and Müller to a public bath. I slipped and fell on the wet floor, injuring my left hip so much that I was unable to rise. After I had been carried to my quarters in the Markgrafen Strasse, two surgeon friends examined my injury. It turned out that I was suffering only from a strong contusion, which threatened to keep me in bed a considerable time. There I lay immovable and helpless while the city teemed with police agents to whom the catching of an insurrectionist from Baden or the Palatinate, who was, moreover, prosecuted on account of other political sins and now engaged in a further mischief, would have been an especial pleasure. My invalid condition lasted two weeks. As soon as I could leave the house again I took up with redoubled zeal my task, the story of which I shall now endeavor to give in a coherent report.

CHAPTER X

IMMEDIATELY after my arrival in Berlin I put myself in communication with several persons, who had been designated to me as trustworthy by Frau Kinkel, and by my democratic friends. I spent some time in studying them carefully, as I could not confide the purpose of my presence in Berlin to anyone of whom I might not be convinced that he would be useful in its accomplishment. After this review I told my secret to one of them only, Dr. Falkenthal, a physician who practiced and lived the life of an old bachelor in the suburb of Moabit. Falkenthal had already been in correspondence with Frau Kinkel. He had an extended acquaintance in Spandau and conducted me there to an innkeeper by the name of Krüger, for whom he vouched as a thoroughly reliable and energetic man. Mr. Krüger occupied in Spandau a highly respected position. He had for several years served his town as a member of the common council; he conducted the best hotel; he was a man of some property, and was also generally liked on account of his honorable character and his amiable disposition. Although much older than myself, we gradually became true friends. I found in him not only qualities of heart and soul thoroughly sympathetic to me, but also clear judgment, great discretion, unflinching courage, and a noble, self-sacrificing devotion. He offered me his hotel as headquarters for my enterprise.

I preferred, however, not to live in Spandau, as the presence of a stranger in so small a town could not well remain a secret. To dwell in the great city of Berlin appeared to me much less dangerous, at least during the long time of preparation which my undertaking would probably require.

From Berlin to Spandau and from Spandau back to Berlin I did not avail myself of the railroad, because at the Berlin station the police examined the passcards of every traveler, even on the way-trains, and if my passport, with the name of Heribert Jüssen, issued in Cologne, appeared too frequently, it might have excited suspicion. I therefore always hired a street cab, a "droschke," and each time a different one, on going and coming to and from Spandau, usually making the short journey during the night.

The first point to be considered was whether it would be feasible to liberate Kinkel by force. I soon convinced myself that there was no such possibility. The armed guard of the penitentiary itself consisted only of a handful of soldiers and the turnkeys on duty. It would therefore have been possible for a number of resolute men to storm the building. But it was situated in the center of a fortified town filled with soldiers, and the first signal of alarm would have attracted an overpowering force. Such a venture would therefore have been hopeless. On the other hand, we knew of cases in which prisoners, even more closely watched than Kinkel was, had escaped by breaking through barred windows and tunneling walls, and then being helped to a safe place by their friends. But this, too, seemed hardly possible in our case for several reasons, among which Kinkel's lack of skill in the use of his hands was not the least serious. In any event, it seemed prudent to try first whether or not one or the other of the officers of the penitentiary could be induced to help us. This sort of business was extremely repugnant to me. But what would I not do to save a dear friend, who had been so badly and cruelly

HERR LEDDIHN

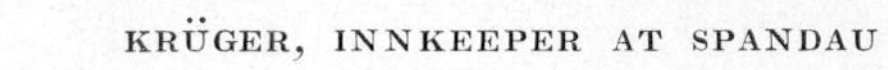

KRÜGER, INNKEEPER AT SPANDAU

treated, and a champion of liberty who might still be so useful to a great cause?

Krüger selected two young men, well known to him, who were in friendly intercourse with some of the officers to be taken into our confidence. Their names were Poritz and Leddihn, vigorous, strong, and true men, who confessed themselves willing to render any aid required of them in so good a work as the liberation of such a prisoner as Kinkel. They agreed to bring to me the one of the penitentiary guards who, they believed, might be most easily persuaded. Thus they introduced to me in a little beerhouse, in which I had a room to myself, a turnkey who had been, like most of his colleagues, a non-commissioned officer in the army and was now supporting a large family upon a very small salary. Poritz and Leddihn had vouched to him for my good faith, and he listened quietly to what I had to say. I presented myself as a traveler for a business house, who was closely related to the Kinkel family. I described to him the misery of the wife and the children, and how anxious they were, lest with the poor convict fare he would gradually waste away in body and mind. Would it not be possible to smuggle into Kinkel's cell from time to time a bit of meat or a glass of wine to keep up in a measure his strength, until the king's grace would take pity on him?

The turnkey thought Kinkel's lot indeed very deplorable. It would be a good work to alleviate it a little—perhaps not impossible, but perilous. He would consider what might be done. At the close of our conversation I slipped a ten-thaler note into his hand with the request that he buy with it some nourishing food for Kinkel if he could transmit it to him without danger. I intimated that business affairs required me to leave Spandau, but that I would return in a few days, to hear what report he could give about the condition of the prisoner. He could be certain of my gratitude.

Thus we parted. Three days later I went again to Spandau and met the turnkey in the same way as before. He told me he had succeeded in handing to Kinkel a sausage and a little loaf of bread, and that he had found the prisoner in comparatively good condition. He was also willing to do still more in a similar way. Of course I did not wish him to do so at his own expense, and therefore gave him a second ten-thaler note which I accompanied with the request that he deliver into Kinkel's hands a few words written on a slip of paper, and bring back to me from Kinkel a word in reply. This too he promised to do. I wrote down a few words without a signature, containing about the following: "Your friends are true to you. Keep up your courage." It was less important to me to inform Kinkel of my presence than to satisfy myself that the turnkey had really carried out my instructions, and whether I could go farther with him.

Again I left to return in a few days. In the same manner as before my man turned up and brought me my slip of paper, which bore a word of thanks in Kinkel's hand. The turnkey had evidently kept his promise, and had thereby taken a step which compromised him greatly. Now it appeared to me time to come to the point. Thus I told him that the thought had crossed my brain what a splendid deed it would be to deliver Kinkel entirely from his dreadful situation, and, that before returning to my home on the Rhine, I thought it my duty to ask him whether this thing could not be accomplished through his aid. The man started and at once exclaimed this would be impossible; with such an attempt he could and would have nothing to do.

The mere suggestion had evidently terrified him, and I

saw clearly that he was not the man whom I needed. Now I had to get rid of him and assure myself at the same time of his silence. I expressed to him my regret at his unwillingness, and added, that if he, who had been represented to me as a compassionate and at the same time courageous man, thought such an attempt hopeless, I had to accept his opinion and abandon the idea. I would therefore without delay depart for my home and not return. Then I hinted to him something about a secret and mysterious power which, if it could not liberate Kinkel, might become very dangerous to those who betrayed him. I succeeded indeed in intimidating him to such a degree that he begged me most earnestly not to bear any ill-will against him. I assured him that if he would bury in silence all that had happened, he might expect me to remain his friend. He might count even upon my further gratitude if, also, after my departure he would continue to furnish Kinkel from time to time with some nourishment. This he promised to do with demonstrative earnestness. Then I handed him another ten-thaler note and took leave of him forever.

So my first attempt had failed. I remained quiet for some days until Krüger, Leddihn and Poritz, who in the meantime had been watching the penitentiary people very carefully, communicated to me their conviction that my man had not disclosed anything. Thereupon my Spandau friends brought to me another turnkey. I began with him in the same manner as with the first, and everything seemed to progress favorably until I put the question whether or not he was willing to lend his hand in an attempt to set Kinkel free. The second man showed no more courage than the first, whereupon I dismissed him. A third man was brought, but he seemed so frightened by the first word that I did not put the decisive question to him at all.

Now it appeared to me prudent to let the affair rest for a while, at least until we could be perfectly assured that the three disquieted souls in the penitentiary had preserved silence. My sojourn in Berlin, too, began to become uncomfortable to me. The number of friends who knew of my presence in the Prussian capital had grown a little too large, and I was confronted too often by the question why I was there and what were my intentions. I therefore requested one of my friends to bid good-bye to the others in my behalf. I had departed not to return. Where I went, nobody knew. In fact, I went for a week or two to Hamburg. There I met my friend Strodtmann and got into communication with some people of our way of thinking. But the most agreeable society could not hold me long. By the end of September I returned to my work, but I did not go back to Berlin, thinking it safer to live with my friend, Dr. Falkenthal, in the suburb of Moabit.

At Spandau I received the report that everything had remained quiet. In general my secret had been well kept. To my friends in Berlin I had disappeared into regions unknown. Only one of them, a law student, by the name of Dreyer, once accidentally ran against me in Moabit. He may have had a suspicion as to what my business was, but I could firmly count upon his discretion. At a later period many persons who were entire strangers to me have stated that they were at that time in confidential relations with me, but such statements were unfounded. Even Dr. Falkenthal and Krüger did not at that time know my true name. To them I was, as my passport indicated, Heribert Jüssen, and among Dr. Falkenthal's neighbors, who sometimes saw me, I passed for a young physician assisting the doctor in his studies. To strengthen this impression I always carried a little kit of surgical instruments with me as they are frequently seen in the hands of physicians. From Moabit I made my nightly excursions as before.

After my return from Hamburg I did not at once succeed in finding among the penitentiary officials the man I wanted. A fourth was introduced to me, but he too would undertake nothing more than to smuggle into Kinkel's cell some eatables and perhaps a written communication. I began to entertain serious doubts as to whether the plan so far pursued could be successfully carried out, for the list of the turnkeys was nearly exhausted. Then suddenly and unexpectedly I found the helper whom I had so long looked for in vain. My Spandau friends made me acquainted with Officer Brune.

At the first moment of our meeting I received from him an impression very different from that which his colleagues had made upon me. He too had been a non-commissioned officer in the army; he too had wife and children and a miserable salary like the others. But in his bearing there was nothing of the servile humility so frequently found among subalterns. When I talked to him of Kinkel and of my desire to alleviate his misery at least a little by conveying to him additional fare, Brune's face expressed none of the pitiable embarrassment of the man who is vacillating between his sense of duty and a ten-thaler note. Brune stood firmly upright like a man who is not ashamed of what he is willing to do. He talked with astonishing frankness without waiting for the gradual advance of my suggestions.

"Certainly," he said, "I will help as much as I can. It is a shame and a disgrace that so learned and worthy a gentleman should sit here among common rogues in this penitentiary. I would gladly help him out myself, if I had not to take care of my wife and children."

His indignation at the treatment Kinkel had received

appeared so honest, and the whole manner of the man expressed so much courage and self-respect that I thought I might come to the point with him without circumlocution. And thus I told him point-blank that if the support of his family was his greatest trouble, I would be able to overcome that difficulty. Assured of this, would he then, I asked, be willing to lend a hand to Kinkel's escape?

"If it can be done," he answered; "but you know it is a difficult and dangerous thing. I will consider whether and how it may be done. Give me three days' time to think it over."

"Good," I replied, "do think it over; to judge from your accent you are a Westphalian."

"Yes, born near Soest."

"Then we are near neighbors; I am a Rhinelander. In three days then."

Those were three long days which I passed in Dr. Falkenthal's quarters. I sought to soothe my impatience by reading Dumas' "Three Musketeers" and a large part of Lamartine's history of the Girondists. But the book would fall again and again into my lap and my thoughts roam abroad.

On the evening of the third day I went again to Spandau and a heavy burden fell from my heart at Brune's first word.

"I have thought it over," he said. "I think we can do it."

I had to restrain myself for joy. Brune explained how some night in the near future, when the watch in the upper story of the penitentiary would be his and a certain other officer would be in the lower story, he might possess himself of the necessary keys and conduct Kinkel to the gate of the building. The plan, as he laid it before me, the details of which I shall return to later, appeared feasible.

But not until the night from the 5th to the 6th of November would the night watches be as he would have them. This suited me, for I too wanted some time for necessary preparations.

Then I informed Brune what provision I would be able to make for his family. A sum of money was at my disposal which was contributed partly by German democrats, partly by personal admirers of Kinkel, among them the Russian Baroness Brüning, of whom I shall have more to say. This enabled me to offer to Brune a decent compensation. Brune was content. The question whether it would be best to ship him and his family to America he rejected at once. Perhaps he hoped to remain undiscovered as a participant in our enterprise or he preferred, in case of discovery, to suffer his punishment and to keep his family in the Fatherland.

Thus we were agreed. Now the important preparations were taken in hand. Frau Kinkel had instructed me to call personally for the sum of money at my disposal at the residence of a lady in Berlin, a friend of hers who was a relative of the celebrated Felix Mendelssohn Bartholdy. It was in the dusk of evening that I arrived at this lady's house. I was received by a somewhat solemn footman to whom I gave my name Heribert Jüssen. He showed me into a large drawing-room, in which everything—furniture, pictures, books, musical instruments—breathed comfort and refinement. I had to wait a little while, and the contrast between my own wild business and these peaceable and elegant surroundings became very sensible to me. At last a lady clad in black entered, whose features I could just discern in the twilight. She was no longer young nor altogether beautiful. But her presence radiated a rare charm. In her hand she carried a large pocketbook.

"You bring me greetings from a Rhineland friend?" she

said with one of those mellow voices that touch the soul like a benefaction.

"Yes, cordial greetings," I replied, "from a friend who asked me to beg you for a package of valuable papers which she had put into your hands for safe-keeping."

"I knew that you would come at about this time," the lady replied. "In this pocketbook you will find all. I do not know your plans, but they must be good. You have my warmest wishes; God protect and bless you." Then she reached out to me her slender hand with a warm pressure, and I felt, after having left her, that her blessing had already become a reality.

That money was a heavy care to me. Never had I borne any responsibility of this kind for the property of others. In order not to expose this precious treasure to any accident, I carried it constantly with me tightly sewed in the inside pocket of my waistcoat.

The difficult task which I had still to perform before the decisive hour consisted in arranging for means of transportation to a safe place of refuge. Where should we turn after the escape of the prisoner? The frontiers of Switzerland, Belgium and France were too far away. We could not venture upon so long a journey through a hostile country. Nothing remained, therefore, but to try to reach the seacoast somewhere in order to cross over to England. After due consideration I concluded that the government would certainly take all precautions to watch every outgoing vessel in the harbors of Bremen and Hamburg. It appeared therefore prudent to choose another seaport, and so I turned to Mecklenburg. We had an influential and true friend in Rostock in the eminent jurist and president of the house of delegates, Moritz Wiggers, with whom I had become personally acquainted at the democratic congress in Braunschweig. I might also hope to reach Rostock more quickly than any other port—for we could not trust ourselves to the railroads—and the journey to Rostock offered the advantage that if we left Spandau about midnight, we might hope to cross the Mecklenburg frontier and thus to be beyond the immediate pursuit by the Prussian police about daybreak. I had also on my list of reliable persons a very considerable number of Mecklenburgers to whom I could apply for assistance.

I now set out to travel along the road which I had resolved to take, in order to make the necessary arrangements as to relays of horses and carriages for the decisive night and the day following. Of course, we could use only private carriages with, if possible, the owners on the box. Until then I had succeeded in keeping my secret within a very narrow circle of participants. But now it was necessary to draw a larger number of persons into confidence, and thus the danger grew in proportion. What I feared most was not malicious treachery, but excessive and indiscreet zeal. Everywhere I was met with hearty cordiality, and this cordiality was not confined to persons of the same political belief.

Of this I had a surprising example. My democratic friends had designated as specially trustworthy and helpful a gentleman living in the interior of Mecklenburg who was not on my list. I visited him and was very kindly received. He also assured me without hesitation of his willing assistance in the arrangement for relays. Then our conversation turned upon politics, and to my indescribable astonishment, my new friend declared to me that he considered our democratic ideas as well meant but as vain phantasies. He became quite eloquent in setting forth his opinion that human society would appear most delightful and would also be most happy if it were as variegated and checkered as possible in its division into estates and classes and ranks and conditions and callings, with princes, knights, merchants, clergymen, tradesmen, peasants, each and all with different rights and duties. Even monasteries he would have preserved with their abbots and abbesses, monks and nuns. In short, of all phases of human civilization the Middle Ages seemed to him the most congenial. "You see," he added with a kindly smile, "I am what you would call a full-blooded reactionary, and I don't believe at all in your liberty and equality and that sort of thing. But that they have put Kinkel, a poet and a sage, into a penitentiary on account of his idealistic imaginings, that is a revolting scandal, and although I am a good conservative Mecklenburger, I am at all times ready to help Kinkel out."

So we parted in the warmest agreement. But after all I did not feel quite comfortable about my new friend, and I talked afterwards with my democratic associates in Mecklenburg of the curious speeches of this gentleman and of my anxiety about him. "Do not borrow any trouble on that score," was the answer. "He is indeed a very curious saint and talks amazing stuff. But when there is a good deed to be done, he is as true as gold." And so he proved to be.

After a journey of several days my relays were arranged, and I could hope that a drive of less than thirty hours would take us from Spandau to Rostock. There we might confide ourselves to our good friends until a vessel should be ready to take us across the sea. To carry us from Spandau to the first relay, Krüger applied to a well-to-do farmer in the neighborhood by the name of Hensel, who had fast horses and would be glad to put them and his carriage and himself as driver at our disposal.

On November 4 I took leave of Dr. Falkenthal. He was acquainted with my plans in general, but I had not thought it necessary to initiate him into all the details. So he did not know the exact night in which the attempt was to be made, and he was also discreet enough not to ask me about it. But in bidding me farewell, he gave me a brace of pistols, which might serve me in close quarters. Arrived in Spandau on the evening of November 4, I had a conversation with Brune, in which we talked over the details of our scheme, in order to assure ourselves that nothing had been neglected. Everything seemed to be in order.

Our programme disposed of, Brune said: "There is one more thing of which I do not like to speak."

I listened with some surprise. "What is it?"

"You have my fullest confidence," Brune continued. "What you have promised to do for my family that you will honestly do—if you can."

"Certainly I can. I have the means in my possession."

"That is not what I mean," Brune objected. "If everything goes well to-morrow night, then I am as sure of the money as if I had it in my pocket. That I know. But maybe all will not go well. The thing is dangerous. Accident may have its play. Something human can happen to you and to me too, in fact, to both of us. And what will then become of my family, my wife and my children?"

He was silent for a moment and so was I. "Now, what further?" I asked.

"Considering the matter calmly," Brune slowly answered, "you will see yourself that the money must be in the hands of my family before I risk my head."

"You tell me yourself that I must consider this thing," I said with some hesitation. "Let me do so and I shall give you my answer as soon as possible. In the meantime will you prepare everything according to our agreement?"

"You may depend upon it."

Then we wished each other good-night.

The hour I spent after this in the solitude of my room in Krüger's hotel, taking counsel with myself, I have never forgotten.

The money, according to my notions an enormous sum, had been confided to me for a specific purpose; should it be lost without having accomplished this purpose, then it was all over with Kinkel, for such a sum could hardly be raised for him a second time. My personal honor would also be lost, for I would then have upon me a suspicion of dishonesty or at least a reproach of guilty recklessness. And was it not really great recklessness to confide this trust fund, upon a mere promise, without further guarantee, to a man who after all was a stranger to me? What did I really know of Brune? Nothing but that his face and his utterances had made upon me a most favorable impression and that he was held in good repute by his acquaintances. And these acquaintances had told me that they would have brought Brune first to me had they not thought that a man like him would hardly consider such a proposition. Indeed, they had added, that if he did it, he might be absolutely trusted. But was not the opportunity to appropriate to himself such a sum of money and then to manifest his official fidelity by delivering me up to the police, to a person in his situation, in the highest degree seductive? And would not he, if he contemplated such a treachery, act exactly as Brune had done? Had he not by the most positive promises and by apparent preparations excited my hopes to the utmost, to the end of inducing me by some clever pretext to deliver to him the money, and then to ruin me all the more easily?

On the other hand, could Brune, were he ever so honest, really act differently? Could he expose his wife and his children to the chance of accident? Was he not obliged in order to secure the future of his family to demand the money in advance? Would I not do the same in his situation? Furthermore, did Brune seem like a traitor? Could a traitor look into my eyes and speak to me as Brune had done? Was his straightforward, frank, candid, even proud bearing that of a man who would entice another into an ambush to rob him? Impossible.

And finally, how could I hope to win if I did not dare? Should I abandon the liberation of my friend because I would deny to Brune the request which everybody else would make to me under similar circumstances? Yes, it was clear, if I would save Kinkel from his dreadful fate, I had to risk if necessary even my honor.

The thought to deposit the money for Brune in a third person's hand had occurred to me, but I rejected it, partly because that might have led to further complications; partly, also, because if I must dare, I preferred to dare in a manner which Brune would take as proof of my absolute confidence in his integrity.

I reminded myself that the war in Schleswig-Holstein was still going on. In the Schleswig-Holstein army, I thought, I might enlist as a volunteer under an assumed name and seek my fate on the field of battle, should the enterprise in Spandau miscarry, and the money be lost, and I at the same time escape. My friends would then at least believe in my honesty. This was the reasoning that led me to the decision to hand over the money to Brune before the fulfillment of his promise. I had just formed this conclusion when Krüger knocked at my door and said that Poritz and Leddihn were below; was there still anything more they could do for me?

"Yes," I answered. "I would ask them to bring Brune

to me once again in a quarter of an hour to the Heinrich Platz."

Brune came with my friends. I took him aside.

"Mr. Brune," I said, "I will not let you go to bed with a load of doubt on your heart. We have spoken about the money. That money is a treasure confided to me. My honor hangs on it. Everything I trust to you—money, honor, freedom, all. You are a brave man. I wish to say to you still this night that to-morrow evening at five o'clock I shall bring the money to your quarters."

Brune was silent for a moment. At last he heaved a sigh and replied: "I would probably have done it without this. To-morrow at midnight your friend Kinkel will be a free man."

I passed the larger part of the following day with Krüger, Leddihn, and Poritz, in going over the chances of our enterprise, in order to make provision for all not yet foreseen accidents. At last the evening came. I put the money for Brune into a cigar box and went to his dwelling. I found him alone in his scantily furnished but neat living-room, and handed the cigar box to him with: "Here it is; count it."

"There you do not know me," he answered; "if between us a mere word were not sufficient, we should not have begun together. What comes from you, I don't count."

"Is there anything to change in our plan?"

"Nothing."

"To-night, then."

"To-night, and good luck!"

Indeed, we had good reason to be confident of the success of our plan, barring incalculable accidents. The penitentiary building was situated in the center of the town, a large, barrack-like edifice, the bare walls of which were pierced by one large gate and a multitude of narrow slits of windows. On all four sides it was surrounded by streets. The entrance was on the main street. It led into a large gateway. Inside of that gateway there was, on the right, a door opening into the official dwelling of the director of the institution, and on the left a door leading into the guardroom of the soldiers on duty in the prison. At the end of the passage a third door opened upon an inner court. A stone staircase leading up from the hall united the lower with the upper stories. High up on the second story was Kinkel's cell. It had a window towards the rear of the edifice. This window was guarded by a screen which opened upwards so that a little daylight fell in from above and only a small bit of sky could be seen, but nothing of the surroundings below. The window was also guarded by strong iron bars, wire lattice and a wooden shutter, which was closed at night—in short, by all the contrivances that are usually employed to shut off a prisoner from all communication with the outside world. Moreover, the cell was divided into two compartments by a strong wooden railing, which reached from the floor to the ceiling. One of the compartments contained Kinkel's bed; in the other, during the day, he did his work. The two compartments were united by a door in the wooden railing, which every evening was securely fastened. The entrance to the cell from the corridor was guarded by two heavy doors, with several locks. In the street, under Kinkel's cell, stood day and night a sentinel. Another sentinel watched during the daytime the door of the building on the main street, but he was transferred to the inner court during the night—a regulation which proved very important to us. Had it not been for this stupid arrangement we would never have attempted what we did. The cell, the doors, the locks on the railings, were all examined several times every twenty-four hours by the turnkeys on duty.

The keys to Kinkel's cell, as well as those to the door in the inside wooden railing, were during the night, after Kinkel had been locked up in his compartment, kept in a locker in the room of the inspector, the so-called Revier room. As Brune had no access to the Revier room during the night, and the key had been confided to another superior officer, he had availed himself of some opportunity to procure a wax impression of that key, from which a duplicate key was made, enabling Brune to enter the Revier room during the night. The key to the locker containing the keys to Kinkel's cell was, as Brune knew, in the evening negligently put on top of that locker, so that without difficulty he could possess himself of the keys to the cell. Thus Brune believed himself fully able to enter the cell during the night and to take the prisoner out. It had been agreed that Brune, who had the watch of the night of the 5th to the 6th of November on Kinkel's corridor, should bring Kinkel down the stairs into the gateway. He was sure that he could take him without danger past the turnkey watching the lower floor. Whether he intended to interest that man in our affair, or to divert his attention in some manner, Brune did not tell me. He only assured me I might depend upon there being no difficulty about this. As soon as Kinkel was conducted into the gateway below, I was to be there to receive him. In one of the wings of the great door that opened upon the main street there was a little postern gate to facilitate the daily passage in and out. Of the key of this postern gate we had also procured a wax impression, and from it a duplicate key. Now, it was to be my task, shortly after midnight, after the town night watchman—for in Spandau there was at that time still a night watchman with spear and rattle—had passed by the building on the street, to open the postern gate, to step into the interior of the gateway, there to await Brune and

Kinkel, to wrap Kinkel up in a cloak, to take him through the postern gate into the street and to hurry with him to Krüger's hotel, where he was to put on a suit of clothes, and then step with me into Hensel's carriage—and away.

I had asked Brune to provide Kinkel with a plentiful supply of food, so that he might be in a good physical condition. But to avoid long excitement, Kinkel was to be informed only on the evening of the 5th of November, the night of the attempt, that something was being done for him, and that he should go to bed at the accustomed hour, rise immediately before midnight, dress himself and be ready for the venture.

On the same day Leddihn and Poritz had entrusted two good, able-bodied friends with the charge of guarding the street corners nearest to the penitentiary during the night and to come to our aid if necessary. About midnight all my people were at their posts, and after the night watchman had passed down the street I approached the door of the penitentiary. I had covered my feet with rubber shoes, so as to make my step inaudible. A second pair of rubber shoes I had with me for Kinkel. In my belt I carried the pistols given to me by Dr. Falkenthal; in one pocket a well-sharpened dirk and in another a slungshot, with which to arm Kinkel in case of stress. I had thrown across my shoulders a large cloak with sleeves, which should serve Kinkel as a first wrap. So equipped I softly opened the postern gate to step into the gateway of the prison. I left that little gate ajar and the key sticking in the lock. The gateway was dimly lighted by a lantern hanging from the ceiling. My first task was to prevent the opening from the inside of the director's door on the right, and of the guardroom door on the left, and I did so by tying the doorhandles to the iron fastening of the bell rope with stout strings. This was the most delicate piece of work I had to do. Nothing moved. My gaze was riveted on the end of the passage opposite where Brune was to appear with Kinkel.

So I waited. One minute elapsed after another, but all remained still. I waited a full quarter of an hour, but nothing stirred. What did this mean? According to all calculations they ought to have joined me some time ago. My situation began to appear to me very precarious. Was Brune after all faithless? I took one of my pistols out of my belt and held it in my left hand ready to fire, and my dirk in the right. But I resolved to remain at my post until I could say to myself that the last chance of success was gone. Half an hour had passed and still everything was quiet as the grave. Suddenly I heard a faint rustle, and at the other end of the gateway I saw a dark figure appear like a specter as if it had stepped out of the wall. My hands closed more tightly on my weapons. The next moment I recognized in the dim light the form of Brune. There he was at last, but alone. He put his finger upon his lips and approached me. I awaited him ready for the worst.

"I am unfortunate," he whispered with his mouth at my ear. "I have tried everything, I have failed. The keys were not in the locker. Come to me to-morrow and get your money back."

I said nothing in reply, but quickly untied the strings from the door handles, right and left, and then stepped out through the postern gate, locked it, and put the key into my pocket. I was hardly on the street when Leddihn and Poritz hastened to join me. With a few words I told them what had happened. "We were afraid you had been trapped," said Leddihn. "You stayed so long inside that we were on the point of coming after you to fetch you out."

Soon we reached Krüger's hotel, where Hensel stood

ready with his carriage to take Kinkel and me away. The disappointment that followed my report was terrible.

"But there is something more to do this night," said I, "for my relays stand on the road deep into Mecklenburg. We must order them off."

I stepped into the carriage, an open vehicle with a top over the back seat. Hensel took the reins, and so we drove away. It was a melancholy journey. We were on the road something over three hours when we observed sparks of fire sputtering from a black object that came toward us. We quickly recognized it to be a carriage. I had steel and flint at hand and also struck sparks. This was the signal of recognition that I had agreed upon with my Mecklenburg friends. The carriage coming toward us stopped and so did we.

"Is this the right one?" asked a voice. This was the concerted question.

"It is the right one," I replied, "but our enterprise has failed. Pray turn back and advise the next relay and request our friends there to pass on the word in this way. But for Heaven's sake keep silent about the rest, lest all may be lost."

"Of course, but what a confounded disappointment! How did the failure happen?"

"Another time. Good-night."

The two carriages turned. We drove back in the direction of Spandau, but very slowly, almost as if a part of a funeral procession, both sitting silent. I tormented myself with the gravest reproaches. Could not the unfortunate accident that had crossed our plan easily have been prevented? Could we not have duplicated the keys to the cell as well as those to the postern gate and the Revier room? Certainly. But why had this not been done? Why had Brune not thought of it? But as Brune had not done so, was it not my duty to see to it? I had neglected that duty. Mine, mine only, was the fault of this terrible miscarriage. Mine the responsibility that Kinkel was not now a free man hurrying to the seacoast behind fleet horses. The fruit of long and dangerous labor had recklessly been jeopardized by my negligence. Would I ever be able again to reknit the torn threads of the scheme? And, if so, was it not probable that through the improvidence of some one of the participants rumors of what had happened would get abroad and Kinkel would be surrounded with the severest measures of precaution and even carried into another and more secure dungeon? But if nothing of this did happen—where was the money entrusted to me? No longer in my possession—in the hands of another man who might keep it if he would, and I perfectly powerless to recover it. And thus Kinkel's horrible lot might be sealed forever through my guilt. Thus my conscience put itself to the rack in that terrible night.

At last Hensel interrupted the silence. "How would it be," he said, "if we stopped for a few hours in Oranienburg? We could there feed our horses, sleep a little, and then comfortably drive on."

I was content. I began to feel very much exhausted; and then, if of last night's happenings anything had got abroad in Spandau and thereby any danger threatened, the prudent and watchful Krüger, I felt sure, would send somebody to find us on the road and to give warning.

It was very dark when we arrived at a hotel in Oranienburg. After I had permitted my thoughts to torment me a little longer, I fell asleep at last. When I awoke light shone through the windows of my room, and with me awoke also the consciousness of the whole weight of our failure, with even greater clearness than during the past night. Such awakenings belong to the unhappiest moments of human life. We breakfasted late, and it was on this occasion that for the first time I saw my companion, Mr. Hensel, in clear daylight. I had met him at Krüger's and on our night drive only in the dark. The stately broad-shouldered figure and the long dark beard had then struck my attention; but I could now see the clear, shrewd, and at the same time bold, sparkle of his eyes, and the expression of his face, which betokened a strong will as well as sincerity and kindness of heart. Hensel observed that I was in low spirits and tried to put a pleasant face upon things. He thought that our friends in Spandau were not only faithful, but also discreet, that the officers of the penitentiary in their own interest would keep silent, and that a new attempt would soon be possible. I willingly agreed with him. In fact I was busily thinking of what was now to be done, and such a thought is always the most effective antidote for discouragements. I have frequently in life had the experience that when we are struck by an especially heavy blow, we can do nothing better than to present to our minds all, even the worst, possible features of trouble that may still be in store for us, and so in our imagination drink the cup of bitterness down to the last drop; but then to turn our thoughts to the future and to occupy them entirely with that which must be done to prevent further misfortune, to repair the damage done, and to replace what has been lost by something equally desirable. This is a sure and rapid cure; for the consequences of the misfortune hardly ever will be as disastrous as imagined. Of course, I do not apply this to the loss of one very dear.

In returning to Spandau we were in no hurry. We even thought that it would be more prudent to arrive there in the dark, and therefore started only after noon at a slow trot. Arrived in Spandau, I learned from Krüger that all had remained quiet. I forthwith went to Brune's rooms. I found him there, evidently expecting me. The little cigar box stood on the table.

"That was cursed ill-luck last night," he said, "but it was not my fault. Everything was in the best of order, but as I opened the locker in the Revier room I could not find the keys to the cell. I searched and searched for them, but they were not there. This morning I learned that Inspector Semmler had accidentally, instead of placing them in the locker, put them into his pocket and carried them with him to his home."

For a moment he was silent. "There is the money," he continued, pointing to the cigar box; "take it; count it first; no thaler is missing."

I could not refrain from shaking the man's hand and in my heart asking his pardon for my doubts.

"What comes from you," I answered, repeating his words of yesterday, "will not be counted. But what now? I do not give up. Must we wait until you have the night watch again?"

"We might wait," he replied, "and in the meantime duplicate all the keys that we need so that this difficulty may not arise again; but," he added, "I have thought over the matter to-day. It is a disgrace that that man should sit in the convict's cell a day longer—I will try to help him this very night, if he has courage enough for a break-neck feat."

"What, this night?"

"Yes, this night. Now listen." Then Brune told me that the officer who during the coming night should have the watch on the upper stories, had been taken ill, and he, Brune, had offered to take his place. Thereupon he had thought he might without much difficulty take Kinkel into the loft under the roof and let him down with a rope from out of one of the dormer windows on the street. To this end he would of course again require the keys to the cell, but after the accident of last night, when the inspector took them home with him through mere thoughtlessness, they would certainly be again in their accustomed place. I should only see to it that the street below was kept free, while Kinkel was let down from the roof, and that he then be promptly received and carried off. "It is a somewhat perilous undertaking," Brune added; "from the dormer window down to the street it may be sixty feet, but if the Herr Professor has courage, I think we may succeed."

"I vouch for Kinkel's courage," I said; "what does not a prisoner dare for liberty?"

The details were rapidly considered and determined upon. I undertook to procure the necessary rope for Brune. He was to wind it about his body under the overcoat and take it into the penitentiary building in that way. About midnight I was to be in the dark recess of the door of the house opposite the gate of the penitentiary, from which I could observe the dormer windows of the building; when in one of them I should see the light of a lantern move up and down perpendicularly, three times, that would be a sign that everything was in order for the descent. If standing in my sheltered place I then struck sparks with my steel and flint, Brune would understand from this signal that everything was in safe order on the street.

With a hearty handshake I took leave of Brune and hurried to Krüger's hotel. Poritz and Leddihn, whom I had quickly sent for, procured at once a rope of the necessary length and strength, and carried it to Brune's dwelling. But after freeing Kinkel how should we get him away from Spandau? I had no relays of horses and carriages on the road; the preceding night everything had fitted in so excellently, but now? Fortunately Hensel was still in Krüger's house. When

I told him what was to happen in the next few hours, he broke out in loud jubilation.

"I will take you with my own horses as far as they can travel," he exclaimed.

"But our nearest friend is in Neu-Strelitz," I replied; "that is a good many miles from here. Will your horses hold out that distance?"

"The devil take them if they don't," said Hensel. We resolved then to risk it and to confide ourselves to benignant fate. A short conversation with Poritz and Leddihn followed about the measures necessary to keep the streets clear of unwelcome intruders, while Kinkel was swinging down on his rope. Those measures were simple. My friends were to occupy the street corners with their stalwart fellows whom they had already employed last night, and if some belated reveler should show himself, they were to simulate intoxication and use all sorts of means to divert the unwelcome person from our path. In case of necessity they were to use force. Poritz and Leddihn vouched for everything.

"Happy coincidence," chuckled Krüger. "This evening some of the officers of the penitentiary are to celebrate a birthday in this hotel. There will be a bowl of punch, and I will make that punch especially irresistible."

"And you will detain those officers long enough?"

"You may be sure of that. Not one of them will cross your way." This prospect put us into the best of humor, and we had a cosy little supper together. Our thoughts were, however, constantly directed to the accidents that might again play mischief with us, and fortunately an important possibility occurred to us.

At the time of Kinkel's descent from the dormer window hanging on his rope, the rubbing of the rope against the edge

KINKEL'S ESCAPE

of the brick wall might easily loosen tiles and brick which then would fall down and produce a loud clatter. We therefore resolved that Hensel should take his carriage immediately after midnight slowly along the street so that the rattle of the vehicle on the rough cobblestone pavement might drown all other noises.

Shortly before midnight I stood, equipped as on the night before, well hidden in the dark recess of the house door opposite the penitentiary. The street corners right and left were, according to agreement, properly watched, but our friends kept themselves as much as possible concealed. A few minutes later the night watchman shuffled down the street and when immediately in front of me swung his rattle and called the hour of twelve. Then he slouched quietly on and disappeared. What would I have given for a roaring storm and a splashing rain! But the night was perfectly still. My eye was riveted to the roof of the penitentiary building, the dormer windows of which I could scarcely distinguish. The street lights flared dimly. Suddenly there appeared a light above by which I could observe the frame of one of the dormer windows; it moved three times up and down; that was the signal hoped for. With an eager glance I examined the street right and left. Nothing stirred. Then on my part I gave the signal agreed upon, striking sparks. A second later the light above disappeared and I perceived a dark object slowly moving across the edge of the wall. My heart beat violently and drops of perspiration stood upon my forehead. Then the thing I had apprehended actually happened: tiles and brick, loosened by the rubbing rope, rained down upon the pavement with a loud clatter. "Now, good Heaven, help us!" At the same moment Hensel's carriage came rumbling over the cobblestones. The noise of the falling tiles and brick was no longer audible. But would they not strike Kinkel's head and benumb him? Now the dark object had almost reached the ground. I jumped forward and touched him; it was indeed my friend, and there he stood alive and on his feet. "This is a bold deed," were the first words he said to me. "Thank God," I answered. "Now off with the rope and away." I labored in vain to untie the rope that was wound around his body.

"I cannot help you," Kinkel whispered, "for the rope has fearfully lacerated both my hands." I pulled out my dirk and with great effort I succeeded in cutting the rope, the long end of which, as soon as it was free, was quickly pulled up. While I threw a cloak around Kinkel's shoulders and helped him get into the rubber shoes he looked anxiously around. Hensel's carriage had turned and was coming slowly back.

"What carriage is that?" Kinkel asked.

"Our carriage."

Dark figures showed themselves at the street corners and approached us.

"For Heaven's sake, what people are those?"

"Our friends."

At a little distance we heard male voices sing, "Here we sit gayly together."

"What is that?" asked Kinkel, while we hurried through a side street toward Krüger's hotel.

"Your jailers around a bowl of punch."

"Capital!" said Kinkel. We entered the hotel through a back door and soon found ourselves in a room in which Kinkel was to put on the clothes that we had bought for him—a black cloth suit, a big bear-skin overcoat, and a cap like those worn by Prussian forest officers. From a room near by sounded the voices of the revelers. Krüger, who had stood a few minutes looking on while Kinkel was exchanging his convict's garb for an honest man's dress, suddenly went out with a peculiarly sly smile. When he returned carrying a few filled glasses, he said, "Herr Professor, in a room near by some of your jailers are sitting around a bowl of punch. I have just asked them whether they would not permit me to take some for a few friends of mine who have just arrived. They had no objection. Now, Herr Professor, let us drink your health first out of the bowl of your jailers." We found it difficult not to break out in loud laughter. Kinkel was now in his citizen's clothes, and his lacerated hands were washed and bandaged with handkerchiefs. He thanked his faithful friends with a few words which brought tears to their eyes. Then we jumped into Hensel's vehicle. The penitentiary officers were still singing and laughing around their punch bowl.

We had agreed that our carriage should leave Spandau through the Potsdam gate which opens upon the road to Hamburg, and then turn in a different direction in order to mislead the pursuit that was sure to follow. So we rattled at a fast trot through the gate, and this ruse succeeded so well that, as we learned later, we were really the next day, in accordance with the report of the guard at the gate, pursued in the direction of Hamburg. Before we reached the little town of Nauen we turned to the right on a field road and reached the Berlin Strelitz turnpike near the Sandkrug. Our bays made the best of their speed.

Only when the keen night air touched his face, Kinkel seemed to come to a clear consciousness of what had happened. "I would like to hold your hand in mine," he said, "but I cannot; my hands are too much torn."

He then put his arm around me and pressed me once and again. I would not let him express his gratitude in words, but told him how the night before everything had been so well arranged, and how our plan had been crossed by an unfortunate accident, and what a mournful ride I had had in the same carriage only twenty-four hours before.

"That was the most terrible night of my life," said Kinkel. "After Brune had instructed me to hold myself ready, I waited for the appointed hour with the most confident expectation. Before midnight I was up. I listened as only an ear practiced in long isolation can listen. Now and then I heard a distinct noise of steps in the corridors, but they would not approach. I heard the clocks outside strike the hours. When midnight was past the thought first rose in me: 'Is it possible that this should fail?' Minute after minute went by, and all remained quiet. Then I was seized by an anguish which I cannot describe. The perspiration dropped from my forehead. Until one o'clock I had still a little hope, but when even then Brune did not come I gave up everything for lost. The most gruesome pictures rose in my imagination. The whole design had surely been discovered. You were in the hands of the police and also imprisoned for many years. I saw myself a miserable wreck in convict's garb. My wife and my children perished in misery. I shook the rails in my cell like a madman. Then I dropped exhausted upon my straw bed. I believe I was nearly insane."

"Well, and this night?"

"Oh, this night," Kinkel exclaimed, "I could hardly trust my eyes and ears when Brune with a lantern in his hand came into my cell and whispered to me, 'Get up quickly, Herr Professor; now you shall get out.' That was an electric shock. In a moment I was on my feet, but do you know that to-night again everything was on the point of going wrong?"

I listened eagerly, and again and again a cold shiver ran down my back as Kinkel proceeded with his story. Half an hour before midnight Brune was in Kinkel's cell. This time he had found the keys in the locker and had opened with two of them the cell doors. After having called Kinkel up, he attempted to open, with a third key, the door in the wooden railing. He tried and tried, but in vain. The key did not fit. Afterwards it appeared that the key with which Brune tried to open the cell door belonged to the window shutters, but that one of the keys for the doors of the cell also opened the door of the wooden railing. Thus Brune had the true key in his hand without knowing it or without thinking of it in the excitement. So Kinkel stood on one and Brune on the other side of the wooden railing, baffled and for a moment utterly bewildered. Then Kinkel grasped with the strength of despair one of the wooden rails, trying to break it by throwing the whole weight of his body against it, but in vain. Brune worked hard with his sword to the same end, also in vain. Then he said: "Herr Professor, you shall get out to-night even if it costs me my life." He left the cell and in a minute returned with an ax in his hand. With a few vigorous blows two of the rails were cut loose. Using the ax as a lever he effected an opening which just permitted Kinkel's broad-shouldered body to pass through. But had not the blows of Brune's ax alarmed the whole house? The two listened with suspended breath. All remained quiet. In fact, Brune had been no less prudent than daring. Before he swung his ax he had carefully closed the two thick doors of the cell. The sound of the blows which filled the interior of the cell was, as to the outside, very much deadened by the thick walls and by the heavy doors. They not only had not wakened any of the sleepers, but had not reached those that were awake, or if they did make any impression, it was as if the noise had come from the outside of the building.

Now Brune left the cell with Kinkel, the doors of which he again locked. Then they had to walk through corridors, up and down various stairways, and even to pass a night watchman. By Brune's clever management they succeeded in doing this. At last they reached the loft under the roof and the dormer window, through which the dangerous ride through the air had to be undertaken. Kinkel confessed to me that he was seized with a dizzy horror when he looked down upon the street below and then upon the thin rope which was to bear him; but when he saw my sparkling signal, the meaning of which Brune explained to him in a whisper, he regained his composure and boldly swung out over the precipice. At once the tiles and bricks began to rain about his head, but none of them struck him, only the hands which at first had taken too high a hold on the rope and through which it had to glide, suffered grievously. That was, however, a slight wound for so hard a struggle and so great a victory.

When Kinkel finished his narrative, Hensel took out of the hamper one of the bottles of precious Rhine wine that Krüger had provided us with for our journey, and we drank to the health of the brave Brune, without whose resoluteness and fidelity all our plans and labors would have come to nothing. It was a happy, enthusiastic moment, which made us almost forget that so long as we were on German soil the danger was not over, and our success not yet complete.

CHAPTER XI

At a sharp trot we sped on through the night. I still hear Hensel's commanding call, "Boom up! Boom up!" as often as on the turnpike we reached a toll gate. Through Oranienburg, Teschendorf, Löwenberg, we flew without stop, but when we approached the little town of Gransee, nearly thirty-five miles from Spandau, it became clear that our two good bays would soon break down unless we gave them rest and some refreshment. So we stopped at a wayside tavern, near Gransee, and fed them—then forward again.

As daylight appeared I could for the first time look at Kinkel with leisure. How he was changed! He whom a little more than a year ago I had known as a youthful man, the very picture of health and vigor! His closely clipped hair was now tinged with gray, the color of the face a dead yellow, the skin like parchment, the cheeks thin and flabby, the nose sharp, and the face deeply furrowed. If I had met him on the street unexpectedly I should scarcely have recognized him.

"They have dealt hard with you," I said.

"Yes, it was the highest time for me to breathe free air again. A year or two more of that kind of life and I should have been burned to ashes, devastated body and soul. Nobody who has not himself suffered it knows what solitary confinement means and the debasement of being treated like a common criminal. But now," he added gayly, "now human life begins once more."

And then he described in his humorous way how at that very moment in the penitentiary in Spandau they would be discovering that Kinkel, like a bird, had escaped from his cell, and how one turnkey after another with a troubled face would run to the director and the whole gang of them would put their heads together and notify the higher authorities; and how they would then examine the guards of the city gates, and how they would hear of a carriage that between twelve and one o'clock had rattled through the Potsdam gate, and how then a troop of mounted constables would be hurried after us in the direction of Nauen and Hamburg, while we were paying a visit to our friends in Mecklenburg.

"I only wish," remarked Hensel anxiously, "that we could make that visit a little more quickly." The sun was up when we greeted the boundary pole of Mecklenburg. Even there we did not by any means feel quite safe, although a little safer than on Prussian territory. The trot of our horses became slower and slower. One of them appeared utterly exhausted. So we had to stop at the nearest Mecklenburg inn, in Dannenwalde. There Hensel washed the horses with warm water, which helped a little, but only for a short time. In the town of Fürstenberg we had to unharness them for a longer stop because they could go no farther, having put over fifty miles behind them. But at last we reached Strelitz safely, where in the person of Judge Petermann, a city magistrate, we had an enthusiastic friend and protector, who already on the preceding night had been on the road with one of the relay carriages.

Petermann received us with so demonstrative a joy that I feared he would not refrain from proclaiming the happy event from the windows of his house to the passersby. In fact, he could not deny himself the pleasure of bringing in some friends. Soon we sat down to a plentiful meal, and with merrily clinking glasses we waited for another carriage and fresh horses. There we took a cordial leave of our friend Hensel.

His two fine bays had lain down as soon as they reached the stable, one of them, as I learned later, never to rise again. Honor to his memory!

Petermann accompanied us on the further drive, which now went on with uninterrupted rapidity. In Neubrandenburg, as well as in Teterow, we changed horses, and by seven o'clock the next morning, the 8th of November, we arrived at the "White Cross Inn," on the Neubrandenburg turnpike near the city of Rostock. Petermann went at once to fetch our friend Moritz Wiggers, whose turn it now was to take the management of affairs. Without delay he sent us in a wagon, accompanied by a Rostock merchant by the name of Blume, to Warnemünde, a seaside resort on a fine harbor, where we were cared for in Wöhlert's Hotel. Petermann, happy beyond measure, that his part of the adventure was so successfully accomplished, turned back to Strelitz. On our journey we had accustomed ourselves to call Kinkel by the name of Kaiser and me by the name of Hensel, and these names we inscribed upon the hotel register.

Wiggers had recommended Warnemünde to us as a place of patriarchal customs and conditions, where there existed police only in name and where the local authorities, if they should discover us, would make it their business to protect, rather than betray us. There, he thought, it would be safe to remain until a more secure asylum or a favorable opportunity to cross the sea could be found. From the shore of Warnemünde for the first time in my life I saw the sea. I had longed for that spectacle, but the first view of it was disappointing. The horizon appeared to me much narrower and the waves which rushed on white-capped, as the northeast wind drove them in, much smaller than I had pictured them in my imagination. I was soon to make better acquaintance with the sea and to learn to look at it with greater respect and higher enjoyment.

However, we were little disposed to give ourselves to the contemplation of nature. Kinkel had spent two, and I three nights in a carriage on the highroad. We were extremely fatigued and in a few minutes lay sound asleep.

The next day Wiggers returned with the news that there was only one brig on the roads, but that she was not ready to sail. A friend of his, Mr. Brockelmann, a merchant and manufacturer, thought it safest to send us across the sea on one of his own ships and to shelter us in his own house until that ship could be started. Thus we left our hotel, and a Warnemünde pilotboat carried us up the Warnow River. We landed near a little village, where Brockelmann awaited us with his carriage.

We saw before us a stalwart man of about fifty years, with gray hair and whiskers, but with rosy complexion and youthful vivacity in expression and movement. He welcomed us with joyous cordiality, and after the first few minutes of our acquaintance, we were like old friends. In him we recognized a self-made man in the best sense of the term, a man who had carved his own fortune, who could look back with self-respect upon what he had accomplished and who found in his successes an inspiration for further endeavor and for an enterprising and self-sacrificing public spirit. His broad humanity, which recognized the right of everyone to a just estimation of his true value and his claim to a corresponding chance of advancement, had made him from his early youth a liberal, and after the revolution of 1848, a democrat. He had practically carried out his principles and theories as far as possible, and he was therefore widely known as a protector of the poor and oppressed. But especially his employees, his working people, of whom there was a large number in his factories, revered and loved him as a father. When he offered us his house as an asylum he could well assure us that he had workingmen enough who at his request would fight for us and in case of need hold possession of our asylum long enough to give us time for escape. However, it would not come to this, he said, as the arrival of such guests as "the Herren Kaiser and Hensel" in his house would attract no attention, and even if our secret were suspected by any of his people, there were no traitors among them. In short, he could vouch for everything. Thus we drove to his house, which was situated in a suburb of Rostock. There we had some days of rest and plenty. Brockelmann, his wife, his eldest daughter, her fiancé, the merchant Schwartz, and a little circle of friends, overwhelmed us with the most lavish attentions. How can I describe the care with which the mistress of the house herself washed Kinkel's wounded hands and bandaged and nursed them! And the meals which, according to Mecklenburg notions of hospitality, were necessary! The indispensable first breakfast and second breakfast and sometimes third breakfast, and the noon repast, and the afternoon coffee with cake, and the suppers, and the "little something" before going to bed, and the nightcaps, which succeeded one another at incredibly short intervals; and the evenings, during which Wiggers played to us Beethoven's sonatas with a masterly hand, reminding Kinkel of the musical language of his Johanna! And the occasional surprises when Brockelmann had the revolutionary hymn, the "Marseillaise," played by a brass band in the house!

With all this, however, the more serious side of our situation was not forgotten. Brockelmann had ordered one of his own vessels, a little schooner of forty tons, which had proved a good sailer, to be prepared for us. The "Little Anna"—this was the name of the schooner—received a cargo of wheat for England, which was put on board as rapidly as possible, and Sunday, the 17th of November, was the day fixed for our departure, if by that time the long-prevailing northeaster should have changed into a more favorable wind.

In the meantime the news of Kinkel's flight had gone through all the newspapers and caused everywhere a great stir. Our friends in Rostock informed themselves with minute care of all that was printed and said and rumored about the matter. The " warrant of capture," which the Prussian Government had published in the newspapers concerning the " escaped convict," Kinkel, our friends brought to us at tea-time, and it was read aloud with all sorts of irreverent comments, amid great hilarity. Of the part I had in the liberation of Kinkel the authorities and the public knew at that time nothing. Especial pleasure we derived from the newspaper reports which announced Kinkel's arrival at several different places at the same time. The liberal Pastor Dulon in Bremen, following a true instinct, described in his journal with much detail when and how Kinkel had passed through Bremen and sailed for England. Some of my friends reported his arrival in Zürich and in Paris. One paper brought a circumstantial report of a banquet that had been tendered to Kinkel by the German refugees in Paris, and even the speech he had made on the occasion. Thus nothing remained untried to confuse the Prussian police and to mislead its searches.

But there were also some alarm signals of a disquieting nature. Wiggers received on the 14th of November a letter, without signature, from the neighborhood of Strelitz in an unknown handwriting, as follows: " Expedite as much as possible the shipment of goods entrusted to you. There is danger in delay." Probably the authorities had discovered our tracks between Spandau and Strelitz, and were pursuing them further. Then on Friday, November 15, a stranger called upon Wiggers, who represented himself to be our friend, " Farmer

Hensel," and inquired whether Kinkel, whom he had taken in his carriage from Spandau to Strelitz, was still in Rostock. Wiggers had indeed heard us speak of him with expressions of the highest confidence, but he apprehended the stranger might not be Hensel himself, but a spy in disguise. So he feigned the utmost astonishment at the news that Kinkel was in Rostock, but promised to gather information, and to communicate the result to the stranger, whom he requested to call again the next day. The occurrence was at once reported to us, and the description given by Wiggers of the appearance of the man persuaded us that the stranger was the true Hensel, who, as he had said to Wiggers, had come to Rostock merely to quiet his anxiety about our safety. Kinkel and I wished very much to see him and to press once more the hand of our brave and faithful friend, but Wiggers, who had become seriously worried by the warning received from Strelitz, counseled the utmost circumspection and promised us to transmit to Hensel, who had said that he was to remain in Rostock until the 18th, our warmest greetings after we should have reached the open sea.

Thus we found in spite of all agreeable surroundings considerable comfort in the report that the northeast wind had gone down; that the "Little Anna" was anchoring at Warnemünde, and that everything would be ready for our departure on the 17th of November.

On a frosty Sunday morning we sailed, in the company of an armed escort, which our friends had composed of reliable men in sufficient numbers, as they believed, to resist a possible attack by the police, in two boats across the bay to the anchorage of the "Little Anna." Arrived on board, Mr. Brockelmann gave the captain, who was not a little astonished at receiving a visit from so large a company, his instructions: "You take these two gentlemen," he said, pointing to Kinkel and myself, " with you to Newcastle. You pass Helsingoer without stopping, and pay the Sound dues on your return. In stress of weather you will beach the vessel on the Swedish shore rather than return to a German port. If the wind suits you better for another harbor than Newcastle on the English or Scottish coast, you will sail there. The important thing is that you reach England as quickly as possible. I shall remember you if you carry out my orders punctually." The captain, whose name was Niemann, may have received these instructions with some amazement, but he promised to do his best.

Some of our friends remained with us until the steam tug hitched to the " Little Anna " had carried us a short distance into the open sea. Then came the leave-taking. As Wiggers tells in an elaborate description of the scene in a German periodical, Kinkel threw himself sobbing into his arms and said: " I do not know whether I shall rejoice at my rescue, or shall mourn that like a criminal and an outcast I have to flee my dear fatherland! " Then our friends descended into the tug, and with grateful hearts we bade them farewell. They fired a salute with their pistols and steamed back to Warnemünde, where, according to Wiggers, they celebrated the accomplished rescue with a joyous feast.

Kinkel and I remained on the poop of our schooner and gazed after the little steamboat that carried our good friends away. Then our eyes rested upon the shore of the fatherland until the last vestige had disappeared in the dusk of the evening. In our halting conversation now and then the question would recur: " When shall we return? " That a victorious uprising of the people would call us back, we both hoped fervently. It was a hope born of ardent desire and nursed by fond illusions. What would we have answered the prophet who at that moment had told us that first I, but only after eleven years, would again put my foot on German soil, and then not as a German, but as the Minister of the United States of America to Spain on my return to my new home, and that Kinkel would have to wait until, after the war between Prussia and Austria in 1866, the former Prince of Prussia and commander of the forces that had taken Kinkel prisoner near Rastatt, now king and president of the North-German Confederation, would open to him once more, by an amnesty, the door of the Fatherland!

We did not quit the deck until it was dark. The cabin of the schooner was very small. Its first aspect destroyed in me a fond imagining. I had until then only once seen a seagoing ship, a brig, which at the time when I attended the gymnasium had been brought from Holland up the Rhine and anchored near Cologne; but I could see that ship only from the outside. My conception of the interior of the ship I had derived from novels and descriptions of maritime wars which I had read as a boy, and so the main cabin of a ship stood before my eyes as a spacious room well-fitted out with furniture and the walls decorated with trophies of muskets and pistols and cutlasses. Of all this there was nothing in the cabin of the "Little Anna." It measured hardly more than eight feet between the two berths, one on each side, and in the other direction hardly more than six. It was so low that Kinkel, standing upright, touched the ceiling with his head. In the center there was a little table screwed to the floor, and behind it a small sofa covered with black haircloth; just large enough to hold Kinkel and me, sitting close together. Above the table was suspended a lamp which during the night faintly illumined the room. The berths, which had been hastily prepared for us, were a foot or two above the floor and open, so that when we were in bed we could see one another. These arrangements appeared to be very different from those of the proud East India ships, or of the frigates which I had found so enticingly described in my books; but when I considered that this was after all an unusually small trading schooner, I found that they were as practical as they were simple.

Captain Niemann, who had so unexpectedly been stirred up from his winter's rest by the sudden order of his master, probably did not know at first what to think of his two remarkable guests on the "Little Anna." One of our friends, who had accompanied us on board, had by some hint given him reason to believe that we were bankrupt merchants forced by unfortunate circumstances to run away from home; but the skipper told us afterwards he could not make his theory agree with the manifestations of respect and of warm, aye, even enthusiastic, attachment with which our friends had treated us. However, he had nothing to do but to execute orders received. In case of necessity he would really have run his vessel on shore at the risk of losing her. In the meantime he took very good care of us. The captain had a crew of seven men: a mate, a cook, a boy, and four seamen. Frau Brockelmann had amply provided us with all sorts of delicacies, foreseeing that the bill of fare of the schooner's kitchen would be very limited.

At first the sea voyage was agreeable enough. A gentle breeze filled the sails, and the ship glided along pleasantly. But as morning dawned, wind and sea became more lively and Kinkel reported himself seasick. The wind increased, the sea ran higher, and Kinkel grew more and more miserable as the day progressed. He gathered himself up to go on deck, but soon returned to his berth. I tried to lift him up, but in vain. After a few hours of acute suffering he became quite desperate in his torment and he felt that he was going to die. He had a mind to tell the captain to carry him to the nearest port. His agony seemed to him intolerable. Had he escaped from prison to die such a wretched death? It is recognized as one of the peculiarities of seasickness that those who do not suffer from it do not appreciate the sufferings of those who do, and that the sufferer considers the indifference of the well person as especially hardhearted and exasperating. That was the case with us. I felt myself uncommonly well. The more the "Little Anna" bobbed up and down in the waves, the higher rose my spirits. I felt an inordinate appetite which did the fullest justice to the accomplishments of our cook. This joyous feeling I could not entirely conceal from Kinkel, although I deplored very sincerely his sufferings, which probably were aggravated through the nervous condition resulting from his long imprisonment. I thought I could raise him up by making fun of his fear of immediate death, but that would not do at all, as Kinkel believed in all seriousness that his life was in danger. My jokes sounded to him like unfeeling recklessness, and I had soon to change my tone in order to cheer him.

In this condition we passed Helsingoer, the toll-gate of the Sound dues, and with it the last place in which our liberty might possibly have been in danger, and so we entered the Kattegat. The sea had been wild enough in the Sound, but in the Kattegat it was much wilder. The winds seemed to blow alternately from all points of the compass, and we cruised two days between the Skagen, the projecting headland of Denmark, and the high rocks of Sweden and Norway, until we reached the more spacious basin of the Skagerack. But there too, and as we at last entered the open North Sea, the "dirty weather," as our sailors called it, continued without change. At times the wind grew so violent that Captain Niemann recognized it as a real gale. Like a nutshell the "Little

Anna" jumped up and down on the angry billows. The sea constantly washed the deck, where I kept myself all the time that Kinkel did not need me below; and in order not to be washed overboard, I had the mate bind me fast to the main-mast. So I gained a vivid impression of the constantly changing grandeur of the sea, which at the first view from Warnemünde had failed to impress me. Now I was fascinated by the sensation to such a degree that I could hardly tear myself away, and every minute I had to stay below appeared to me like an irretrievable loss.

Kinkel continued seasick several days, but he gradually became aware of how much seasickness a man can endure without fatal result. By degrees his suffering diminished; he went on deck with me and began to appreciate the poetry of the sea voyage and then forgave me that I had refused to believe in the deadly character of the malady. The bad weather continued without interruption ten days and nights. At times the fury of the elements made cooking impossible. The most that could be done was to prepare some coffee, and beyond that we lived on biscuits, cold meats and herring, but we remained in good spirits and began to enjoy the humor of our situation. Two things impressed me especially—the one repeated itself every morning during the stormy time: Shortly after daybreak the mate regularly came to the cabin to bring us our coffee while we were still lying in our berths. When the sea thundered furiously against the sides of the ship and crashed down on the deck so that we could hardly hear our own words, and when then the "Little Anna" bounced up and down and rolled to and fro, like a crazy thing, so that we had to hold on to something in order not to be tumbled out of our berths, the brave seaman stood there in a dripping suit of oilskin, spread his legs far apart, held on with one hand to the little table, and balanced in the other, with astonishing skill, a bowl of coffee without spilling a drop, and screamed at us to the utmost of his power to make us understand the surprising intelligence that the weather was still bad and we could not expect to have any cooking done. We had therefore to be satisfied with what he then offered us. Thirty years later, when I was Secretary of the Interior in the government of the United States, I visited, during the presidential campaign of 1880, the town of Rondout on the Hudson, where I had to deliver a speech. After the meeting I crossed the river on a ferryboat in order to take the railroad train to New York at the station of Rhinebeck opposite. In the dusk of the evening a man approached me on the ferryboat and spoke to me in German. "Excuse me," he said, "that I address you. I should like to know whether you recognize me."

I regretted not being able to do so.

"Do you not remember," he asked, "the mate on the 'Little Anna,' Captain Niemann, on which you and Professor Kinkel, in November, 1850, sailed from Rostock to England?"

"What!" I exclaimed, "do I remember the mate who every morning stood in the cabin with his bowl of coffee and executed such wonderful dances? Yes."

"And you always made such funny remarks about it which set me laughing, if I could understand them in the terrible noise. That mate was I."

I was much rejoiced, and we shook hands vigorously. I asked how he was doing and he replied, "Very well, indeed."

I invited him to visit me in Washington, which he promised to do. I should have been glad to continue the conversation longer, but in the meantime we had reached the eastern bank of the Hudson. My railroad train stood ready and in a few minutes I was on the way to New York. The mate did not keep his promise to visit me in Washington and I have never seen him again.

The other picture still present to my mind was more serious in its involuntary ludicrousness. While we were driven about on the North Sea by violent gales the sky was constantly covered with dense clouds, so that no regular observation could be had to determine where we were. The captain indeed endeavored to ascertain our whereabouts as well as he could by the so-called dead reckoning; but after we had been so going on for several days he declared to us quite frankly that he had only a very vague idea of our latitude and longitude. Now we saw him frequently in the cabin sitting on the little sofa behind the table with his head bent thoughtfully over his chart, and as the matter was important to us, too, we tried to help him in his calculations. Kinkel, after he had overcome the seasickness, and myself spent almost the whole day on deck in spite of the storm, and as we had observed the drifting of the vessel from its true course we formed an opinion on that matter, to which the captain listened with great apparent respect; and when during the night he sat under the lamp over his chart, Kinkel and I stuck our heads out of our berths, holding fast to some object so that we could not fall out, and looking at the chart in this position, discussed with the captain the question of latitude and longitude, of the force of the wind, of the current, of the water, and so on. Finally we would agree upon some point at which the ship ought to be at that time, and that point was then solemnly marked with a pencil on the chart. Then the "navigation council," as we called it, adjourned. The captain mounted again to the deck and Kinkel and I crept back into our berths to sleep.

On the tenth day of our voyage the sky cleared at last,

and the first actual observation showed that our calculations had not been so very wrong and that three or four days would bring us to the English coast. So we headed for the port of Newcastle. Kinkel had in the meantime recovered all his bright humor, and would not permit me to remind him of his outbreaks of seasick despair. We were of good cheer, but rejoiced with our whole hearts when we saw the first strip of land rising above the horizon. Then the wind turned toward the south and the captain declared that we would have to cruise a considerable time against it in order to reach the port of Newcastle. The navigation council therefore met once more and resolved to steer in a northerly direction toward Leith, the harbor of Edinburgh. This was done, and the next evening we saw the mighty rocks that guard the entrance of that port. Then the wind suddenly died away and our sails flapped. Kinkel and I quoted for our consolation various verses from Homer: how the angry gods prevented the glorious sufferer Odysseus, by the most malicious tricks, from reaching his beloved home, Ithaca, but how at last, while he was asleep, he was wafted by gentle breezes to the hospitable shores of his island. And so it happened to us. After we had gone to bed in a somewhat surly state of mind, a light wind arose that carried us with the most gentle movement toward the long-wished-for port, and when we awoke next morning the "Little Anna" lay at anchor.

Now the good captain, Niemann, learned for the first time what kind of passengers he had carried across the North Sea under the names of Kaiser and Hensel. He confessed to us that the matter had appeared to him from the beginning quite suspicious, but he expressed in the heartiest manner his joy that, even ignorantly, he had contributed his part to Kinkel's liberation. Kinkel and I were impatient to get to land. Fortunately Mr. Brockelmann had not only given us letters to his correspondent in Newcastle, but also to a merchant in Leith, by the name of McLaren. These letters we wished to present at once, but the captain reminded us that the day was Sunday, on which a Scottish merchant would certainly not be found in his counting-house, and he did not know how we could find his residence. This difficulty we recognized. However, we were heartily tired of the "Little Anna," with its narrow cabin and its many smells. We resolved, therefore, to make our toilet and to go ashore, in order at least to take a look at Edinburgh. We also hoped to find shelter in some hotel. It was a clear, sunny winter morning. What a delight as we ascended the main street of Leith to feel that we had at last firm ground under our feet again and that we could look everyone in the face as free men! At last—all danger past, no more pursuit, a new life ahead! It was glorious. We felt like shouting and dancing, but bethought ourselves of the probable effect such conduct would have on the natives. We wandered from the harbor up into the streets of Edinburgh. These streets had on their Sunday look. All the shops closed; not a vehicle breaking the stillness. The people walked silently to church. We soon noticed that many of the passersby looked at us with an air of surprise and curiosity, and before long a troop of boys collected around us and pursued us with derisive laughter. We looked at one another and became aware that our appearance contrasted strangely indeed with that of the well-dressed church-goers. Kinkel had on his big bearskin overcoat, which reached down to his feet; his beard, which he had permitted to grow, looked like a rough stubblefield—and at that time a full beard was, in Scotland, regarded as an impossibility among respectable people. On his head he wore a cap like that of a Prussian forester. Regulation hats we did not possess. I was in a long brown overcoat with wide sleeves and a hood lined with light blue cloth, a garment which in Switzerland a tailor had evolved from my large soldier's cape. We suddenly became conscious of making very startling figures on a Sunday morning on the streets of this Scottish capital, and were no longer surprised at the astonishment of the sober church-goers and the mockery of the boys. However, there we were. We could make no change, and so sauntered on without troubling ourselves about the feelings of the others.

We looked up the celebrated Walter Scott monument and several of the famous edifices, and then went on and up to the castle, where the first view of soldiers in the splendid Scottish Highland uniform burst upon us. We enjoyed to our hearts' content the aspect of the city and its wonderfully picturesque surroundings. In short, we found Edinburgh beautiful beyond compare. In the meantime it had become high noon, and we began to feel that the contemplation of the most magnificent view does not satisfy the stomach. The imperious desire for a solid meal moved us to descend from the castle and to look about for a hotel, or at least a restaurant. But in vain. From the outside some buildings looked like public houses, but nowhere an open door. One or two we tried to enter, but without success. Now our utter ignorance of the English language became very embarrassing. Of words of English sound we knew only two—"beefsteak" and "sherry." We addressed some of the passersby in German and also in French, but they all responded after a long and astonished stare in an idiom entirely unintelligible to us, although we both had remarked that when we heard these Scottish people talk at a distance, their language sounded very much like German. When we pronounced our two English words, "beefsteak" and "sherry," those whom we addressed pointed toward the harbor. Our situation became more and more precarious, as the sun was setting. We were very tired from our long wanderings, and hunger began to be tormenting. Nothing seemed to remain to us but to return to the "Little Anna."

So we walked back to the harbor. Unexpectedly we came upon a large house in the main street of Leith, the front of which bore the inscription "Black Bull Hotel," and an open door. We entered at once, and ascended a flight of stairs to the upper story. There we reached a spacious hall with several doors, one of which was ajar. We looked through it into a little parlor lighted by an open coal fire. Without hesitation we entered, sat down in comfortable armchairs near the fireplace, pulled the bell-rope and waited for further dispensations of fate. Soon there appeared in the door a man in the dress of a waiter, with a napkin under his arm. When he saw the two strange figures sitting near the fireplace, he started and stood a moment, mute and immovable, with staring eyes and open mouth. We could not keep from laughing and when we laughed, he too smiled, but with a somewhat doubtful expression. Then we pronounced our two English words: "Beefsteak, sherry!" The waiter stammered an unintelligible reply. He then moved back toward the door and disappeared. Soon he returned with another man, also a waiter. Both stared at us and exchanged a few words between themselves. We laughed and they smiled. Then one of them said something in English which sounded like a question. Again we spoke our two words—beefsteak and sherry. Thereupon both nodded and both left the room. After a little while a third man appeared, who wore a double-breasted coat—evidently the landlord. He examined our appearance with a knowing look and talked to us in a friendly tone. Again we repeated our speech about beefsteak and sherry and tried to signify by gestures that we were hungry. At the same time Kinkel had the fortunate idea of putting his hand in his pocket and taking out a few gold pieces, which he showed to the landlord on his open palm. The landlord smiled still more, made a little bow, and took himself away.

After a while the waiter whom we had first seen set the table in fine style. Now we sat down at the hospitable board. Thereupon the waiter lifted the silver cover from the soup tureen he had brought in, with a mighty swing, pointed a forefinger of his other hand into the open dish, and said slowly and emphatically, seeming to give a dab to the contents of the tureen with each syllable, " ox—tail—soup." Then he looked at us triumphantly and stepped behind Kinkel's chair. This was my first lesson in English. Judging from the similarity with German words, we could well imagine what the words " ox " and " soup " signified, but the meaning of the word " tail " became clear to us only when we saw the contents of the tureen on our plates. We found the soup delicious, and thus our English vocabulary had been enriched by a valuable substantive. The landlord had been sensible enough not to confine himself to beefsteak and sherry in the execution of the desire we expressed, but to give us a complete dinner, to which, after our long sea voyage and the Sunday walk in the Scottish capital, we did full justice.

By all sorts of ingenious gestures we made our landlord understand that we wanted paper and ink and pens, and that we would then wish to go to bed. All our requests were understood and complied with. We now added postscripts to the letters, which we had written to our families during the last days of our voyage on the " Little Anna," giving further news of our happy arrival on British soil. Kinkel invited his wife to meet him in Paris, and then wrote a long letter to my parents, in which he said to them many kind things about me.

After this was done the waiter conducted us into a spacious sleeping apartment with two beds, the enormous size of which astonished us. The next morning we bade farewell to our kind host, grateful to him for having tolerated in his house two such uncanny looking guests, without luggage and with a vocabulary of only two English words.

Now we called at the counting-house of Mr. McLaren, in whom we found a very pleasant and polite gentleman, speaking German fluently. Letters from Mr. Brockelmann had told him everything about Kinkel and myself; he therefore greeted us with much cordiality, insisted on having our luggage taken from the "Little Anna" to his residence, and upon devoting himself entirely to us so long as we might choose to remain in Edinburgh. In McLaren's counting house we took leave of the good Captain Niemann. I have never seen him again, but many years afterwards I learned that he had perished on the North Sea in a heavy winter gale.

After having bought some presentable clothing and decent hats, thus acquiring an appearance similar to that of other men, we accepted Mr. McLaren's invitation to see Holyrood and to dine at his house, whereupon we took the night train for London.

There we were accredited by Brockelmann to the banking house of Hambro & Son. The chief of the house placed one of his clerks at our disposal, a young gentleman from Frankfurt, Mr. Verhuven, who during our sojourn in London was to devote his whole time to us. He was an exceedingly agreeable companion, and with him we hurried during several days from morning until night from place to place to see the great sights of London. In this way we missed the many visitors who left their cards at our hotel, the "London Coffee House." Among these we found that of Charles Dickens. His acquaintance we should have been especially proud to make, but to our great regret we did not find him at home when we returned his visit.

In those days I received the first distinct impression of the English language, an impression, which now, after long acquaintance with it, I can hardly explain to myself.

The celebrated tragedian Macready was playing several Shakespearian parts in one of the London theaters. We saw him in "Macbeth" and "Henry VIII." Although I did not understand the spoken words, I was sufficiently conversant with those dramas to follow the dialogue, but I had hardly any enjoyment of it, as the impure vowels and the many sibilants, the hissing consonants, in fact, the whole sound and cadence of the English language, fell upon my ear so unmusically, so gratingly, that I thought it a language that I would never be able to learn. And, indeed, this disagreeable first impression long prevented me from taking the study of English seriously in hand.

After a few days of overfatiguing pleasure we started for Paris. To witness the meeting of Kinkel and his wife, after so long and so painful a separation, was hardly less delightful to me than it was to them. But with this delight our arrival in Paris imposed upon me also a heavy burden, which consisted in sudden "fame." Although I had received in Rostock, in Edinburgh, and in London, in small circles of friends, praise of the warmest kind, I was not a little astonished and embarrassed when I learned in Paris of the sensation created by the liberation of Kinkel. While Kinkel and I had been crossing the North Sea in the cabin of the "Little Anna," holding navigation councils with Captain Niemann, it had become generally known that I, a student of the university of Bonn, had taken a somewhat important part in that affair. The details of it were of course still unknown to the general public, but that sort of mystery is notoriously favorable to the formation of legends, and the Liberal newspapers in Germany had vied with one another in romantic stories about the adventure. The favorite and most accredited of those fables represented me like Blondel before the dungeons of Richard Cœur de Lion, attracting the attention of the imprisoned friend, not indeed with the lute of a troubadour, but in my case with a barrel organ, and thus detecting the window of his cell, and then effecting his escape in a marvelous way. Another myth brought me in communication with a Prussian princess, who, in a mysterious, and to herself very perilous, manner, had advanced my undertaking. Several newspapers put before their readers my biography, which consisted in great part of fantastic inventions, inasmuch as there was but little to say of my young life. I even became the subject of poetic effusions, which celebrated me in all sorts of sentimental exaggeration. My parents, as they afterwards wrote me, were fairly flooded with congratulations, which in great part came from persons entirely unknown to them.

Of course, the praise I received from my parents and the gratitude expressed by Frau Kinkel and her children were a real and a great satisfaction to me, but the extravagances which I had to read in German papers and to hear in the constantly extending circle of our acquaintance in Paris, disquieted me seriously. What I had done had appeared to me as nothing so extraordinary as to merit all this ado. Then there was also constantly present to my mind the thought, that without the help of a group of faithful friends, and especially without Brune's bold resolution at the decisive moment, all my efforts would have been in vain. And of Brune, who in those days was subject to a sharp and dan-

A MYTHICAL PORTRAIT OF SCHURZ

gerous investigation, I could not speak without seriously compromising him. Thus I felt in submitting to praise as one who accepts credit for some things, at least, done by others, and this feeling was in a high degree painful to me. Moreover, in every company in which I showed myself I was asked time and again: "How did you succeed in carrying out this bold stroke? Tell us." Inasmuch as I could not tell the whole truth, I preferred to tell nothing. New legends were invented which if possible were still more fantastic than the old ones. This was so oppressive to me that I became very much averse to going into society, and I fear that I sometimes repelled those who came to me and pressed me with questions in an almost unfriendly manner.

To bring the narrative of this episode to a conclusion, I must add something about the further fortunes of those who coöperated with me in the Kinkel rescue. On the day after Kinkel's escape from Spandau, suspicion fell at once upon Brune. He was forthwith arrested and subjected to close examination. At first nothing could be proved against him; but then, so it was reported, they placed with him in his cell a detective whom he did not suspect and to whom in a careless way he confided his story. He was thereupon tried and condemned to three years' imprisonment. After he had served his term he removed with his family to his old home in Westphalia, where, with the money he had received from me, and which had not been discovered, he could comfortably live with his family, and where he enjoyed the respect of his neighbors. When in 1888 I visited Germany I was informed by a friend of Brune's, that Brune was at the time a janitor in a great iron-works in Westphalia, that he was doing well, although he began to feel the infirmities of old age, and that he would like to know something about me. I answered at once, giving him all the desired information about myself, and asked him for his photograph. The same friend wrote again that my letter had given Brune much pleasure, but that he was in his old age still more stubborn than he had been before, that he had always refused to be photographed, and that he even now could not be moved to do it. I desired much to see him again and had already made arrangements for the journey when, to my intense regret, uncontrollable circumstances prevented it. In 1891 I received in America a letter from Brune's daughter in which she informed me of the death of her brave father.

My friends in Spandau had rejoiced so much at the success of our enterprise that they could not conceal their joy; and so Krüger was involved in the investigation and was brought to trial. It has been reported that he willingly confessed the reception he had accorded to me in his hotel, remarking at the same time that it was his business as a hotel-keeper to open his house to all decently appearing strangers who could pay their bills; that he could not always investigate who those strangers might be, and what were their circumstances and their intentions. For instance: immediately after the revolution in Berlin on the 18th of March, 1848, a very stately looking gentleman with some friends had arrived in a carriage at the door of his inn. Those gentlemen had been in great excitement and hurry, and he had noticed several extraordinary things in their conduct. In great haste they had departed, as he had afterwards heard, for England. It had not occurred to him for a single moment to deny to them as unknown people the hospitality of his house. Only later he had been informed that the most distinguished looking of these gentlemen had been His Royal Highness, the Prince of Prussia (later Emperor William I.). This narrative, recounted with the quiet smile peculiar to Krüger, is said to have put the audience present at the trial into the gayest humor, which even the court could not entirely resist. Krüger was pronounced not guilty, continued to live quietly in Spandau, and died in the seventies, much esteemed and mourned by all his fellow-citizens.

Poritz, Leddihn, and Hensel also were acquitted, there being no conclusive proof against them. Poritz and Hensel died not many years afterwards. I saw Leddihn again in 1888 in Berlin. He had been living for several years in the capital, was a well-to-do citizen and a member of the city council. Three years afterwards the newspapers reported his death.

It is remarkable how the memory of that adventure has remained alive in various parts of Germany. Hardly a year has passed since 1850 without bringing me in newspaper articles or letters new versions of the old story, some of them extremely fantastic. When early in this century the penitentiary building in Spandau in which Kinkel had been imprisoned was taken down to make room for another structure, some citizens of Spandau sent me a photograph of it, showing the part of the building from which Kinkel escaped, Kinkel's cell, and his and my portrait, taken from a daguerreotype made in Paris, in December, 1850. In January, 1903, nearly fifty-three years after our drive from Spandau to Rostock, I received a pictorial postal card signed by a member of the German Reichstag and several other gentlemen, who sent me cordial greetings and a picture of the "White Cross Inn," near Rostock, marked "Kinkel's Corner," where we had stopped in our flight, and where the room in which we took an early breakfast still seems to be pointed out to guests.

CHAPTER XII

THE Kinkel family resolved to settle down in England. Kinkel occupied himself for a little while with the study of the most important architecture, picture galleries, and other art collections in Paris, and then left for London. I preferred to stay in Paris for a while, partly because I hoped there to find special facilities for continuing my favorite studies, partly for the reason that Paris was regarded as the great focus of liberal movements on the continent, and I believed it was the most convenient point for one wishing to work as a newspaper correspondent. Thus we parted.

Now I had to begin an orderly method of life and active self-support. My journalistic connections in Germany were quickly resumed, and I found that I could earn 180 francs a month by letter-writing for newspapers. I resolved to limit my regular expenses to 100 francs a month, and thus to lay by a little reserve for emergencies. This presupposed a careful economy, but I soon learned with how little money a person may decently get along in Paris. This school of economy has always remained useful to me. I shared the quarters of my friend, Strodtmann, who had already been in Paris for some time and who occupied a spacious room in a hotel garni in the Faubourg Montmartre. But this common housekeeping did not last long. Strodtmann was not able to preserve order among his things, and as I, too, had my weaknesses in that direction, our room, which served at the same time as a living and sleeping apartment, often presented the picture of most wonderful confusion. It is an old experience, that a person who is not himself very orderly finds the disorderliness of another sometimes quite unendurable. So it was with us. Of course it appeared to me that Strodtmann was the greater sinner, and in this I was not altogether wrong. He was somewhat of a gourmet; he would study the delicacies exposed in the show-windows of restaurants with great enthusiasm and discernment, and he imagined that he himself could prepare fine dishes. He therefore made on our grate-fire all sorts of experiments in roasting and frying and filled the room with very unwelcome odors. He insisted also on preparing our coffee, for he was sure that he knew much better to do that than I or anybody else. To this assumption I should have offered no resistance whatever; but as he handled the burning alcohol of his machine very carelessly it happened that he set on fire papers and clothes that were lying around everywhere, and finally he burnt a big hole into the most valuable article of my wardrobe, namely, that large cloak with the hood, belonging to my Baden officer's period. We laughed together about his awkwardness, but after this catastrophe we agreed in the most amicable spirit that there was not room enough in one apartment for two persons as disorderly as ourselves. I therefore rented a room on the Quai Saint-Michel, No. 17, and Strodtmann settled down in the Latin Quarter in my neighborhood.

The house No. 17 Quai Saint-Michel was kept by a widow, Mme. Petit, and her daughters, two unmarried ladies no longer young. The house was in all things decent, respectable, and strictly regulated. In this regard it distinguished itself advantageously from most of the hotel garnis in the Latin Quarter. Those of Mme. Petit's tenants whose conduct was especially correct were rewarded with invitations, from time to time, to take tea in her little salon, where the presence of the two faded daughters and some friends of the family created an atmosphere of extraordinary dullness. After having gone through that experience once we avoided a repetition. My room in the house was, according to my notions, quite comfortable. To be sure, the windows did not open on the side of the Seine, but they looked into a narrow and dirty side street. In order to reach my room I had to go up several stairs and to go down several other stairs, and to wander through a long, dark corridor and to turn various corners; but that did not disturb me. It was rather spacious, had a floor of red tiles, upon which there were a few diminutive pieces of carpet, several chairs fit for use, a round table, a fireplace, a wardrobe for my clothes, and even a piano, which was indeed very old and bad, but might have been worse. My bed stood in an alcove, and by means of chintz curtains I could hide it from the gaze of visitors, so that my room looked not like a bedchamber, but like a little salon, which I was quite proud of. For this dwelling I had to pay a rent of thirty francs a month, a sum rather high for me; but I thought that the character of the house would otherwise help me to save. My first breakfast consisted of a cup of coffee, which I prepared myself, or a glass of wine and a piece of bread, sometimes with butter. After having worked at my writing-table until noon I took a second breakfast or lunch that never was to exceed one-half franc in cost, in some restaurant of the Latin Quarter, and in the evening I dined in an eating-house kept in the Rue Saint-Germain l'Auxerois near the Louvre, that was kept by a socialistic association of cooks, the Association Fraternelle des Cuisiniers réunis. Cooks, waiters, and guests addressed one another according to the model of the French Revolution, "Citoyen," and this pride of civic equality showed itself also in the circumstance that the citoyen-waiter accepted no tip from the citoyen-guest. These citoyens furnished for one franc a very simple but very substantial and good meal, including even a "confiture" as a dessert and a glass of wine. The company was mixed, but this made it easier for us to imagine ourselves during the meal as living in the ideal state of general fraternity.

Other expenses, of laundry and of an occasional fire in my room, brought the amount of the whole budget to not quite three francs a day, less than sixty cents in American money, or ninety to ninety-three francs a month. I could permit myself even some luxuries: the purchase of a few books, some of which are still in my possesion; also occasional tickets for the parterre in the Odéon or in a Faubourg theatre; now and then a cup of coffee on the Boulevard and—only now and then, to be sure—I could afford to see Rachel at the Théâtre Français. Thus I managed to incur no debts, to save a small reserve, to be obliged to nobody for anything, and to feel myself quite independent and comfortable.

Of course I could not, under such circumstances, indulge in expensive social enjoyments. Aside from an occasional visit to the salon of the Countess d'Agoult, the well-known friend of Franz Liszt, my intercourse remained mainly confined to German exiles, some students and young artists who pursued their studies in Paris, and also some young Frenchmen who attended lectures at the Sorbonne or other institutions of learning, and in this circle I found very agreeable companions. We had every week a "musical evening"; sometimes in my room, in which young musicians—among them Reinecke, who afterwards became the famous director of the well-known "Gewandhaus Concerts" in Leipzig—reviewed the most recent composers, and now and then produced their own compositions, while I and others served as an enthusiastic public. On such occasions we used to drink a punch which, for reasons of economy, left nothing to be desired in point of weakness.

In this circle my good comrade, Adolph Strodtmann, was

a general favorite. He had at that time plunged deep into the socialistic poetry of that period, in which he saw a promising symptom of a new mental and moral revival of the human race. Some French poems of that kind he translated with extraordinary skill into sonorous German verse, which he read to us at our social meetings to our great delight. He was also a generous listener, and although very deaf, professed great interest in our musical performances, giving his sometimes startling judgment in a thundering voice. We all loved him for his high enthusiasms, his ardent sympathies, the frank honesty of his nature and the robust ingenuousness with which he promulgated his occasionally very eccentric opinions of men and things. At times his oddities afforded us much amusement, which he good-naturedly shared, frequently laughing loudest with childlike astonishment at the queer exhibitions he had made of himself. He might well have served as the original to many caricatures of the "absent-minded professor," who is a favorite subject of funny pictures in German periodicals.

Now and then he was seen on the street smoking a long German student's pipe, as he had done in Bonn. In Paris the passersby would stand still with amazement when they beheld so unaccustomed an apparition, and soon he was known in the Latin Quarter as "l'homme à la longue pipe." One day he came into my room with a hairbrush under his arm, and when I asked him, "Strodtmann, what are you carrying there?" he looked at the thing at first with great surprise, and then laughed boisterously and said, with his loud voice, "Why, this is my hairbrush. I thought it was a book from which I wished to read to you." Another time when he visited me I noticed that his face bore the expression of extraordinary seriousness, if not trouble. "I have only one pair of boots," he said; "one of the boots is still pretty good, but the other, you see"—and here he pointed to his right foot—" the other is bursting in the seams. Have you not a boot that you can lend me?" Indeed, I possessed two pairs, and it so happened that of one pair one boot was a little damaged and the other in a perfectly serviceable condition. This sound boot I gladly put at Strodtmann's disposal. When we undertook to make the exchange we noticed at once that the two good boots, his and mine, belonged to two different fashions. His was pointed at the toe and mine was broad-cut, and both were for the left foot. These unfortunate circumstances did not disturb Strodtmann in the least, and although he may have suffered at times considerable inconvenience, he walked about in these two left boots, one of which was pointed and the other broad, until his own footgear had had the necessary repairs.

I felt the necessity of perfecting myself in the French language in order to speak and write it with ease, and with that delicacy which constitutes one of its characteristic charms. One of my friends recommended to me a teacher who bore the high-sounding name of Mme. La Princesse de Beaufort. According to rumor, she belonged to an old noble family, but was impoverished to such a degree by the political revolutions, that she had to earn her bread as a teacher of language. Whether this was all true in reality I do not know, but when I sought her out I found her in a modest apartment of a hotel garni, an elderly lady of very agreeable features and a quiet, refined and somewhat courtly manner that permitted me to believe she had really moved in distinguished circles. She accepted me as a pupil and declared herself willing to give me two lessons a week, each of which should cost one franc. We began the next day. My teacher allowed me the choice of the method of instruction, and I proposed to her, instead of following the usual custom of memorizing rules of grammar, that I would write for her little letters or essays on subjects that interested me. She was then to correct my mistakes and to instruct me in the idiomatic forms of speech. In following this method we were to have a grammar at hand for the purpose of pointing out the rules which I had violated. This pleased her, and as I was already able to make myself somewhat understood in French, we set to work without delay.

This method proved very successful. My letters or short essays treated of real happenings that had occurred to me, or of what I had seen in museums, or of books, or of the political events of the day. Now, as I did not merely link together grammatically constructed sentences as the pupils of so many educational institutions usually do when writing their Latin themes, but as I set forth my experiences and my views with great freedom and thereby tried to give my exercises some intrinsic interest, my teacher did not confine herself to the mere correction of my grammatical mistakes, but she entered into animated conversations with me, in which she encouraged me further to enlarge upon the subjects narrated or discussed in my papers. These conversations, in which she showed, aside from a thorough knowledge of French, much independent thought and comprehension, became to both of us so agreeable that not seldom the passing of the hour escaped our attention, and when I rose to take leave she insisted that I stay in order to pursue the discussion a little farther. Aside from these lessons I read much and never permitted myself to skip over words or forms of speech which I did not understand. My progress was encouraging, and after a few weeks it happened sometimes that my teacher returned my paper to me with the assurance that she found nothing in it to correct.

This way of learning a foreign language proved no less effective than agreeable. One may begin the attempts of free expression, and thus an independent use of the language, with a comparatively small vocabulary. Conscientious reading and well-conducted conversations will then quickly enlarge the vocabulary and develop the facility of expression. But I cannot lay too much stress upon the fact that the free and exact rendering of one's own thoughts *in writing* is the most efficient exercise in acquiring a language. In mere conversation we are apt to skip over difficulties by permitting ourselves vaguenesses and inaccuracies of expression which would sternly demand correction—and correction, too, easily kept in mind—when the written word looked us in the face. To quicken the efficacy of this exercise requires, of course, a teacher able not only to pound grammatical rules into the head of the pupil, but also to stir up, through study of the language, a mentally active interest in the subjects spoke or written about. Mme. La Princesse de Beaufort filled these requirements to a high degree, and the hours which I passed with her have always remained with me an especially agreeable memory.

Another similarly effective method of acquiring foreign languages without a teacher I will explain later in connection with my study of English. Thanks to my teacher, I rapidly acquired such fluency and ease in the French language, that I could, and did, write short letters to French journals, which were published without correction. I regret to say that in the course of time I have lost some of that facility in consequence of a want of practice. For this I reproach myself, because one may without difficulty, also without constant opportunity for conversation, retain a complete possession of a language once learned by simply reading to one's self every day aloud a few pages of some good author.

I continued with zeal to study French history, especially that of the time of the great revolution, and as France was still regarded as the revolutionary leader, and we expected the most important results from the developments there, I took a lively interest in French politics and pursued with the intensest concern the struggle going on at that time between the Republicans and the President, Louis Napoleon, who was suspected of usurpatory designs. But I had to confess to myself that many of the things which, as a critical observer, I witnessed around me seriously modified my conception of the grandeur of the events of the revolutionary period, and shook my faith in the historic mission of France as to the future of the civilized world. I frequently visited the gallery of the National Assembly when debates of importance were announced. I had studied the history of the " Constituent Assembly " of 1789, of the " Legislative Body " and of the " Convention " of the first revolution with great diligence and thoroughness, knew by heart some of the most celebrated oratorical performances of Mirabeau and others, was well acquainted with the parliamentary discussions of that period, and hoped now to hear and see something similar to that which had moved me so powerfully in reading and which lived in my imagination as a heroic drama. My disappointment in visiting the National Assembly with this expectation was great. Indeed, high-sounding speeches and scenes of stormy and tumultuous excitement were not lacking; but with all this, as it seemed to me, there was too little of an earnest and thoughtful exchange of opinions between eminent men, and too much of theatrical attitudinizing and of declamatory phrasemongery. It happened to me—as it frequently happens —that the disappointment of expectations which had been pitched too high, will, in the conclusions we draw, lead us to underestimate the character and value of existing things and conditions as we see them before us. What in fact I did witness was the French way of doing things. That way did not correspond with my ideals; but it was, after all, the French way, which, with all its histrionic superficialities, had in the past, especially in the great revolution, proved itself very real and serious and had produced tremendous results.

However, what I saw of political action on the public stage had a sobering effect on me, and this effect was intensified and confirmed by my observations in the Latin Quarter and in public places of amusement of the dissoluteness of student life—the habitual life of young men who might be considered the flower of French youth. I shall never forget the impression made upon me and my friends by a masked ball at the opera which some of us young Germans visited during the carnival season of 1851. Everybody was admitted who could pay for his ticket and provide himself with the prescribed attire, that is to say, the ordinary evening dress or some fancy costume. The ball began about midnight. The multitude present consisted of all ranks and conditions, among whom I recognized a good many students living in the Latin Quarter, with their grizettes or " petites femmes," and of other persons who had come, not all to take part in the dance, but to witness this characteristic spectacle of Parisian life. The anterooms were teeming with women in dominos, who approached men walking about in a very confidential way. The great auditory of the opera and the stage were arranged as a ballroom. Dancing began in comparatively decent manner, but degenerated soon into the ordinary cancan. Police agents moved through the room to prevent the grossest violations of decency. At first they seemed to succeed in a degree—at least the dancers seemed to keep themselves in check in their immediate presence. But as the hours advanced, the temperature of the room rose, and the blood of the dancers became heated, the business of the guardians of order grew more and more hopeless. At last all restraint was at an end and bestiality would have its own way. Men and women, some of whom in the fury of the dance had torn their clothing from their shoulders, raved like crazed beings. The scene beggared description. The programme announced as the last dance a galop, called the "Hell Galop." The orchestra played an especially furious measure, accompanied with the ringing of bells. In truth, the crowd whirling in the wildest reel of sensuality looked very much like a pandemonium rushing straight into the bottomless pit. While this galop was going on—it was about four o'clock in the morning—the rear of the big room filled itself with soldiers, who formed in line. Suddenly the music of the orchestra was drowned by a rattling roll of drums, and the infantry line, bayonets fixed but arms trailed, advanced slowly, step by step crowding the dancers and the onlookers out of the hall.

To drink the cup to the dregs, we went to one of the restaurants on the Boulevard near by to take some refreshments—" petit souper," as it was called. The spectacle we beheld there surpassed all we had seen before. The most unbridled fancy could not imagine a picture more repulsive.

I had often tarried in the gallery of the Luxembourg in contemplation of Couture's great canvas, called "La decadance des Romains," which so eloquently portrays the moral decline of a mighty people and a great civilization; but what we here saw before us lacked even the reminiscence of past greatness, which in Couture's picture is so impressive. It was moral decay even to putrescence in its most vulgar form, its most repulsive aspect, its most shameless display.

My friends and myself consoled ourselves with the reflection that we had seen the worst, an exceptional extreme, and that this could not possibly be representative of the whole French people; and to this thought we clung all the more readily as our hopes of the new democratic revival in Europe hung upon the part which we expected the French Republic to play.

But I had to confess to myself that on the whole the atmosphere of Paris was not congenial to me, and with sincere pleasure I accepted an invitation of the Kinkel family, urging me to visit them in London and to spend at least a week or two in their happy home.

Here I must mention an occurrence which at the time caused me astonishment. Strodtmann had made me acquainted with a marine painter by the name of Melbye, a Dane. He was much older than we, an artist of considerable skill, who talked about his art as well as various other things in an agreeable manner. He was greatly interested in clairvoyance, and told us he knew a clairvoyante whose performances were most extraordinary. He requested us several times to accompany him to a "séance" and to convince ourselves of her wonderful abilities. At last an evening was fixed for this entertainment, but it so happened that at about the same time I received an invitation from Kinkel, which I resolved to accept without delay. When I packed my valise Strodtmann was with me in my room and he expressed his regret that I could not attend the séance that evening. He went away for a little while, to return to my room later in the day and to accompany me to the railroad station. In the meantime the thought struck me that I might furnish a means for testing the powers of the clairvoyante. I cut off some of my hair, wrapped it in a piece of paper and put this into a letter-envelope, which I closed with sealing-wax. Then I tore a little strip from a letter I had received that morning from the Hungarian General Klapka, the celebrated defender of the fortress Komorn, and put this strip containing the date of the letter also into a folded paper and enclosed it likewise in an envelope sealed with wax. When

Strodtmann had returned to me I gave him the two envelopes, without informing him of their contents, and instructed him to place them in the hands of the clairvoyante, with the request that she give a description of the appearance, the character, the past career and the temporary sojourn of the person from whom the objects concealed in the envelopes had come. Then I left for London.

A few days later I received a letter from Strodtmann, in which he narrated the results of the séance, as follows: The clairvoyante took one of my envelopes in her hand and said this contained the hair of a young man who looked thus and so. She then described my appearance in the most accurate way, and added that this young man had won notoriety by his connection with a bold enterprise, and that at the present time he was on the other side of a deep water, in a large city and in the circle of a happy family. Then she gave a description of my character, my inclinations and my mental faculties, which, as I saw them in black and white, surprised me greatly. Not only did I recognize myself in the main features of this description, but I found in it also certain statements which seemed to give me new disclosures about myself. It happens sometimes when we look into our own souls that in our impulses, in our feelings, in our ways of thinking, we find something contradictory, something enigmatical, which the most conscientious self-examination does not always suffice to make clear. And now there flashed from the utterances of this clairvoyante gleams of light which solved for me many of those contradictions and riddles. I received, so to speak, a revelation about my own inner self, a psychological analysis which I had to recognize as just as soon as I perceived it.

What the clairvoyante said about the other envelope, which contained Klapka's writing, was hardly less astonishing. She described the writer of the letters and figures contained in that envelope as a handsome, dark-bearded man, with sparkling eyes, who had once governed a city full of armed men and besieged by enemies. The description of his person, of his past, and also of his character as far as I knew it, was throughout correct; but when the clairvoyante added that this man was at the time not in Paris, but in another city, where he had gone to meet a person very dear to him, I thought we had caught her in a mistake. A few days later I returned to Paris, and had hardly arrived there when I met General Klapka on the street. I asked him at once whether, since he had written his last letter to me, he had been constantly in Paris, and I was not a little amazed when he told me that he had a few days ago made an excursion to Brussels, where he had stopped not quite a week, and the "dear person" whom he was to have seen there, I learned from an intimate friend of Klapka, was a lady whom it was said he would marry. The clairvoyante was therefore right in every point.

This occurrence mystified me very much. The more I considered the question, whether the clairvoyante could possibly have received knowledge of the contents of my envelopes, or whether she could have had any cue for guessing at them, the more certain I became that this could not be. Strodtmann himself did not know what I had put into the envelopes. Of Klapka's letter to me he had not the slightest information. He also assured me that he had put the envelopes into the hands of the clairvoyante, one after the other, in exactly the same condition in which he had received them, without for a moment confiding them to anybody else and without telling to anyone from whom they came; and I could absolutely depend upon the word of my thoroughly honest friend. But even if—which was quite unthinkable to me—there had been some collusion between him and the clairvoyante, or if he had, without knowing it, betrayed from whom the envelopes had come, it would not have solved the riddle how the clairvoyante could have described my character, my inclinations, my impulses, my mental qualities, much more clearly and truthfully and sagaciously than Strodtmann or Melbye ever could have done. In fact, Melbye knew me only very superficially. In our few conversations he had always done the most talking; and a deep insight into the human soul did not at all belong to Strodtmann's otherwise excellent abilities. In short, I could not in the whole incident find the slightest reason for the suspicion that here we had to do with a merely clever juggler. The question arose: Was not here a force at work which lay outside of the ordinary activity of the senses and which we could indeed observe in the utterance of its effects, and which we perhaps could also set in motion, but which we could not define as to its true essence or its constituent elements? In later years I have had similar experiences, which I intend to mention in their proper places.

I shall now return to my visit in London. Kinkel had rented in the suburb of St. John's Wood a little house, where I was most heartily welcomed as a guest. He had already found a profitable field of work as a teacher, and Frau Kinkel gave music lessons. I found the whole family in a very cheerful state of mind, and we spent some happy days together. In fact I felt myself so much at home that Kinkel could easily persuade me to give up Paris and to come over to London, where I, as it seemed to me, would be able to make a comfortable living as a teacher without great difficulty. I then returned to Paris, as I thought only for a few weeks but my departure from the French capital was to be delayed by an unexpected and very disagreeable incident.

One afternoon I accompanied on a walk the wife of my

friend Reinhold Solger, a fellow-German refugee, a man of great knowledge and acquirements, who later was to occupy a respected position in the service of the United States. We were in the neighborhood of the Palais Royal when an unknown man stopped me and asked to have a word with me aside, as he had something very confidential to communicate to me. As soon as we were out of the hearing of Mrs. Solger he told me that he was a police agent, ordered to arrest me and to take me at once to the "Prefecture de Police." I excused myself to Mrs. Solger as best I could and accompanied the unwelcome stranger.

He conducted me first to a police commissioner, who inquired after my name, my age, my nativity, and so on. I was astonished that the police, who seemed to know my name, did not know where I lived. I declared to the commissioner that I had absolutely no reason for concealing anything, and acquainted him with the number of the house in which I lived, as well as with the place in my room where the keys to all my belongings could be found; but I wished to know for what reason I had been taken into custody. The commissioner mysteriously lifted his eyebrows, talked of higher orders, and thought I would learn of this soon enough. Another police agent then conducted me to the "Prefecture de Police." There I was turned over to a jailer, who after I had surrendered the money I had with me and my pocket-knife to a subordinate turnkey, took me into a cell and locked me in. To the question whether I would not soon be informed of the reason of my arrest I did not receive any answer. My cell was a little bare room, sparingly lighted by a narrow window with iron bars high up in the wall. There were two small, not very clean, beds, two wooden chairs and a little table.

I expected every moment to be called to a hearing, for I

thought that in a republic, such as France was at that time, they would not incarcerate anybody without telling him the reason therefor at once; but I waited in vain. Evening came and the turnkey informed me that I might have a supper, consisting of various dishes which he enumerated, if I were able and willing to pay for it; otherwise I would have to be content with the ordinary prison fare, which he described to me in a manner not at all alluring. I ordered a modest meal, and in eating it I thought with melancholy longing of my good Citoyens in the Rue Saint-Germain l'Auxerois.

Late in the evening, when I had already gone to bed, another prisoner was brought to my cell. In the dim light of the turnkey's lantern I saw in the newcomer a man still young, in shabby clothes, with a smooth-shaven face and dark, restless eyes. He at once began a conversation with me and informed me that he had been accused of theft, and upon that accusation had been arrested. The charge, however, was entirely unfounded, but as he had been arrested before on similar suspicions, the authorities would not accept his assurances of innocence. I thus had a common thief as my companion and roommate. He seemed to see in me a fellow-laborer in the vineyard, for he asked me in a rather confidential tone what accident I had been caught in. My short and entirely truthful response did not appear to satisfy him; he may have even regarded it as unfriendly, for he did not say another word, but lay down upon his bed and was soon in a profound sleep.

During the still night I thought over my situation. Had I really done anything in Paris that might have been considered punishable? I examined all the corners of my memory and found nothing. Of course the reason for my arrest could only be a political one, but however my opinions and sentiments might displease the government of President Napoleon,

I certainly had not taken part in any political movement in France. In Paris I had only been an observer and a student. I did not doubt that while I was in prison the police would search the papers in my room, but that could not disquiet me, as I knew that nothing could be found there except some historical notes, a few literary sketches and some letters from friends of an entirely harmless nature. All the papers which might in any way have been considered questionable, as well as the pistols which I had carried with me during the Kinkel affair, I had been cautious enough to entrust to one of my friends for safekeeping. Nothing remained but the suspicion that I had been taken into custody at the instance of the Prussian government. But would the French Republic be capable of surrendering me to Prussia? This I deemed impossible; and thus I looked the future calmly in the face. But I was stung by a feeling of the degradation inflicted upon me by shutting me up in the same room with a common thief. It revolted my self-respect. And this could happen in a republic!

My indignation rose the following morning when I still failed to receive information about the cause of my arrest. At an early hour the thief was taken out of the cell and I remained alone. I asked the turnkey for paper, pen and ink, and in my best French I wrote a letter to the prefect, in which, in the name of the laws of the country, I demanded that I be informed why I had been deprived of my liberty. The turnkey promised to transmit the letter, but the day passed without an answer, and so another day, and still another. Neither did I receive a word from my friends, and I hesitated to write to any of them, because the receipt of a letter from me might have embarrassed them. In those few days I learned to understand something of the emotions which may torment the soul of a prisoner—a feeling of bitter wrath against the brutal power that held me captive; the consciousness of complete impotency which rose in me like a mockery of myself; the feverish imagination that troubled me with an endless variety of ugly pictures; a restless impetus that compelled me to run up and down for hours in my cell like a wild animal in its cage; then a dreary emptiness in mind and heart which finally ended in dull brooding without any definite thought.

On the morning of the fourth day I addressed a second letter to the prefect still more vehement and pathetic than the first, and shortly afterwards the turnkey told me that I would be taken to the bureau of the chief. In a few minutes I found myself in a comfortably furnished office-room and in the presence of a stately gentleman, who kindly asked me to sit down. He then complimented me elaborately upon the correctness of the French of my letters, which he called quite remarkable, considering my German nationality; and he expressed in the politest phrases his regret that I had been incommoded by my arrest. There was really no charge against me. It was only desired by the government that I select a place of residence for myself outside of the boundaries of France, and to this end leave Paris and the country as soon as might be convenient to me. In vain I tried to move this polite gentleman to a statement of the reasons which might make my removal from France so desirable. With constantly increasing politeness he told me that it was so desired in higher places. At last I thought to appease his evident trouble about my lacerated feelings by the remark that in fact the desire of the government did not incommode me at all, inasmuch as I had intended to go to London, and that my arrest had only delayed me somewhat in my preparations for departure. The polite gentleman was enchanted at this happy coincidence of my intentions with the desire of his government, and he told me finally not to be in too great a hurry with my preparations for leaving. He would be delighted if I felt myself under his especial protection while in Paris, where I might still remain two, three, four, even six weeks, if that would amuse me. He would then put at my disposal a passport for any foreign country; but after my departure he hoped that I would not embarrass him by returning to Paris without his special permission. Then he bade me farewell with a friendliness bordering on actual affection, and I left him with the impression that I had made the acquaintance of the politest and most agreeable police tyrant in the world.

I hurried back to my quarters and found the Petit family in great tribulation on my account. Madame and the two faded daughters told me in a shrill trio how a few days ago two police agents had searched my room and examined my papers, but had left everything behind them in the best of order. The police had also tried to inform themselves of my conduct by putting questions to the Petit family, and I might be assured that the Petit family had given me the most excellent character; but then the Petit family had become very much disquieted about my lot, and had informed my friends who had called upon me of all that had happened, and requested them to set in motion every possible influence that might help me. Subsequently I learned, indeed, that several of my friends had made proper efforts in my behalf, and it is quite possible that this had hastened my discharge from imprisonment.

The reason of my arrest, however, soon became quite clear to me. Louis Napoleon had begun the preparations for his coup d'état which was to do away with the republican form of government and to put him in possession of monarchical power. While the republicans deceived themselves about the danger that was looming up, and tried to ridicule the pretender as an "inane ape" of his great uncle, this man set all means in motion to win the army and the masses of the people for himself and his schemes. The Napoleonic propaganda was organized in all parts of the country in the most varied forms, and this agitation fell especially with the peasant population on very fertile soil. The legend of the Napoleonic Empire, with its wars and victories, and its tragic end, was the heroic lay of the country people, in the glamor of which every peasant family sunned itself and felt itself great. Each could tell of some ancestor who at Rivoli, or at the Pyramids, or at Marengo, or at Austerlitz, or at Jena, or at Wagram, or at Borodino, or at Waterloo, had fought under the eyes of the mighty chief, and in this heroic epic there stood the colossal figure of the Great Emperor enveloped in myth, like a demigod, unequaled in his achievements, gigantic even in his fall. Every cabin was adorned with his picture, which signified the great past history of power and glory embodied in this one superior being. And now a nephew of the Great Emperor presented himself to the people, bearing the name of the demigod and promising in this name to restore the magic splendor of that period. Numberless agents swarmed through the country, and pamphlets and hand-bills passed from house to house and from hand to hand, to make known the message of the nephew and successor of the great Napoleon, who stood ready to restore all the old magnificent grandeur. Even the barrel-organ was pressed into the service of that agitation to accompany songs about the Emperor and his nephew in the taverns and the market-places of the country. The more intelligent populations of the cities did indeed not reverence the Napoleonic legend with the same naïve devotion; but that legend had, even before the nephew began his career as a pretender, been nourished in a hardly less effective manner. Beranger's songs and Thiers' "History of the Consulate and the Empire" had stimulated the Napoleonic cult, and even the government of Louis Philippe had paid its homage to it, by transporting Napoleon's remains with great pomp from St. Helena to the Church of the Invalides. The field so prepared was incessantly tilled by Louis Napoleon, while he stood as president at the head of the executive power. As the barrel-organ did service in the country districts, the theater was made to serve in the cities. I remember a spectacular drama, which was produced on one of the Faubourg stages with great pomp and startling realism. It was called "La Barrière de Clichy," and represented the campaign of 1814, the exile of Napoleon on the Isle of Elba, and his return to France in 1815. Napoleon appeared on the boards in an excellent mask, on foot and on horseback, and all the engagements of that campaign in which he was successful passed before the eyes of the multitude; the French infantry, cavalry, and artillery in the historic uniforms of the Empire; the enemies, Prussians and Russians, barbarous-looking fellows, uncouth and rude, and constantly running away from French heroism. Blücher appeared in person as a boisterous barbarian, indulging in the most horrible blackguardism, constantly smoking a short pipe, blowing forth tremendous clouds of smoke, and incessantly spitting around him. The enemies were regularly defeated, so that it was difficult for the impartial beholder to understand why Napoleon, after all these splendid victories, succumbed, and was forced to go into exile. At any rate, he soon returned amid the enthusiastic acclamation of the people. The army went over to him promptly, and this piece concluded with his triumphal entry into Grenoble. The public applauded with enthusiasm, and the cry of "Vive l'Empereur" was heard, not only on the stage, but not seldom also in the galleries, in the parterre, and in the boxes. Thus the city populations were being labored upon.

The so-called "Prince-President" sought to win the army by appearing at parades and maneuvers in a general's uniform, by showing the soldiers all possible favors, and by drawing to himself the most adventurous spirits among the officers. In the spring of 1851 he began also to prepare the prospective battlefield of the intended "coup d'état." The bourgeois of Paris were made to apprehend that the city was full of the most dangerous elements from which every moment an attempt at a complete subversion of the social order was to be feared; that "society" was in imminent danger and must be "saved." The "Prince-President," so the word went forth, was ready to undertake that work of salvation, but the parliamentary power sought to bind his hands. However, he was doing what he could, and would first undertake to deliver Paris of the dangerous characters infesting it. One of the measures taken to that end consisted in the driving away from the city all foreigners who might be suspected of an inclination to take part in forcible resistance to the intended "coup d'état," and in that category I too was counted.

A police agent, who described the threatening dangers in a pamphlet written for the purpose of terrifying the timid bourgeois, called me an especially daring revolutionist, who in his old fatherland had already committed the most frightful outrages. To illustrate this, he narrated the liberation of Kinkel, describing him with the most fabulous fabrications as an uncommonly detestable criminal. To these circumstances I owed my arrest and my exile from France, in spite of my modest and retired conduct during my stay there. It is indeed not at all improbable that if I had been in Paris at the time of the coup d'état I should have seen in the popular resistance to the Napoleonic usurpation the decisive struggle for and against liberty in Europe, and I might have taken up the musket and fought with the republicans on the barricades on the 2d of December. So it may be, that, if it had otherwise been my intention to remain in Paris, the police saved me from participating in a hopeless enterprise, and possibly from a miserable end.

The last weeks of my sojourn in Paris were devoted to visits to galleries, museums, and interesting architectures, and to merry conviviality with my friends. To one of them, a young Frenchman from Provence who had studied medicine in Paris, my departure was especially hard. I had made his acquaintance as one of the lodgers of the Petit house, and I mention him because he furnished a remarkable example of the effect of German philosophy upon a French brain, which I would not have deemed possible had I not personally witnessed it. Soon after we had become acquainted he attached himself to me and to several others among my German friends, and as he was a modest, agreeable, and able young man taking life seriously, we reciprocated his friendly feelings. He loved Germans, so he said, because they were the nation of thinkers. He had made the acquaintance of some products of German literature in translations, and tried to possess himself of the language, mainly for the purpose of studying the works of German philosophers; but he seemed to find it very difficult. Thus he had to content himself with French renderings of German philosophical works, and he frequently came to us for the explanation of phrases which he did not understand. Sometimes we could give him such explanations, but many of the dark expressions we did not understand ourselves. Suddenly we became aware that our young Provençal, whose conduct of life had always been very regular and irreproachable, visited the German beerhouses, of which there were a great many in Paris, and drank heavily. This went so far that one day Mme. Petit and her daughters asked me to visit him in his room, as he had come home the night before much intoxicated, and was now, it seemed, seriously ailing. I complied with this request at once and found my friend in that condition which at the German university is designated as a deep "Katzenjammer." The young man confessed to me that he was heartily ashamed of his behavior, but he thought if I knew the cause of it I would not think so ill of him. Then he told me, with great gravity, that he had for some time tried to study the German philosopher Hegel, and he had found in his works many things that had tormented him with doubts as to the soundness of his own mind. Therefore he had tried to amuse himself, and as the Germans, of whom he believed that Hegel's philosophical works were their favorite reading, liked to drink beer, he had also made an effort to facilitate the Hegel studies by accustoming himself to the same beverage. The good boy talked so seriously and so honestly that I refrained from laughing, and assured him with equal seriousness that many a German, too, had nearly become insane in studying Hegel, and that the drinking of beer did not help them. Now, if Hegel, in the German language, produced such effects upon German heads, what effect could be expected upon my friend of a French decoction of Hegel? This seemed to quiet my good Provençal very much. I advised him now to give up Hegel, as well as the excessive drinking of beer, and to devote himself again to the study of medicine, like the well-behaved, serious, and diligent man he had been before. He promised this, and he did it really; and on the day of my farewell from Paris we took leave of one another with the sincerest regret. As this story may seem somewhat extravagant and improbable, I cannot refrain from concluding it with the assurance that it is literally true.

CHAPTER XIII

ABOUT the midle of June I arrived in London. Kinkel had already selected rooms for me on St. John's Wood Terrace, not far from his house, and he had also found pupils for me to whom I was to give lessons in the German language and in music, the proceeds of which would be more than sufficient to cover my modest wants. The well-known paradox that you can have more in London for a shilling and less for a pound, than anywhere else, that is to say, that you can live very cheaply and comparatively well in modest circumstances, while life on a grand scale is very expensive, was at that time as well founded as undoubtedly it still is. I could have found a great many more pupils if I had been able to speak English. But, strange as this appeared to myself in later life, my musical ear still rebelled against the sound of the English language, and could not conquer its repugnance. The peculiar charm of its cadence I began to appreciate only as I learned to speak it with fluency. In the social circles to which I was admitted, and of which I shall say something later, German and French were sufficient. In teaching German to others the Princess De Beaufort's method in teaching me French proved of great use to me.

Some of my pupils took a very lively interest in old German literature, and requested me to read with them the Nibelungenlied; and, as not seldom happens, in my rôle of teacher I learned more of the subject I had to teach than I had known before, and than I would have learned otherwise. I taught and learned with real enthusiasm, for—I may permit myself here to remark, by the way—the Nibelungenlied is, in my opinion, certainly not in elegance of diction, but surely in dramatic architecture, the grandest and most powerful epic presented by any medieval or modern literature.

In my social intercourse, the Kinkel family occupied naturally the first place. Their house was small, and modestly furnished. But in this house dwelled happiness. Kinkel had regained the whole cheerful elasticity of his being. His hair and beard were, to be sure, touched with gray, but the morbid pallor which his imprisonment had imparted to his face had yielded to the old fresh and healthy hue. With cheerful courage he had undertaken the task of founding for his family in a foreign country a comfortable existence, and his efforts were crowned with success. To the private lessons he gave were added lectures and other engagements at educational institutions. During the first months he had earned enough to give his wife an Erard grand piano, and Frau Kinkel won in a large social circle an excellent reputation as a teacher of music. The four children promised well as they grew up. There could have been nothing more pleasant and instructive than to see Frau Kinkel occupied with the education of her two boys and two girls. They not only began to play on the piano as soon as they were physically able, but they also sang with perfect purity of tone and naïve expession, quartets composed by their mother especially for them.

The joy I felt when I observed the new life of this family I cannot well describe. I learned to understand and appreciate one great truth: there is no purer or more beautiful happiness in this world than the consciousness of having contributed something toward the happiness of those one loves, without demanding any other reward than this consciousness.

The gratitude of Kinkel and his wife was so sincere and

untiring that it frequently embarrassed me. They constantly were looking for something that they could do to please me. At the time when I was thinking of settling down in London it was hard work for me to induce them to accept my declination when they uttered the wish that I should live in their house. Now I had at least to consent to their pressing proposition that my youngest sister should come over from Germany to be educated in their home, like a child of the family. This turned out happily, as my sister was also blessed with that cheerful Rhenish temperament that radiates sunshine. Then Frau Kinkel insisted upon giving me further lessons upon the piano, and I resumed my musical studies with renewed zest. My teacher taught me fully to appreciate Beethoven, Schubert, and Schumann, and conducted me through the enchanted gardens of Chopin. But more than that, she familiarized me with the rules and spirit of thorough-bass and thereby opened to me a knowledge which in the course of time I learned to value as an enrichment of musical enjoyment. Then she put at my disposal her Erard grand piano, which was reverenced in the family like a sacred thing, and upon which, aside from herself, I was the only one privileged to practice and to improvise, although there was, for such things, another instrument of less value in the house.

The Kinkels, naturally, introduced me also in the social circles which were open to them. Of course my ignorance of the English language I felt as a great drawback. But I had the good fortune of establishing relations of something like friendship with several English families in which German or French was spoken. There I learned to understand how much sincere warmth of feeling there may be hidden in English men and women who often appear cold, stiff and formal. I was soon made to feel that every word of friendly sympathy addressed to me, and every invitation to more intimate intercourse—words which with other people pass as mere superficial expressions of politeness—was to be taken as perfectly honest and seriously meant. Theirs was true hospitality, without pretension and without reserve, in which one breathed the atmosphere of assured confidence. I have also not infrequently been surprised in such friendly intercourse with persons who at first acquaintance seemed to be rather dull, by the reach of thought, the treasures of knowledge, the variety of experiences, and the comprehensive views of life and of the world, which came forth in familiar talks.

At that period, the German language was much in fashion in England, probably owing to the circumstance that the popularity of Prince Albert, whose merit as the patron of the great International Exposition of 1851 was universally recognized, had reached its highest point. It had become a widespread custom to sing German songs at evening parties and the German "Volkslieder," seemed to be especial favorites. I could not but be amused when in great company a blushing miss was solemnly conducted to the piano "to give us a sweet German folk song," and she then, in slow time and in a tone of profound melancholy, which might have indicated a case of death in the family, sang the merry German tune, "Wenn i' komm, wenn i' komm, wiederum komm," etc., etc.

In later years I have often regretted that at that time I did not take more interest in the political life of England and did not seek acquaintances in political circles. But even without this, I received a deep impression of the country and the people. How different was the restless commotion in the streets of London in its mighty seriousness and its colossal motive power, from the gay, more or less artistically elegant, but more than half frivolous activity that entertains the visitor on the streets of Paris; and how different from the half military, half philistine appearance presented by Berlin, which at that time had not yet become a world city! How well justified, how natural, appeared to me the national pride of the Briton, when in Westminster Hall I beheld the statues and busts, and in the Abbey the tombs of the great Englishmen, which stood there as monuments of mighty thoughts and deeds! How firmly founded appeared to me the free institutions of the people to whom civil liberty was not a mere phrase, a passing whim, or a toy, but a life-principle, the reality of which the citizen needed for his daily work, and that lived in the thoughts and aspirations of every Englishman as something that is a matter of course! I saw enough of the country and of the people to feel all this, although we refugees in London lived separate lives as on an island of our own in a great surrounding sea of humanity.

A large number of refugees from almost all parts of the European continent had gathered in London since the year 1848, but the intercourse between the different national groups —Germans, Frenchmen, Italians, Hungarians, Poles, Russians—was confined more or less to the prominent personages. All, however, in common nourished the confident hope of a revolutionary upturning on the continent soon to come. Among the Germans there were only a few who shared this hope in a less degree. Perhaps the ablest and most important person among these was Lothar Bucher, a quiet, retiring man of great capacity and acquirements, who occupied himself with serious political studies, and whom I was to meet again in later life as Bismarck's most confidential privy-councilor. In London, as in Switzerland, the refugees zealously discussed the question to whom should belong the leadership in the coming revolution. Of course this oversanguine conception of things gave rise to all sorts of jealousies, as will always happen among people similarly situated, and the refugees therefore divided into parties which at times antagonized one another with considerable bitterness.

When Kinkel arrived in London he occupied, naturally, a very prominent position among the refugees and became, so to speak, the head of a large following. But he also had his opponents who would recognize in him only a poet, a learned man and a political dreamer, but not a " practical revolutionist " fit to be a real leader in a great struggle. Many of these opponents gathered, strange to say, around Arnold Ruge, a venerable and widely known philosopher and writer, to whom the name of a mere learned man and political dreamer might have been applied even more justly. Then there were groups of socialistic workingmen who partly gathered around Karl Marx and partly around August Willich; and finally, many neutrals, who did not trouble themselves about such party bickerings, but went individually each his own way.

Kinkel certainly was not free from ambition, nor from illusory hopes of a speedy change in the Fatherland. But his first and most natural aim was to make a living for his family in London. This claimed his activity so much that he could not, to so great an extent as he might have wished, take part in the doings of the refugees, a great many of whom had no regular occupation. Neither was it possible for him to keep open house for his political friends and to put his working hours at their disposal, and to make the home of his family the meeting place of a debating club for the constant repetition of things that had been told many times before.

Kinkel was therefore reproached with giving to the cause of the revolution too little, and to his family interests too much of his time and care, and it was said that he was all the more to blame, as he owed his liberation in a high degree to the helpfulness of his democratic friends. However unjust such a reproach, it touched Kinkel deeply. He was in this state of mind when a scheme was proposed to him, characteristic of the feverish imagination of the political exiles. The scheme was to raise a "German National Loan," of I do not remember how many million thalers, to be redeemed at a certain time after the establishment of the German Republic. The money thus raised was to be at the disposal of a central committee to be expended in Germany for revolutionary ends. To expedite the levying of that national loan Kinkel was to go to America without delay, and by means of public agitation, in which his personal popularity and eminent oratorical gifts were expected to prove highly effective, induce the Germans living in America, and also, if possible, native Americans, too, to make liberal contributions. In the meantime some of his friends were, through personal efforts, to win the assent of other prominent refugees to this plan, and thus, if possible, to unite all refugeedom in one organization. But Kinkel was to leave for America forthwith without exposing the project to the chance of further consultation, so that the refugees, who otherwise might have doubted or criticised the plan, would have to deal with it as an accomplished fact.

In later years it must have appeared to Kinkel himself as rather strange, if not comical, that he could ever have believed in the success of such a plan. At any rate this project was one of the most striking illustrations of the self-deception of the political exiles. But there can hardly be any doubt that the reproaches directed against Kinkel, as to his giving more care to the well-being of his family than to the revolutionary cause, and as to his owing a debt of gratitude to one of his friends in further efforts for the revolutionary movement, was to him one of the principal motives for accepting this plan without hesitation. Only a few days after the matter had been resolved upon in a confidential circle Kinkel broke off his activity as a teacher in London—a very great sacrifice for him thus to expose his family to new hazards—and departed for America. I, being still quite young and inexperienced, was sanguine enough to consider the success of such an undertaking possible, and went into it with zeal. I was considered capable of doing some diplomatic service and therefore charged with the task of traveling to Switzerland in order to win the assent of the prominent refugees living there, and so to prepare the foundation for a general organization. This task I assumed with pleasure, and on the way paid a visit to Paris, of which I did not, however, advise the polite prefect of police, and soon met my old friends in Zürich.

For these, I had become, because of the liberation of Kinkel, an entirely new person since my departure a year before. They now attributed to me a great deal more insight and skill than I possessed, and my diplomatic mission, therefore, met with but little difficulty—that is to say, the prominent refugees, in the expectation that a national loan would, through Kinkel's agitations in America, turn out a great success, readily declared their willingness to join the proposed movement.

The most important man, and at the same time the most stubborn doubter, I found there, was Loewe von Calbe. As the last president of the German National Parliament he had gone in the spring of 1849 with the remnant of that assembly from Frankfurt to Stuttgart and there he had, arm in arm with the old poet Uhland, led the procession of his colleagues to a new meeting place, when it was dispersed by a force of Würtemberg cavalry. He was a physician by profession, and had acquired a large treasure of knowledge in various directions by extensive studies. He made the impression of a very calm, methodical

GOTTFRIED KINKEL AND CARL SCHURZ

thinker, who also possessed the courage of bold action. There was something of well-conditioned ease in his deportment, and when the sturdy, somewhat corpulent man sat down, looked at the listener with his uncommonly shrewd eyes, and then exposed his own opinion in well-formed, clear sentences, pronounced in slow and precise cadence, he made the impression of authority, the very presence of which was apt to convince, even before the argument had been conducted to its last conclusions. Loewe was not nearly as sanguine as most of us with regard to the possibility of a speedy change of things in Germany, although even he was not entirely untouched by the current illusions of the exiles' life. He expressed to me his doubts as to the chances of the projected national loan; but as he did not altogether repel the plan, and as I was anxious to win him for this enterprise by further conversations about it, I accompanied him on a tramp through the "Berner Oberland."

Until then I had seen the snowy heads of the Alps only from afar. Now for the first time I came near to them and, so to speak, sat down at their feet. We walked from Bern to Interlaken and then by way of Lauterbrunnen and the Wengern Alp to Grindelwald; then we ascended the Faulhorn, and finally turned to the lakes by way of the Scheideck. We stopped at the most beautiful points long enough to see the finest part of this range. Of all the wonderful things that I saw, the deepest impression was produced upon me not by the vast panoramas, as from the top of the Faulhorn, where large groups and chains of the Alps are embraced in one view, but it was the single mountain peak reaching up into the blue sunny ether from a bank of clouds that separated it from the nether world, and standing there as something distinct and individual. It was the image of the eternally firm, unchangeable, certain, looking down as from a throne in serene sunlight upon the eternally unstable and untrustworthy. This picture became especially impressive when behind a veil of cloud the dull mysterious thunder of the plunging avalanches was heard. As we were favored by constantly beautiful weather I enjoyed this spectacle frequently and always with a feeling that I cannot designate otherwise than devotional.

I was so deeply touched by all this magnificence that I envied every peasant who could spend his life in such surroundings. But my enthusiasm was sobered by an enlightening experience. On the village street of Grindelwald I noticed one day a man of an intelligent face, who was saluted by the children playing on the street, with especial interest. From his appearance I concluded that he must be the schoolmaster of the village, and I was not mistaken. I stopped and asked him for some information about local conditions, and found him amiably communicative. He told me that in the Valley of Grindelwald, a valley covering hardly more than four or five square miles, there were people who had never passed its boundaries. The whole world as seen by them was therefore enclosed by the Schreckhorn, Mönch, Eiger, Jungfrau and Faulhorn. In my enthusiasm I remarked that the constant sight of so magnificent a landscape might perhaps satisfy the taste of any man. The schoolmaster smiled and said that the ordinary peasant was probably least conscious of this grand beauty. He saw, in the phenomena of nature which he observed, rather that which was to him advantageous or disadvantageous, encouraging or troublesome, or even threatening. The cloud formations, which caused us a variety of sensations and emotions, signified to him only good or bad weather; the thunder of the avalanches reminded him only that under certain circumstances they might do a great deal of damage; he saw in the fury of the mountain hurricane, not a grand spectacle, but destructive hail storms and the danger of inundations, and so on.

I asked the schoolmaster whether it was not true what we frequently heard of the famous Swiss' homesickness, that those born and reared in these mountains could not be satisfied or happy elsewhere, and if forced to live in foreign parts, were consumed by a morbid longing for their mountain home. The schoolmaster smiled again and thought such cases of homesickness did occur among the Swiss, but not in larger number nor with greater force than with the inhabitants of other regions. Everywhere he supposed there might be people that adhere to the habits and conditions of life of their homes with a warm and even morbid attachment. But he knew also of a large number of Swiss who in foreign countries, even on the flat prairies of America, had settled down and felt themselves well satisfied there.

" Am I to understand from you," I asked, " that as a rule the Swiss himself does not appreciate the beauty of his country?"

" No, not that," answered the schoolmaster; " the more educated people know everywhere how to appreciate the beautiful because of its beauty; but the laboring man, who here is always engaged in a struggle with nature, must be told that the things which are to him so often troublesome and disagreeable, are also grand and beautiful. When his thought has once been directed to that idea, he will more and more familiarize himself with it, and the Swiss," added the schoolmaster with a sly smile, " also the uneducated Swiss, have now learned to appreciate the beauty of their country very highly."

This sounded to me at first like a very prosaic philosophy, but as I thought about it, I concluded that the schoolmaster was right. The perception of natural beauty is not primitive, but the result of education, of culture. Naïve people seldom possess it or at least do not express it. The aspects of nature, mountain, valley, forest, desert, river, sea, sunshine, storm, etc., etc., are to them either beneficent, helpful, or disagreeable, troublesome, terrible. It is a significant fact that in Homer with all the richness of his pictures there is no description of a landscape or of a natural phenomenon from the point of view of the beautiful. We remark the same in the primitive literature of other countries. In the same spirit spoke the farmer from one of the flat prairies of the west of America, who once traveled on a steamboat on the magnificent Hudson, and when he heard an enthusiastic fellow-traveler exclaim, "How beautiful these highlands are," answered dryly, "It may be a pretty good country, but it's a little too broken."

My diplomatic mission in Switzerland was quickly accomplished. I soon had the assent of almost all the prominent exiles to the plan of the national loan and I thought I had done a good service to the cause of liberty. Then I returned to London. Frau Kinkel asked me to live in her house during the absence of her husband, and I complied with her wish, but life in that house was no longer as cheerful as before Kinkel's departure. I then felt how great the sacrifice was that Kinkel had made by undertaking the mission to America. Frau Johanna had seen him go with sadness and anxiety. She could not be blamed for thinking that the burden imposed upon her by the political friends was all too heavy. She accepted her lot, but not without serious dejection. Her health began to suffer, and conditions of nervousness appeared, and it is probable that then the beginning of that heart disease developed which a few years later brought her to an early grave. The news which we received from Kinkel, was indeed, as far as he himself was concerned, very satisfactory; but it did not suffice to cheer the darkened soul of the lonely woman, however heroically she tried to seek courage in her patriotic impulses and hopes.

Kinkel had much to tell in his letters of the cordiality with which the Germans in America had welcomed him. Wherever he appeared his countrymen gathered in large numbers to listen to the charm of his eloquence. As he traveled from city to city one festive welcome followed another. The enthusiasm of the mass meetings left nothing to be desired. Although Kinkel at that period spoke English with some difficulty, he was obliged to make little speeches in that tongue, when native Americans took part in the honors offered to him. So he visited all the important places in the United States, north, south, east, and west. He also paid his respects to President Fillmore and was received with great kindness. These happenings he described with bubbling humor in his letters, which breathed a keen enjoyment of his experiences, as well as a warm interest in the new country. In short, his journey was successful in all respects, except in that of the German National Loan. Indeed, committees were organized everywhere for the collection of money and for the distribution of loan certificates; but the contributions finally amounted only to a few thousand dollars, a small sum with which no great enterprise could be set on foot. Kossuth, who visited the United States a few months later for a similar purpose, and who enjoyed a greater prestige, and was received with much more pomp, had the same experience. And it was really a fortunate circumstance that these revolutionary loans miscarried. Even with much larger sums hardly anything could have been done but to organize hopeless conspiracies and to lead numbers of patriotic persons into embarrassment and calamity without rendering any valuable service to the cause of liberty.

At that time, however, we thought otherwise. Emissaries

were sent to Germany to investigate conditions there and to build up the revolutionary organization—that is to say, to find people who lived in the same illusions as the exiles, and to put these in correspondence with the London Committee preparatory to common action. Some of these emissaries exposed themselves to great dangers in traveling from place to place, and most of them returned with the report that there was general discontent in Germany and that an important disturbance might soon be looked for. That there was much discontent in Germany was undoubtedly true. But of those who really dreamed of another general uprising there were only a few. The revolutionary fires had burned out; but the exile was so unwilling to accept this truth as to be inclined to look upon everybody that expressed it as a suspicious person. He therefore worked steadily on.

At that time I was favored by what I considered a mark of great distinction. One day I received a letter from Mazzini, written in his own hand, in which he invited me to visit him. He gave me the address of one of his confidential friends who would guide me to him. His own address he kept secret, for the reason, as was generally believed, that he desired to baffle the espionage of monarchical governments. That the great Italian patriot should invite me, a young and insignificant person, and so take me into his confidence, I felt to be an extraordinary distinction. Mazzini was looked upon in revolutionary circles, especially by us young people, as the dictatorial head of numberless secret leagues, as a sort of mysterious power which not only in Italy, but in all Europe, was felt and feared. Wonderful stories were told of his secret journeys in countries in which there was a price on his head; of his sudden, almost miraculous, apearance among his faithful followers here and there; of his equally miraculous disappearance, as if the earth had swallowed him; and of the unequaled skill with which he possessed himself of the secrets of the governments, while he knew how to conceal his own plans and acts. By us young men he was regarded as the embodied genius of revolutionary action, and we looked up to his mysterious greatness with a sort of reverential awe. I therefore felt, when I was called into his presence, as if I were to enter the workshop of the master magician.

The confidential friend designated by Mazzini conducted me to the dwelling of the great leader, situated in an unfashionable street. In the vicinity of his house we met several black-eyed, bearded young men, manifestly Italians, who seemed to patrol the neighborhood. I found Mazzini in an extremely modest little apartment, which served at the same time as drawing room and office. In the middle of the room there was a writing table covered with an apparently confused heap of papers. Little models of guns and mortars served for paper weights; a few chairs, and, if I remember correctly, a hair-cloth sofa, completed the furniture. The room as a whole made the impression of extreme economy.

Mazzini was seated at the writing table when I entered, and, rising, he offered me his hand. He was a slender man of medium stature, clad in a black suit. His coat was buttoned up to the throat, around which he wore a black silk scarf, without any show of linen. His face was of regular, if not classic, cut, the lower part covered with a short, black beard, streaked with gray. The dark eyes glowed with restless fire; his domelike forehead topped with thin, smooth, dark hair. In speaking, the mouth showed a full, but somewhat dark row of teeth. His whole appearance was that of a serious and important man. Soon I felt myself under the charm of a personality of rare power of attraction.

Our conversation was carried on in French, which Mazzini spoke with perfect ease, although with some of the accent peculiar to the Italians. He was constantly smoking while he spoke. He developed even in this confidential conversation between two men an eloquence such as in my long life I have hardly ever heard again—warm, insinuating, at times vehement, enthusiastic, lofty, and always thoroughly natural. The three greatest conversationalists with whom it has been my good fortune to come into touch were Mazzini, Dr. Oliver Wendell Holmes and Bismarck. Of these Dr. Holmes was the most spirited in the "bel esprit" sense; Bismarck the most imposing and at the same time the most entertaining in point of wit, sarcasm, anecdote, and narratives of historical interest, brought out with rushing vivacity and with lightning-like illumination of conditions, facts and men. But in Mazzini's words there breathed such a warmth and depth of conviction, such enthusiasm of faith in the sacredness of the principles he professed, and of the aims he pursued, that it was difficult to resist such a power of fascination. While looking at him and hearing him speak I could well understand how he could hold and constantly augment the host of his faithful adherents, how he could lead them into the most dangerous enterprises and keep them under his influence even after the severest disappointments.

Mazzini had undoubtedly given up, if not formally, yet in fact, his membership in his church. But there was in him, and there spoke out of him, a deep religious feeling, an instinctive reliance upon a higher Power to which he could turn and which would aid him in the liberation and unification of his people. That was his form of the fatalism so often united with great ambitions. He had a trait of prophetic mysticism which sprung from the depths of his convictions and emotions, and was free of all charlatanism, and all affectation, all artificial solemnity. At least that was the impression made upon me. I never observed in him any suggestion of cynicism in his judgment of men and things—that cynicism in which many revolutionary characters pleased themselves. The petty and usually ridiculous rivalries among the leaders of the exiles did not seem to touch him; and discord and quarreling among those who should have stood and worked together, instead of eliciting sharp and offensive criticism on his part, only called from him expressions of sincere and painful regret. The revolution he aimed at was not merely the attainment of certain popular rights, not a mere change in the constitution of the state, not the mere liberation of his countrymen from foreign rule, not the mere reunion of all Italy in a national bond; it rather signified to him the elevation of the liberated people to higher moral aims of life. There vibrated a truthful and noble tone in his conception of human relations, in the modest self-denying simplicity of his character and his life, in the unbounded self-sacrifice and self-denial which he imposed upon himself and demanded of others. Since 1839 he had passed a large part of his life as an exile in London, and in the course of this time he had established relations of intimate friendship with some English families. It was undoubtedly owing to the genuineness of his sentiments, the noble simplicity of his nature, and his unselfish devotion to his cause, not less than to his brilliant personal qualities, that in some of those families a real Mazzini-cult had developed which sometimes showed itself capable of great sacrifices.

The historic traditions of his people, as well as the circumstance that to the end of liberating his fatherland he had to fight against foreign rule, made him a professional conspirator. As a young man he had belonged to the "Carbonari," and then there followed—instigated and conducted by him—one conspiracy upon another, resulting in insurrectionary attempts which always failed. But these failures did not discourage him; they rather stimulated his zeal to new efforts. In the course of our conversation he gave me to understand that he had preparations going on for a new enterprise in upper Italy, and as he probably considered me a person of influence in that part of German refugeedom which would control the disposition of our prospective national loan, he wished to know whether we would be inclined to support his undertaking with our money. At any rate, he evidently desired to create among us a disposition favorable to such coöperation. He no doubt took me for a more influential person than I was. I could only promise him to discuss the matter with Kinkel and his associates, after his return from America. But I did not conceal from Mazzini that I doubted whether the responsible German leaders would consider themselves justified in using moneys which had been collected for employment in their own country for the furtherance of revolutionary uprisings in Italy. This remark gave Mazzini an opportunity for some eloquent sentiments about the solidarity of peoples in their struggle for liberty and national existence. At that time neither of us knew yet how small would be the result of the agitation for a German national loan.

I was honored with another meeting that has remained to me hardly less memorable. In October, 1851, Louis Kossuth came to England. After the breakdown of the Hungarian revolution he had fled across the Turkish frontier. His remaining on Turkish soil was considered objectionable by the Austrian government, and unsafe by his friends. The Sultan, indeed, refused his extradition. But when the republic of the United States of America, in general sympathy with the unfortunate Hungarian patriots, offered them an American ship-of-war for their transportation to the United States that offer was unhesitatingly accepted. But Kossuth did not intend to emigrate to America for the purpose of establishing there his permanent residence. He was far from considering his mission as ended and the defeat of his cause as irretrievable. He, too, with the sanguine temperament of the exile, dreamed of the possibility of inducing the liberal part of the old and also of the new world to take up arms against the oppressors of Hungary, or at least to aid his country by diplomatic interference. And, indeed, could this have been accomplished by a mere appeal to the emotions and the imagination, Kossuth would have been the man to achieve it. Of all the events of the years 1848 and 1849, the heroic struggle of the Hungarians for their national independence had excited the liveliest sympathy in other countries. The brave generals, who for a time went from victory to victory and then succumbed to the overwhelming power of the Russian intervention, appeared like the champions of a heroic legend, and among and above them stood the figure of Kossuth like that of a prophet whose burning words kindled and kept alive the fire of patriotism in the hearts of his people. There was everything of heroism and tragic misfortune to make this epic grand and touching, and the whole romance of the revolutionary time found in Kossuth's person its most attractive embodiment. The sonorous notes of his eloquence had, during the struggle, been heard far beyond the boundaries of Hungary in the outside world. Not a few of his lofty sentences, his poetic illustrations and his thrilling appeals had passed from mouth to mouth among us young people at the German universities. And his picture, with thoughtful forehead, the dreamy eyes and his strong, beard-framed chin, became everywhere an object of admiring reverence.

When now, delaying his journey to America, he arrived

in London the enthusiasm of the English people seemed to know no bounds. His entry was like that of a national hero returning from a victorious campaign. The multitudes crowding the streets were immense. He appeared in his picturesque Hungarian garb, standing upright in his carriage, with his saber at his side, and surrounded by an equally picturesque retinue. But when he began to speak, and his voice, with its resonant and at the same time mellow sound, poured forth its harmony over the heads of the throngs in classic English, deriving a peculiar charm from the soft tinge of foreign accent, then the enthusiasm of the listeners mocked all description.

Kossuth had been offered the hospitality of the house of a private citizen of London who took an especial interest in the Hungarian cause; and there during his sojourn in the British capital he received his admirers and friends. A kind of court surrounded him; his companions, always in their Hungarian national dress, maintained in a ceremonious way his pretension of his still being the rightful governor of Hungary. He granted audiences like a prince, and when he entered the room he was announced by an aide-de-camp as "the Governor." All persons rose and Kossuth saluted them with grave solemnity. Among the exiles of other nations these somewhat undemocratic formalities created no little displeasure. But it was Kossuth's intention to produce certain effects upon public opinion, not in his own, but in his people's behalf, and as to that end it may have seemed to him necessary to impress upon the imagination of the Englishmen the picture of Hungary under her own Governor, and also to illustrate to them the firm faith of the Hungarians themselves in the justice of their cause, it was not improper that he used such picturesque displays as means for the accomplishment of his purpose.

Our organization of German refugees also sent a deputation to Kossuth to pay their respects, and of that deputation I was one. We were ushered into the reception-room in the customary way and there salutued by aides-de-camp with much gold lace on their coats—handsome fellows, with fine black mustaches and splendid white teeth. At last Kossuth appeared. It was the first time that I came near to him. The speaker of our deputation introduced us each by name, and as mine was called Kossuth reached out his hand to me and said in German: "I know you. You have done a noble deed. I am rejoiced to take your hand." I was so embarrassed that I could not say anything in response. But it was, after all, a proud moment. A short conversation followed, in which I took but small part. A member of our deputation spoke of the socialistic tendencies of the new revolutionary agitation. I remember distinctly what Kossuth answered. It was to this effect: "I know nothing of socialism. I have never occupied myself with it. My aim is to secure for the Hungarian people national independence and free political institutions. When that is done my task will have been performed."

On public occasions, wherever Kossuth put forth his whole eloquence to inflame the enthusiasm of Englishmen for the Hungarian cause, his hearers always rewarded him with frantic applause; but his efforts to induce the British government to take active steps against Russia and Austria in behalf of Hungary could not escape sober criticism, and all his attempts to get the ear of official circles and to come into confidential touch with the Palmerston ministry came to nothing. In fact, the same experience awaited him in the United States: great enthusiasm for his person and for the heroic struggles of his people, but then sober consideration of the traditional policy of the United States, and an unwillingness to abandon that traditional policy by active intervention in the affairs of the old world.

Before Kossuth began his agitation in America, Kinkel had returned from there. He had much to tell of the new world that was good and beautiful, although he was obliged to confess to himself that the practical result of his mission was discouragingly trifling. With robust energy he resumed his interrupted activity as a teacher, and with him the old sunshine returned to the Kinkel home.

CHAPTER XIV

IN the autumn of 1851 the refugees in London, especially the Germans, found a common meeting-place in the drawing-room of a born aristocrat, the Baroness von Brüning, née Princess Lieven, from one of the German provinces of Russia. She was then a little more than thirty years old; not exactly beautiful, but of an open, agreeable, winning expression of face, fine manners and a stimulating gift of conversation. How, with her aristocratic birth and social position, she had dropped into the democratic current I do not know. Probably the reports of the struggles for liberty in Western Europe, which crossed the Russian frontier, had inflamed her imagination, and her vivacious nature had indulged itself in incautious utterances against the despotic rule of the Emperor Nicholas. In short, she found life in Russia intolerable, or, may be, she was in danger of arrest had she not left her native country. For some time she lived in Germany and in Switzerland, and there became acquainted with various liberal leaders. She had also corresponded with Frau Kinkel and contributed a portion of the money which was employed in Kinkel's liberation. But on the European continent she believed herself constantly pursued by Russian influences; and no doubt the police, at least in Germany, made itself quite disagreeable to her. So she sought at last refuge on English soil, and in order to be in constant contact with persons of her own way of thinking she settled down in the midst of the Colony of German refugees in the suburb of St. John's Wood. She was most cordially received by the

Kinkel family, and attempted to manage the social part of their establishment. This, however, soon proved impossible. The rich woman, reared in affluent circumstances, could hardly understand that a family obliged to work for its daily living with the most strenuous activity had to husband its time as well as its means with the strictest economy, and could allow itself the luxury of an agreeable social intercourse only to a limited extent. The industry and devotion to duty of the Kinkels could hardly accord with the well-meaning but somewhat extravagant intentions of Baroness Brüning. She hired a spacious house on St. John's Wood Terrace, opened her salon with great hospitality to her friends, and a numerous circle of refugees met there almost every evening.

The Baroness was surrounded by her husband and her children, and the sociability of her house was that of agreeable family life. Baron Brüning indeed did not seem to feel himself quite at home with the friends that visited his drawing-room. He was a distinguished-looking, quiet gentleman, of fine breeding and manners, who, if his ideas did not harmonize with the political principles and teachings that found voice around him, did not make the guests of his house feel his dissent. When the political opinions uttered in his presence happened to be too extreme a somewhat ironical smile would play about his lips; and he met the constantly recurring prophecy, that soon all dynasties on the European Continent would be upset and a family of republics take their place, with the quiet question: "Do you really think that this will soon happen?" But he was always pleasant and obliging, and never failed to fill his place in the social circle and welcomed everybody who was welcome to his wife. The more thoughtful among the guests, and those who had mental interests outside of revolutionary politics, recognized it as a matter of good breeding to reciprocate the amiability of the Baron with every possible attention; and they found in him a well-meaning and well-informed man, who had read much and had formed very clear opinions about many subjects. Thus relations of a certain confidentiality developed themselves between him and some of his guests, of whom I was one; and if he ever talked about his domestic conditions the impression was conveyed that he looked upon the democratic enthusiasms of his wife, with all its consequences, as a matter of fate which must be submitted to. The cause of his compliance with all her eccentricities was by some of us supposed to be that the fortune of the family had come from her side, but it is just as likely that it was the usual helplessness of the weaker will against the stronger, and that the Baron permitted himself to be whirled from place to place and from one social circle to another, although undesirable to him, because the power of resistance was not one of his otherwise excellent qualities. However, the two spoke of one another always with the greatest and most unaffected esteem and warmth, and the Baron made the education of his children the special object of his care and endeavor.

Baroness Brüning was almost entirely absorbed with the society of the exiles. She was not a woman of great mental gifts. Her knowledge was somewhat superficial and her thinking not profound. She possessed the education of "good society," and with it true goodness of heart in the most amiable form. As is usually the case with women whose views and opinions spring more from the emotions of the heart than from a clear and sober observation of things and proper conclusions drawn by the understanding, she devoted her enthusiasms and sympathies more to persons than to principles, endeavors and objects. Such women are frequently accused of an inordinate desire to please, and it may indeed have flattered the Baroness to be the center of a social circle in which there were many men and women of superior mind and character, but her enthusiastic nature was so genuine, her desire to offer a home to the exiles so indefatigable, her sympathy with every case of suffering so self-sacrificing, and her character, with all the freedom of personal intercourse, so perfectly spotless and unassailable, that she would easily have been forgiven much greater vanity. For many of the refugees she was really a good fairy. One she enabled at her own expense to send for his long-betrothed bride from Germany; for another she procured a decent dwelling, and made a secret agreement with the landlord according to which she paid part of the rent; she ran about to procure occupation as a teacher for a third; for a fourth, an artist, she got orders; to a fifth she was the sister of mercy in illness. With watchful providence she sought to learn from one what the other might want and what she might do to help, for she was always careful to hide the helping hand. Her self-sacrificing lavishness went so far that she imposed upon herself all sorts of privations to help others with her savings. Thus she had only one gown in which to appear in the salon. This was of purple satin and had in bygone times doubtless appeared very elegant; but as she constantly wore it there was visible on it not only threadbare spots, but even patches. Some of the ladies of our circle talked to her about it, and she replied: "Ah, yes, it is true I must have a new gown; I have been frequently on my way to a dressmaker, but every time something more necessary occurred to me and I turned back." The old gown had therefore to do service throughout another entire winter. There could have been nothing more charming than the zeal with which in her drawing-room she sought to cheer the depressed and to minister consolation and courage to the downcast, and I still see her, as with her sparkling blue eyes she sat among us and talked eloquently about the great change that was to take place and the good time which must inevitably soon come, and would triumphantly carry us all back into the fatherland. And with all this she was tormented with a disease of the heart which caused her sometimes great suffering and the foreboding of an early death. One day, when I accompanied her on a walk, she suddenly stood still and clutched my arm. Her breath seemed to stop. I looked at her in terror. She had closed her eyes with an expression of pain. At last she opened her eyes again and said: "Did you hear my heart beat? I shall soon die. I can live hardly more than a year. But do not tell anybody. I did not mean to speak of it, but it has just now escaped me." I tried to quiet her apprehensions, but in vain. "No," she said, "I know it, but it does not matter. Now let us talk about something else." Her presentiment was to come true only too quickly.

In the circle of the Brüning house there were some interesting and able men who had already proved their worth or were destined to prove it in later life. There was Loewe, who, shortly after I had met him in Switzerland, had left the Continent and sought a secure asylum in England. There was Count Oscar von Reichenbach of Silesia, a man of much knowledge and a thoroughly noble nature. There was Oppenheim, a writer of uncommon wit and large acquirements. There was Willich, the socialist leader, and Schimmelpfennig, two future American generals. The good Strodtmann, who had followed us to London, was frequently seen there. We also met there birds of passage of a different kind. One day a Frenchman from Marseilles, by the name of Barthélemi, was introduced, I do not remember by whom, in the Brüning salon and pointed out as a specially remarkable personage. His past had indeed been remarkable enough. Already before the revolution of 1848 he had taken part in a secret conspiracy, the so-called "Marianne," had, after being designated by lot, killed a police officer, and had been sentenced to a term in the galleys. In consequence of the revolution of 1848 he was set free, then fought on the barricades in the socialist rising in Paris, in June, 1848—the bloody "June Battle"—whereupon he succeeded in escaping to England. It was said of him that he had killed several persons: some in duels, some without that formality. Now he passed as a "workingman," whose principal occupation was that of the professional conspirator. He stands before my eyes now as he entered the Brüning salon and took his seat near the fireplace: a man of a little more than thirty years, of sturdy figure, a face of dusky paleness with black mustache and goatee, the dark eyes glowing with piercing fire. He spoke in a deep, sonorous voice, slowly and measuredly with dogmatic assurance, waving off contrary opinions with a word of compassionate disdain. With the greatest coolness he explained to us his own theory of the revolution, which simply provided that the contrary minded without much ado be exterminated. The man expressed himself with great clearness, like one who had thought much and deliberately upon his subject and had drawn his conclusions by means of the severest logic. We saw before us, therefore, one of those fanatics that are not seldom produced in revolutionary times—men perhaps of considerable ability, whose understanding of the moral order of the universe has been thoroughly confused by his constant staring at one point; who has lost every conception of abstract right; to whom any crime appears permissible, nay, as a virtuous act, if it serves as a means to his end; who regards everybody standing in the way as outside of the protection of the law; who consequently is ever ready to kill anybody and to sacrifice also his own life for his nebulous objects. Such fanatics are capable of becoming as cruel as wild beasts and also of dying like heroes. It was quite natural that several of those who listened to Barthélemi in the

Brüning salon felt uneasy in his company. Never was Barthélemi seen there again. A few years later, in 1855, he came to a characteristic end. He had been living constantly in London, but retired more and more from his friends because, as was said, he lived with a woman to whom he was passionately attached. It was reported also that he was acquainted with a wealthy Englishman whom he often visited. One day he called at the house of that Englishman with the woman mentioned. He carried a traveling satchel in his hand, like one who was on his way to a railroad station. Suddenly the report of a pistol shot was heard in the apartment of the Englishman, and Barthélemi, pursued by the cries of a woman servant, ran out of the house with his mistress. The Englishman was found dead in a pool of blood in his room. A police officer who tried to stop Barthélemi on the street also fell mortally wounded by Barthélemi's pistol. A crowd rapidly gathering stopped the murderer, disarmed him and delivered him to the authorities. The woman escaped in the confusion and was never seen again. All attempts to make Barthélemi disclose his curious relations with the murdered Englishman were vain. He wrapped himself in the deepest silence, and, so far as I know, the mysterious story has never been cleared up. There was only a rumor that Barthélemi had intended to go to Paris and kill Louis Napoleon, that the Englishman had promised him the necessary money, but had refused it at the decisive moment, and that at their last meeting Barthélemi had shot him, either in order to get possession of the money or in a rage at the refusal. Another rumor had it that the woman was only a spy of the French government, sent to London with instructions to watch Barthélemi and finally to betray him. Barthélemi was tried for murder in the first degree, sentenced to death, and hanged. He met death with the greatest composure, and exclaimed, in the face of the gallows, "In a few moments, now, I shall see the great mystery!" and then died with calm dignity.

My dear old friend, Fräulein Malwida von Meysenbug, has told the story with great warmth in her remarkable book, "The Memoirs of an Idealist." The reader will find there a very striking example of the impression which a personality like Barthélemi's, whatever the cool judgment of the understanding and the voice of justice about him may be, could make upon the soul of a woman of a superior mind and of a susceptible imagination. The execution of Barthélemi revolted her feelings and moved her to tears, but nothing could be more certain than that if a pardon had liberated him his insane fanaticism which made him speak of a murder as of a breakfast would have led him to other bloody deeds, and would finally again have placed him in the hands of the hangman.

Malwida von Meysenbug was one of my most valued friends in the Brüning circle. She was the daughter of Herr von Meysenbug, a minister of the Elector of Hesse-Cassel, who, probably unjustly, had been regarded as a stiff aristocrat and absolutist. After long inward struggles, in which a profound attachment to a young democrat, the brother of my friend, Friedrich Althaus, played an important part, Malwida openly declared herself an adherent of democratic principles; found it impossible to remain longer with her family; went in the year 1849-50 to Hamburg to co-operate with some kindred spirits of liberal sentiments in founding a high school for young women; came into some conflict with the police through her acquaintance and correspondence with democrats, and, especially attracted by the Kinkels, landed in London in our circle. She has herself described her development and the vicissitudes of her life with characteristic frankness and in an exceedingly interesting fashion in the book already mentioned—"The

Memoirs of an Idealist." When we met in London she may have been about thirty-five, but she looked older than she really was. In point of appearance, she had not been favored by nature, but her friends soon became accustomed to overlook that disadvantage in the appreciation of her higher qualities. She had read much and had many opinions, which she maintained with great energy. With the most zealous interest she followed the events of the time on the political as well as on the literary, scientific and artistic field. She was animated by an almost vehement and truly eloquent enthusiasm for all that appeared to her good and noble and beautiful. She felt the impulse, wherever possible, to lend a hand, and pursued her endeavors with a zeal and an earnestness which made her occasionally a severe judge of what seemed to her a light-minded or frivolous treatment of important things. Her whole being was so honest, simple and unpretending, the goodness of her heart so inexhaustible, her sympathies so real and self-sacrificing, her principles so genuine and faithful, that everybody who learned to know her well readily forgave her that trait of imaginative eccentricity which appeared sometimes in her views and enthusiasms, but which really was to be attributed to the excitability of her temperament and the innate kindness and nobility of her heart. The tone of conversation in the Brüning salon did not always please her. When she carried on serious discourse with a member of our circle about important subjects the lighthearted merriment of others was apt to jar upon her. The Baroness herself could not follow her much in the grave treatment which Malwida bestowed upon all questions of consequence, but their personal sympathies still held them together.

The books written by Malwida von Meysenbug, long after the time of which I speak, reveal a human soul of the finest instincts and impulses, and, in spite of many disappointments, of touching faithfulness to high principles and aspirations. One of them, the "Memoirs of an Idealist," owed to its exquisite charms of noble sentiment and genuine sincerity the rare good fortune of reappearing in literature after a long period of seeming oblivion. She lived to a high old age, the last thirty years in Rome, as the center of a large circle of friends, many of them distinguished characters, who clung to her inspiring personality with singular affection. We remained warm friends to the end.

Now to return to my narrative—an event occurred which essentially darkened the horizon of refugeedom, and which also gave to my fate an unexpected and decisive turn.

The reports which we had received from our friends in Paris made us believe that Louis Napoleon, the president of the French republic, was an object of general contempt, that he played a really ridiculous figure with his manifest ambition to restore the empire in France and to mount the throne, and that every attempt to accomplish this by force would inevitably result in his downfall and in the institution of a strong and truly republican government. The tone of the opposition papers in Paris gave much color to this view. Suddenly, on the 2d of December, 1851, the news arrived in London that Louis Napoleon had actually undertaken the long-expected coup d'état. He had secured the support of the army, had occupied the meeting-place of the national assembly with troops, had arrested the leaders of the opposition, as well as General Changarnier, who had been intrusted by the national assembly with its protection, had laid his hand upon several other generals suspected of republican sentiments, had published a decree restoring universal suffrage, which had been restricted by the national assembly, and issued a proclamation to the French people. In this he accused the parliamentary parties of criminal selfishness and demanded the establishment of a consulate, the consul to hold office for ten years. Exciting reports arrived in rapid succession. Members of the national assembly had met in considerable numbers and tried to organize resistance to the coup d'état, but were soon dispersed by military force. At last the news came that the people, too, were beginning to "descend into the streets" and to build barricades. Now the decisive battle was to be fought.

It is impossible to describe the state of mind produced among the exiles by these reports. We Germans ran to the meeting-places of the French clubs, because we expected to receive there the clearest and most reliable tidings, perhaps from sources which might not be open to the general public. In these clubs we found a feverish excitement bordering upon madness. Our French friends shouted and shrieked and gesticulated and hurled opprobrious names at Louis Napoleon and cursed his helpers, and danced the Carmagnole and sang "Ça Ira." All were sure of a victory of the people. The most glorious bulletins of the progress of the street fight went from mouth to mouth. Some of them were proclaimed by wild-looking revolutionary exiles, who had jumped upon tables, and frantic screams of applause welcomed them. So it went on a night, a day and again a night. Sleep was out of the question. There was hardly time for the necessary meals. The reports of victory were followed by others that sounded less favorable. They could not and would not be believed. They were "the dispatches of the usurper and his slaves"; "they lied"; "they could not do otherwise than lie"; but the messages continued more and more gloomy. The barricades which the people had erected in the night of the 2d and 3d of December had been taken by the army without much trouble. On the 4th a serious battle occurred on the streets of the Faubourgs St. Martin and St. Denis, but there, too, the troops had remained masters of the field. Then the soldiery rushed into the houses and murdered without discrimination or compassion. At last there was the quiet of the graveyard in the great city. The popular rising had been comparatively insignificant and powerless. The usurper who had but recently been represented as a weak-minded adventurer, the mere "nephew of his uncle," had succeeded in subjugating Paris. The departments did not move; there was no doubt the Republic was at an end, and with its downfall vanished also the prospect of the new revolutionary upheaval, which, on the impulse coming from France, was expected to spread over the whole European continent.

Stunned by all these terrible reports, and mentally as well as physically exhausted, we quietly returned to our quarters. After I had recuperated from this consuming excitement by a long sleep I tried to become clear in my mind about the changed situation of things. It was a foggy day, and I went out because I found it impossible to sit still within my four walls. Absorbed in thought, I wandered on without any definite aim, and found myself at last in Hyde Park, where, in spite of the chilly air, I sat down on a bench. In whatever light I might consider the downfall of the republic and the advent of a new monarchy in France, one thing seemed to me certain: All the efforts connected with the revolution of 1848 were now hopeless; a period of decided and general reaction was bound to come, and whatever the future might bring of further developments in the direction of liberal movement must necessarily have a new starting-point.

With this conviction my own situation became equally clear to me. It would have been childish to give myself up to further illusory hopes of a speedy return to the Fatherland. To continue our plottings and thereby bring still more mischief upon others, appeared to me a reckless and wicked game. I had long recognized the exile's life to be empty and enervating. I felt an irresistible impulse not only to find for myself a well-regulated activity, but also to do something really and truly valuable for the general good. But where, and how? The fatherland was closed to me. England was to me a foreign country, and would always remain so. Where, then? "To America," I said to myself. "The ideals of which I have dreamed and for which I have fought I shall find there, if not fully realized, but hopefully struggling for full realization. In that struggle I shall perhaps be able to take some part. It is a new world, a free world, a world of great ideas and aims. In that world there is perhaps for me a new home. Ubi libertas ibi patria—I formed my resolution on the spot. I would remain only a short time longer in England to make some necessary preparations, and then—off to America!

I had sat perhaps half an hour on that bench in Hyde Park, immersed in my thoughts, when I noticed that on the other end of the bench a man was sitting who seemed likewise to be musingly staring at the ground. He was a little man, and as I observed him more closely I believed I recognized him. Indeed, I did. It was Louis Blanc, the French socialist leader, a former member of the provisional government of France. I had recently in some social gathering been introduced to him, and he had talked with me in a very amiable and animated way. Indeed, I had found him uncommonly attractive. When I was through with my own thoughts I arose to go away without intending to disturb him, but he lifted his head, looked at me with eyes that seemed not to have known sleep for several nights, and said, "Ah, c'est vous, mon jeune ami! c'est fini, n'est ce pas? C'est fini!" We pressed one another's hands. His head sank again upon his breast, and I went my way home to inform my parents at once, by letter, of the resolution I had taken on that bench in Hyde Park. Some of my fellow-exiles tried to dissuade me from it, picturing to me all sorts of wonderful things which would happen very soon on the European continent and in which we refugees must take an active part; but I had seen too thoroughly through the unreality of these fantastic imaginings to be shaken in my resolve.

Now something happened that infused into my apparently gloomy situation a radiance of sunshine and opened to my life unlooked-for prospects. A few weeks previous to Louis Napoleon's coup d'état I had some business to transact with another German exile, and visited him in his residence in Hampstead. I vividly remember how I went there on foot, through rows of hedges and avenues of trees, where now, probably, is a dense mass of houses, not anticipating that a meeting of far greater importance than that with him was in store for me. My business was soon disposed of and I rose to go, but my friend stopped me and called out into an adjacent room, "Margaretha, come in, if you please, here is a gentleman with whom I wish you to become acquainted. This is my sister-in-law," he added, turning to me, "just arrived from Hamburg on a visit." A girl of about eighteen years entered, of fine stature, a curly head, something childlike in her beautiful features and large, dark, truthful eyes. This was my introduction to my future wife.

On the 6th of July, 1852, we were married in the parish church of Marylebone in London. I have put down in writing how it all came to pass in those otherwise gloomy days; but that part of my story naturally belongs to my children only and to our inner home circle.

In August we were ready to sail for America. Before my departure Mazzini invited me to visit him once more. He con-

CARL SCHURZ AND HIS WIFE

fided to me the secret of a revolutionary enterprise which he had in hand and which, as he said, promised great results. There was to be a new uprising in Lombardy. With his glowing eloquence he pictured to me how the Italian soldiers of liberty would crowd the Austrians into the Alps, and how then similar movements would spring from this victorious insurrection in all other countries of the European Continent, and that then such young men as I should be on the spot to help carry on the work so prosperously begun. "All this will happen," he said, "before you will reach America, or shortly after. How you will wish not to have left us! You will take the next ship to return to Europe. Save yourself this unnecessary voyage." I had to confess to him that my hopes were not so sanguine as his; that I did not see in the condition of things on the Continent any prospect of a change soon to come, which might call me back to the Fatherland and to a fruitful activity; that, if in the remote future such changes should come they would shape themselves in ways different from those that we now imagined, and that then there would be other people to carry them through. Mazzini shook his head, but he saw that he could not persuade me. Thus we parted, and I never saw him again.

A short time after my arrival in America I did indeed hear of the outbreak of the revolutionary enterprise which Mazzini had predicted to me. It consisted of an insurrectionary attempt in Milan, which was easily suppressed by the Austrian troops and resulted only in the imprisonment of a number of Italian patriots. And Mazzini's cause, the unity of Italy under a free government, seemed then to be more hopeless than ever.

Kossuth returned from America a sorely disappointed man. He had been greeted by the American people with unbounded enthusiasm. Countless multitudes had listened to his enchanting eloquence and overwhelmed him with sympathy and admiration. The President of the United States had reverentially pressed his hand and Congress had received him with extraordinary honors. There had been no end of parades and receptions and festive banquets. But the government of the United States, with the approval of the American people, steadfastly maintained the traditional policy of non-interference in European affairs. Kossuth's appeal for " substantial aid " to his country in its struggle for independence had been in vain. When he returned to England he found that the popular enthusiasm there, which had greeted him but a few months before, was burned out. He still tried to continue the advocacy of his cause by delivering addresses in various English cities, and was listened to with the most respectful and sympathetic attention as a very distinguished lecturer. When he appeared on the streets he was no longer cheered by multitudes surging around him. Persons recognizing him would take off their hats and whisper to one another: " There goes Kossuth, the great Hungarian patriot." His cause, the independence of his country, seemed to be dead and buried.

Mazzini and Kossuth—how strangely fate played with those two men! Mazzini had all his life plotted, and struggled, and suffered for the unification of Italy under a free national government. Not many years after the period of which I speak the national unity of Italy did indeed come, first partially aided by the man Mazzini hated most, the French Emperor Louis Napoleon, and then greatly advanced by the marvelous campaign of Garibaldi, which is said to have been originally planned by Mazzini himself, and which reads in history like a romantic adventure of the time of the Crusades. Finally the unification of Italy was fully achieved under the auspices of the dynasty of Savoy; and Mazzini the republican at last died in an obscure corner in unified Italy, where he had hidden himself under a false name, an exile in his own country.

Kossuth had agitated with his wonderful eloquence and then conducted a brilliant though unfortunate war for the national independence of Hungary. A defeated man, he went into exile. In the course of time, much of the political autonomy, of the substantial independence of Hungary as a self-governing country, was accomplished by peaceable means, and the Hungarian people seemed for a while to be contented with it. But it was accomplished under the kingship of the house of Hapsburg; and Kossuth, who never would bow his head to the Hapsburg, inflexibly resisted every invitation of his people calling him back to his country whose legendary national hero he had not ceased to be; and he finally died as a voluntary exile at Turin, a very old and lonely man.

A large part of what those two men had striven for was at last won—but it then appeared in a form in which they would not recognize it as their own.

The German revolutionists of 1848 met a similar fate. They fought for German unity and free government and were defeated mainly by Prussian bayonets. Then came years of stupid political reaction and national humiliation, in which all that the men of 1848 had stood for seemed utterly lost. Then a change. Frederick William IV., who more than any man of his time had cherished a mystic belief in the special divine inspiration of kings—Frederick William IV. fell insane and had to drop the reins of government. The Prince of Prussia, whom the revolutionists of 1848 had regarded as the bitterest and most uncompromising enemy of their cause, followed him, first as regent and then as king—destined to become the first emperor of the new German Empire. He called Bismarck to his side as prime minister—Bismarck, who originally had been the sternest spokesman of absolutism and the most ardent foe of the revolution. And then German unity, with a national parliament, was won, not through a revolutionary uprising, but through monarchical action and foreign wars.

Thus, if not all, yet a great and important part of the objects struggled for by the German revolutionists of 1848 was after all accomplished—much later, indeed, and less peaceably and less completely than they had wished, and through the instrumentality of persons and forces originally hostile to them, but producing new conditions which promise to develop for the united Germany political forms and institutions of government much nearer to the ideals of 1848 than those now existing. And many thoughtful men now frequently ask the question—and a very pertinent question it is—whether all these things would have been possible had not the great national awakening of the year 1848 prepared the way for them.

But in the summer of 1852 the future lay before us in a gloomy cloud. In France, Louis Napoleon seemed firmly seated on the neck of his submissive people. The British government under Lord Palmerston had shaken hands with him. All over the European Continent the reaction from the liberal movements of the past four years celebrated triumphant orgies. How long it would prove irresistible nobody could tell. That some of its very champions would themselves become the leaders of the national spirit in Germany even the most sanguine would in 1851 not have ventured to anticipate.

My young wife and myself sailed from Portsmouth in August, 1852, and landed in the harbor of New York on a bright September morning. With the buoyant hopefulness of young hearts, we saluted the new world.

END OF VOLUME I